Exploring Identity Work in Chinese Communication

Also available from Bloomsbury

Cultural Memory of Language, by Susan Samata
Japanese Questions, by Lidia Tanaka
Language, Identity and Symbolic Culture, edited by David Evans
Pragmatic Particles, by Jieun Kiaer
Teaching Pragmatics and Instructed Second Language Learning, by Nicola Halenko

Exploring Identity Work in Chinese Communication

Xinren Chen

BLOOMSBURY ACADEMIC
LONDON • NEW YORK • OXFORD • NEW DELHI • SYDNEY

BLOOMSBURY ACADEMIC
Bloomsbury Publishing Plc
50 Bedford Square, London, WC1B 3DP, UK
1385 Broadway, New York, NY 10018, USA
29 Earlsfort Terrace, Dublin 2, Ireland

BLOOMSBURY ACADEMIC and the Diana logo are trademarks
of Bloomsbury Publishing Plc

First published in Great Britain 2022
This paperback edition published 2023

Copyright © Xinren Chen, 2022

Xinren Chen has asserted his right under the Copyright, Designs and
Patents Act, 1988, to be identified as Author of this work.

All rights reserved. No part of this publication may be reproduced or transmitted in any
form or by any means, electronic or mechanical, including photocopying, recording,
or any information storage or retrieval system, without prior permission
in writing from the publishers.

Bloomsbury Publishing Plc does not have any control over, or responsibility for, any
third-party websites referred to or in this book. All internet addresses given in this
book were correct at the time of going to press. The author and publisher regret any
inconvenience caused if addresses have changed or sites have ceased to exist, but
can accept no responsibility for any such changes.

A catalogue record for this book is available from the British Library.

A catalog record for this book is available from the Library of Congress.

Names: Chen, Xinren, 1967-author.
Title: Exploring identity work in Chinese communication / Xinren Chen.
Description: London; New York, NY: Bloomsbury Academic, 2021. |
Includes bibliographical references and index.
Identifiers: LCCN 2021023762 (print) | LCCN 2021023763 (ebook) |
ISBN 9781350169326 (hardback) | ISBN 9781350273214 (paperback) |
ISBN 9781350169333 (pdf) | ISBN 9781350169340 (epub)
Subjects: LCSH: Communication–China–Psychological aspects. | Identity
(Psychology)–China. | Pragmatics. | Discourse analysis–Social
aspects–China. | Communication and culture–China.
Classification: LCC BF637.C45 C477 2021 (print) |
LCC BF637.C45 (ebook) | DDC 153.60951–dc23
LC record available at https://lccn.loc.gov/2021023762
LC ebook record available at https://lccn.loc.gov/2021023763

ISBN: HB: 978-1-3501-6932-6
PB: 978-1-3502-7321-4
ePDF: 978-1-3501-6933-3
eBook: 978-1-3501-6934-0

Typeset by Newgen KnowledgeWorks Pvt. Ltd., Chennai, India

To find out more about our authors and books visit
www.bloomsbury.com and sign up for our newsletters.

Contents

List of Figures	vi
List of Tables	vii
Preface	viii
1 Introduction	1
2 Defining key terms	9
3 Generative mechanism of identity work	33
4 Discursive practices of identity work	57
5 Taxonomies of identity work	85
6 Identity work strategies	119
7 Identity work in interpersonal communication	141
8 Identity work in institutional communication	167
9 Identity work in public communication	197
10 Conclusion	217
Notes	223
References	227
Index	243

Figures

3.1	Performing identity work in context	34
3.2	Contextual correlates (based on Verschueren 1999: 76)	53
4.1	The reciprocal relationship between discursive practices and identities (based on Tracy 2002: 23)	58
7.1	Modified model of rapport management (X. R. Chen 2018b: 9)	147

Tables

2.1	Subcategories, Definitions and Connotations/Illustrations of Identity	14
3.1	Categorization of Metapragmatic Awareness	51
4.1	Discursive Practices of Identity Construction	60
4.2	Domains of Identity Work	61
7.1	Identity Work and (Im)politeness Assessment	145
8.1	Mediation Steps in *Gold Medal of Mediation*	177
8.2	Information for Episodes Involving the Legal Mediator	179
8.3	Information for Episodes Involving the Psychotherapeutic Mediator	180
8.4	Discursive Practices Used for Identity Construction	181
8.5	Discursive Practices Used by the Legal Mediator to Construct or Highlight His Professional Identity	183
8.6	Discursive Practices Used by the Psychotherapeutic Mediator to Construct or Highlight Her Professional Identity	189
9.1	Types and Distribution of the Identities Constructed	209

Preface

Pragmaticians have come to understand that a communicator's identity is often (de)constructed and negotiated purposefully and has an impact on communicative outcomes. While previous endeavours tend to focus on the aspects or types of identity that are constructed and the ways in which they are discursively realized, much less systematic effort has been devoted to exploring why identities are constructed, what principles or maxims constrain their construction, what factors determine their appropriateness and effectiveness, and suchlike. To the best of my knowledge, no systematic accounts have been proposed in English-medium publications to explain the generative mechanisms of identity work in communication. This book serves to fill these important knowledge gaps.

Central to the current pursuit of this book are a number of views on identity that have been gaining popularity within the field of pragmatics and beyond. Amongst others, communication involves dynamic choices and identity shifts by discursive means; the identity chosen in communication is not the steady entirety of one's identity but rather is fragmental, temporary and changeable; discursively constructed identity can be pre-existing or non-pre-existing, default or deviant, appropriate or inappropriate; identity is a resource that communicators can exploit to facilitate the realization of their communicative needs; there may be a mismatch between the identity of self and other that is made manifest or is newly constructed by the speaker and that perceived and accepted/rejected/deconstructed by the hearer; a mismatch between the identity of self and other which is adopted or construed by the interlocutors can be consequential; and identity is intersubjective in the sense that it can be accepted, challenged or even deconstructed.

I have termed the form of identity conceived above 'pragmatic identity'. By proposing this term, I purport to highlight the type of dynamic identity that the speaker/writer adopts or constructs at the juncture of producing the current utterance(s) or the whole discourse in the communicative context concerned, as well as the identity that the hearer/reader is supposed to adopt when interpreting the utterance(s) or the whole discourse. It is communication-bound, discourse-bound and, more specifically, utterance-bound. Most importantly, underlying (the hearer's response to) the speaker's choice of pragmatic identity, we can recognize, generalize and rationalize various types of identity work. By identity work, I refer to the discursive effort (the hearer perceives or assumes) which the speaker invests for some pragmatic purpose in a communicative context by making manifest a default, pre-existing identity of self or other, constructing a new, deviant, non-pre-existing identity of self or other, or challenging, rejecting or even deconstructing an identity of self or other that the interlocutor has made manifest or constructed. In view of the immense communicative values or implications of such identity work, this book develops a pragmatic approach to communicative practices, with special reference to real-world and virtual Chinese communication.

By adopting a pragmatic approach, this book does not explore identity and its discursive construction for their own sake, as is often pursued in disciplines such as social psychology, communication studies and cultural studies. Rather, it undertakes a description and explanation of how and why Chinese communicators perform various types of identity work in different domains of communication. It also seeks to address how Chinese communicators, through dynamic construction, negotiation or even deconstruction of the identity of self or other, and the way in which the dynamic construction of identity is perceived by the hearer/reader, have an impact on communicative outcomes. Hopefully, it will help to raise the reader's awareness of the various types of identity work, by bringing to the fore the goals, strategies and linguistic choices of Chinese communicators in the course of their communication.

Upon completion of the book, I wish to acknowledge with gratitude the assistance of the following people: Professor Ziran He, from Guangdong University of Foreign Studies, for his unfailing support and encouragement; my former or current students, including Mengxin Li, Wenjing Feng, Jie Li, Jia Qiu, Kun Yang, Yingzhe Jin, Hao Liu, Jie Xia, Xiaohong Liu and others for their assistance in the preparation of the book with respect to indexing, proofreading and much more; Andrew Wardell, senior commissioning editor of Bloomsbury Academic, who kindly approached and entrusted me with a contract to write this book; Becky Holland, from the same press, who offered her assistance and granted me an extension to enable the completion of the book; and Judith Heaney for her professional copy-editing. I would also like to acknowledge the support of my research project entitled 'On Pragmatic Identity' from the National Social Sciences Fund of China.

The author and publisher gratefully acknowledge the permission granted to reproduce copyright material in this book. Every effort has been made to trace copyright holders and to obtain their permission for the use of copyright material. The publisher apologizes for any errors or omissions, and would appreciate being notified about any such mistakes so that they can be corrected in future reprints or editions of this book.

This book is dedicated to Ms Jing Chen, and to many of my doctoral and MA students, who have all contributed to the development of my pragmatic approach to identity and identity work over the years.

1

Introduction

1.1 Orientation of the book

Identity is a topic of increasing academic interest in a variety of disciplines. In the PsychINFO database, the number of hits for the keyword 'identity' is 233 for the 1950s, 775 for the 1960s, 2,896 for the 1970s, 6,901 for the 1980s, 15,106 for the 1990s, and over 12,000 for the first five years of the 2000s (Côté 2006: 3–4; see also Chen and Chen 2020: 1). Similarly, in humanities such as history, literature and cultural studies, 'the number of dissertation abstracts involving the use of the word "identity" has been growing almost three times from the mid-1980s to the mid-1990s' (Fearon 1999: 1, n.1). The same is also true for many fields of social sciences, as indicated by Côté's (2006) search of SocAbs, a sociological abstract database. More relevantly, the number of publications involving the use of 'identity' as a keyword, which include journal publications, PhD dissertations, papers or chapters in edited volumes as well as authored books, reached 20,986 in December 2019 (Chen and Chen 2020: 1), as evidenced by the search of the Linguistics and Language Behavior Abstracts database, a much greater number than other familiar terms such as 'politeness' (3,974) and 'speech acts' (8,950) in the field of pragmatics.

Broadly speaking, there are two contrasting views of identity. One is essentialist, treating identity as a set of pre-existing (hence stable and static) attributes or expectations, and the other is constructionist, treating identity as a set of emergent (hence fluid and fragmented) properties.[1] By and large, the former view is held by some social scientists (e.g. Erikson 1968; Marcia 1980; Perry 1975; Rorty 1976; Stryker 1987; Tajfel 1974, 1981, 1982), who believe that individuals are moulded in, and by, society by forming, developing and eventually obtaining various social expectations (Chen and Chen 2020). In contrast, the latter view, often described as a discursive turn or postmodern turn (Benwell and Stokoe 2006: 4), is embraced by some scholars from fields such as psychology (e.g. Widdicombe 1998), communication studies (e.g. Tracy 2002; Tracy and Robles 2013), interactional sociolinguistics or conversation analysis (e.g. Heritage and Clayman 2010; Zimmerman 1988, 1992, 1998) and linguistics (e.g. Blommaert 2005; Butler 1990; X. R. Chen 2013a, 2014, 2018a; De Fina 2003; Dolón and Todolí 2008; Grad and Rojo 2008; Ho 2010; Locher and Hoffmann 2006; Ren 2012; Spencer-Oatey 2007, 2009; Yuan and Chen 2013), in which identity is discursively constructed, represented and interpreted. These scholars cross disciplinary boundaries and collaborate on edited identity-related books (e.g. Antaki and Widdicombe 1998; Benwell and Stokoe 2006; Bucholtz and Hall 2004, 2008, 2010; De Fina, Schiffrin and Bamberg 2006), demonstrating the trend of disciplinary convergence on the theme of identity.

This book partly subscribes to the less radical view that identity is both pre-existing and emergent. Ochs (1990, 1993, 2012), for example, proposes the notion of identity-indexing, arguing that for a linguistic structure used in discourse to symbolically index a certain identity, we must view the latter's existence as independent of the former. In other words, although she explores the process of identity construction interactionally, she assumes the pre-existing nature of identity (Chen and Chen 2020: 1). However, while acknowledging the interrelation of language/discourse and identity, this book departs from her view in two significant directions: for one thing, we will go beyond the view that language use is merely identity-indexing; rather, we will argue that language users can, for good or bad, use language (together with other semiotic resources) to construct an identity that does not necessarily (pre-)exist (cf. Zhong and Zeng 2020) for the person concerned. For another, while acknowledging the fact that language use sometimes merely indexes identity, identity construction is at other times a conscious motivated social or interactional practice. In other words, we do not often use a linguistic structure just to index a certain identity; more importantly, we often 'use words of identity to do things' (X. R. Chen 2018a). Furthermore, this book will endorse the view that identity is often non-unidirectional; in other words, it can be an interactional outcome, jointly constructed by the co-participants, especially the interlocutors of a social interaction (e.g. Bucholtz and Hall 2005: 587; Kroskrity 2000). Finally, this book also endorses the view that identity can be a participant resource (e.g. Antaki and Widdicombe 1998; X. R. Chen 2013a, 2014, 2015, 2018a; Ho 2010; Wang 2013; Widdicombe 1998; Yuan 2012).

It is these departures, alongside these endorsements, that distinguish the current enterprise from most, if not all, of the discourse-bound/based studies on identity, as found in the fields of discourse analysis, conversation analysis, interactional sociolinguistics and pragmatics. We shall not confine our attention to the identities that communicators index or represent via their use of language, and how these identities are transmitted and interpreted by their interlocutors. Rather, we will explore further why they construct these identities, real or false, in order to accomplish their interactional goals. For this reason, to capture the shift of attention on identity as 'a pragmatic turn', we will adopt the term 'pragmatic identity' (X. R. Chen 2013a, 2014, 2018a) to refer specifically to the type of identity explored in this book. Chapter 2 will offer a detailed definition of the term. This turn, which is by and large in line with a rhetorical approach to identity (cf. Tracy 2002), provides the foundation for the proposal of 'identity rhetoric' (Yuan 2020), as exemplified by the use of various strategies based on identity (de)construction (listed in Chapter 5 and illustrated in Chapters 7, 8 and 9).

Thus, central to the current book are a number of views that have gained popularity in the field of pragmatics and beyond. Among others, I deem the following: (i) at times, communication involves dynamic choices and identity shifts by discursive means; (ii) the discursively constructed identity can be based on a pre-existing or non-pre-existing identity, and is therefore default or deviant; (iii) the constructed identity can be appropriate or inappropriate; (iv) the constructed identity is a resource used by communicators to facilitate the realization of their communicative needs, transactional and/or interpersonal; (v) identity work occurs in various domains of communication; and (vi) identity is intersubjective in that it can be accepted, questioned, challenged or even deconstructed.

1.2 Aims of the book

With the conceptual basis of the current approach to identity established, let us now state the manifold aims of this book.

To begin with, this book aims to introduce an explicit and operable theoretical framework for conducting the pragmatic exploration of identity in communication. Specifically, we wish to establish logical links between the identity choices made by communicators, and hence their discursive choices, on the one side, and their interactional needs and contexts on the other. We will argue and demonstrate that to fulfil certain communicative needs in a given context, language users can choose to (de)construct a certain identity of theirs, or that of others, by making appropriate discursive choices (X. R. Chen 2013a,

2018a). In this sense, identity (de)construction at an interactional moment in the interactional space is a means to an end. To capture this pragma-rhetorical approach, a systematic construal of the pragmatic decision process is inevitable. However, despite the numerous studies on identity (de)construction published in international English-medium journals, few have undertaken a theoretical study of the process. Furthermore, no study has explored and described the range of possible strategies for performing identity work for communicative purposes. It is because of this theoretical gap that we seek to present a working framework for conducting pragmatic research on identity work.

Second, following on from the first aim, we would like to highlight the point that current and future pragmatic research on the relationship between identity and communication may need to focus more on how and why communicators (de)construct a certain identity or even shift from one identity to another. A brief survey of related literature indicates that the majority of researchers concentrate on what (type of) identity or identities have been constructed, negotiated, challenged or even deconstructed, or on what discursive choices are made in the process (e.g. Chiles 2007; Clifton and Van De Mieroop 2010; Ho 2010; Jiang and Liu 2014; Moody 2014; Schnurr 2009). While these studies are most definitely necessary and beneficial, they need to be complemented by studies that further address the motivations and influencing factors of identity construction.

Third, we wish to exemplify various forms of identity strategies and related discursive practices with real-life Chinese data, thus providing a useful window through which the Chinese people and their culture can be understood. While we are not entitled to claim that the various pragmatic phenomena of identity work are unique to Chinese communicators, it is safe to say that they are highly characteristic of them.

A last, but not necessarily least, aim is related to the Chinese language. As Chen and Chen (2020) have already done, we wish to make studies, written by Chinese scholars on the topic and published in the Chinese language over the last decade or so, more available and accessible. As summarized and advanced in X. R. Chen (2018a), research on identity studies has been a favourite topic of academic pursuit for Chinese pragmaticians, leading to a rich amount of literature. However, as the majority of these works are written in Chinese and published in China, they are inaccessible to non-Chinese-speaking readers. The current book and the special issue of *East Asian Pragmatics* (2020, issue 5.1) represent our efforts to improve this situation.

In summary, this book endeavours to raise the reader's awareness of the diverse identity work performed by Chinese people during the course of communication. For this purpose, it will bring to the fore the goals, strategies and discursive practices that underlie their identity work. It echoes the growing sense among pragmaticians that identity is often (de)constructed and negotiated purposefully and has an impact on communicative outcomes. While related existing endeavours in the field of pragmatics are primarily concerned with the aspects or types of identity that are constructed and the ways in which they are discursively constructed, there has been relatively little effort to explore the identity strategies that are adopted, the reasons why identities are constructed, what principles or maxims constrain their construction and what factors determine their appropriateness and effectiveness. In other words, no pragmatic theory has been developed, in a fairly systematic manner, to account for the generative mechanisms of identity in communication. This book serves to fill these important knowledge gaps by analysing data from Chinese communication.

1.3 Methodological considerations

Primarily, this book adopts a discursive approach to identity, in the sense that the judgement and recognition of identity that is (de)constructed in situated contexts of Chinese communication will be based on the nuanced analysis of discursive or interactional data. A discursive analysis will draw on the intrinsic interrelationship between discursive practices and identity construction (X. R. Chen 2013a, 2018a; Tracy 2002; Tracy and Robles 2013). We will present the details in Chapter 4.

The data used in this book were obtained from a variety of sources: (i) field notes taken from real-life dialogues among friends, colleagues and family members; (ii) a self-built database consisting of transcribed reality TV (RTV) texts, novels, advertisements and social media messages/dialogues; (iii) ready-made corpora such as the Contemporary Chinese Language Corpus; and (iv) examples from published articles. While some illustrative data used to explain key concepts may appear to be sporadic, other data used to investigate why some identities are constructed are more systematic.

For our empirical research on motivated identity (de)construction in Chinese communication, both qualitative and quantitative analyses will be conducted for different reasons. In particular, the qualitative dimension of the analysis will employ applied conversation analysis, which often enables us to specify 'the precise point at which an identity emerges' (Chen and Chen 2020: 3). In addition, we will also profit from multimodal pragmatic analysis (MPA) (Chen and Qian 2011), under the assumption that the (de)construction of identity is often accompanied by the use of multiple semiotic resources.

1.4 Structure of the book

The book can be divided into four main parts. The first chapter is a general introduction. Chapters 2–6 form the second part of the book, and are intended to be a theoretical exploration and preparation for later chapters. Chapters 7–9 constitute the third part of the book, and describe the application of theoretical ideas to the analysis of real-life data in different domains of communication. Finally, Chapter 10 provides a conclusion. The chapters are detailed below.

This introductory chapter introduces the rationale for, and objective of, the book. Its content includes a synopsis of previous research related to the study of identity in general and the pragmatic approach to identity in particular, thereby establishing a niche for the current book; an outline of the main goals of this book, with a view to highlighting the novelty and contribution of the current effort; a description of the methodology used in the book, covering the data and analytical methods used in different parts of the research reported in the book; and an overview of the chapters, specifying the layout of the entire book.

Chapter 2 defines a couple of key terms that are crucial to the development and understanding of subsequent chapters. It will be made clear that both the notion of identity and the related term 'identity work' are to be interpreted/understood from a pragmatic point of view as something that communicators dynamically choose and discursively (re/de)construct for communicative purposes, in the sense of a deployable resource rather than the sociological or demographic sense of an individual. Identity work, then, is the deliberate discursive effort as well as the process of deploying an identity resource in the situated communicative event.

Chapter 3 addresses the core issue of how the performance of identity work is motivated by certain communicative needs and is constrained or shaped by situational and sociocultural factors. The Maxim of Identity is proposed as a complement to the existing maxims of quality, quantity, relevance and manner of Grice's (1975) Cooperative Principle (CP). This new maxim is required to detect identity work as the extra effort made by communicators. Meanwhile, I will employ the Balance Principle (X. R. Chen 2004a) to interpret identity work as giving rise to additional 'pragmatic strength' to satisfy the communicative needs at a particular moment. Contextual factors will also be discussed as having a strong bearing on the enactment of identity work to maintain communicative equilibrium.

Chapter 4 demonstrates how identity work is discursively accomplished, as manifested in the self-built Chinese database. The exploration encompasses seven domains, which are summarized by enriching Spencer-Oatey's (2005, 2008) domains of rapport management on the basis of the data. We will find not only some discursive practices that frequently occur in different languages but also some that appear to be more prevalent in Chinese than in many European languages.

Chapter 5, on the basis of the self-built database, categorizes and illustrates identity work from a number of different aspects, ranging from directions, targets, rapport orientations and dimensions. While the categorization may be incomplete, it fairly adequately depicts commonly observed identity work in the Chinese data, adding to our understanding of how the 'manipulation' of the identity of self or other in situated contexts can help satisfy various communicative needs.

Chapter 6, also on the basis of the self-built database, categorizes and illustrates the 'rhetoric' of identity work in terms of strategies. This categorization is not meant to be exhaustive and allows alternative characterizations, while showcasing an array of strategic ways in which Chinese communicators frequently 'play' with their own identity, or that of their interlocutors, or others.

Chapter 7 explores the ways in which Chinese individuals (jointly) perform identity work with one another in daily life, as a means of relating and rapport management. It will be shown that identity work can contribute to the fulfilment of illocutionary goals by managing interpersonal rapport. Using first-hand dinner-table interactional data of toasting in the Chinese context, the chapter ends with an empirical study of the identity work that emerges in this context, how it is performed and the reasons it is performed in the manner observed.

Chapter 8 explores identity work as a means of exercising and suspending power in institutional communication. It exemplifies how identity work can serve to increase or decrease the extent or degree of power, and thus facilitate the transactional goals at hand. The chapter ends with a case study of the identity work performed by two mediators during a Chinese RTV program. It will be demonstrated how the mediator can balance the construction of professional power and the management of impression by shifting between different identity options.

Chapter 9 examines how identity work is used in various public spheres of communication as a rhetorical means of persuasion. Specifically, it will discuss how the enactment of identity work can enhance the persuasiveness of three genres of public discourse: public declarations, public notices and public slogans. Finally, based on a sizable number of randomly collected real-estate advertisements from Chinese urban areas, the chapter reveals the various types of identity work that are conducted by the designers of the advertisements, and discusses how such identity work can help to persuade or even trick potential buyers into action.

Chapter 10, the final chapter, winds up the book by summarizing the content and findings of the previous chapters. It discusses some remaining issues and recommends future areas of research, before acknowledging some limitations of the current study.

2

Defining key terms

2.1 Identity

Identity matters! Without an identity, we would be nothing. But what exactly is identity? How many definitions does it have? Which definition is the best? Actually, these questions do not really matter as they probably do not have a single answer.

What is important is that identity should be defined in a way that is appropriate to our purpose, rather than considering all the definitions that are available in the literature. For this reason, the current research will draw on Simon's (2004) conceptualization of identity, which combines sociological, psychological and sociocognitive approaches. According to his Self-Aspect Model of Identity, one's concept about self includes various ideas about one's attributes or properties such as

- psychological characteristics or traits (e.g. introverted);
- physical features (e.g. curly hair, slim);
- roles (e.g. husband);
- abilities (e.g. be poor at dancing);
- tastes (e.g. preference for liquor);
- attitudes (e.g. against abortion);
- behaviours (e.g. get up early); and
- explicit group or category membership (e.g. female, scholar).

(Simon 2004: 45)

These attributes, while capable of defining who we are, are not exhaustive of all aspects of identity that are relevant to communication. Based on a survey of existing literature, this book proposes a new characterization of identity to enable our later categorization and discussion of identity work.

Identity as a set of social attributes

Originating from sociological concepts of identity, this dimension of identity, as a set of social attributes, concerns the demographics of an individual or social group, that is, social attributes such as nationality, ethnicity, gender and language background. In some ways, it is captured by the notion of 'master identity', a term proposed by Tracy (2002). In daily life, the identity of individuals as a set of social attributes influences their discursive practices, which in turn provide clues for identifying their social attributes. For example, in sociolinguistics, Labov (1966) examined the interrelationship between language variation and a variety of social factors (e.g. gender, age, education, profession, ethnicity, class) by conducting an elaborate field investigation of civic dialects. In pragmatics, some scholars have discussed gender differences when performing speech acts such as requesting (e.g. Blum-Kulka, House and Kasper 1989; Macaulay 2001), complimenting (e.g. Parisi and Wogan 2006; Rees-Miller 2011), expressing gratitude (e.g. Eisenstein and Bodman 1986; Karafoti 2007) and apologizing (e.g. Chamani 2014; Holmes 1995; Tannen 1990).

Identity as membership

Identity as membership refers to an individual belonging to a group, an organization or a community, and is similar to the 'collective self' (Brewer and Gardner 1996) or 'collective identity' (Brewer and Gardner 1996; Tracy and Robles 2013). An individual's membership could be endowed by a number of groups such as a family, a community and a club. It could be stably rooted in a social structure or temporarily assigned (e.g. group membership of a game by drawing lots, or that of a panel discussion). Membership can overlap with social attributes. For example, a teacher can be a female individual and a member of a female club. With 'identity as membership', individuals recognize that they have similarities with other members of the same group and they highlight their collective identity when required by the occasion.

Identity as identification

As a sense of identification, identity concerns an individual's sense of belonging or acceptance: interlocutors choose or construct specific identities for the purpose of approaching or distancing others. Identity as identification has been the focus of many socio-psychological studies (Yuan and Fang 2008), for example, the self-categorization theory (Turner et al. 1987). Furthermore, sociopsychologists (e.g. Tajfel 1981; Tajfel and Turner 1986) also propose the Social Identity Theory (SIT), which considers identity to be an in-group identification tendency: once an individual in society tends to identify with a specific group, he/she will maintain his/her prior dignity as a member of it. Likewise, Bucholtz and Hall (2005: 586) regard identity as 'the social positioning of self and other'. On the basis of the above ideas, identification in this study is not only concerned with one specific group but also involves identification with the other interlocutor(s) or a third party; it is a psychological or emotional positioning and is manifested in the form of identity construction for the other interlocutor(s) or the third party. The speaker sees identity as identification when emphasizing the same attributes, sense of belonging, roles, stances, images, personalities and so on, while he/she states identity as an attribute when only source information is given.

Identity as a role

In the 1960s, role identity theory defined identity as one's 'imaginative view of himself as he likes to think of himself being and acting as an occupant of that position' (McCall and Simmons 1978: 65) or the role played by people in society (Stryker 1980/2002). This theory focuses on the influence of role identity on human acts and the importance of negotiation with others in certain situations. Identity as a role focuses on the individual's position in a social structure or social relationship, that is, the sociality of the identity, which is similar to 'interactional identity' (Tracy 2002), such as teacher/student and husband/wife.

Identity as a doer

Identity as a doer concerns the issue of 'who I am in a situated activity or task'. This dimension of identity is closely related to the genre of utterances that the interlocutors are engaged in, which concerns the various participants of an event, such as the host, the speaker and questioners in a lecture. In some ways it corresponds to the 'situated identity' raised by Zimmerman (1998). The interlocutors adopt suitable identities within categorized activities and perform actions related to a series of categories (Chen et al. 2013).

Identity as status

The concept of identity is related to status when certain features of the interlocutor, such as his/her position or qualifications, are highlighted during the course of an interaction to emphasize that individual's position in the social hierarchy, such as 'you are a person of high rank' ('你是个有身份的人'). According to He (2015: 12), identity, in its traditional sense, refers to 'the social status (the interlocutor possesses) in a specific situation, occasion, or event'.[1] In this sense, identity has been heatedly debated by scholars of sociology, psychology, rhetoric and culturology. In these fields, the concepts of identity and social status are integrated (He 2015: 13).

Identity as a stance

Identity as a stance involves an individual's attitude or tendency towards a given topic: interlocutors present their identity features by conveying their specific stances on certain topics or interlocutors. Bucholtz and Hall (2005) refer to identity as the stance manifested by means of linguistic reference in interactions. Tracy and Robles (2013) discuss three types of linguistic practices involving stance, holding that stance can define the speaker as a certain type of person by the presentation of his/her opinions and attitudes. Therefore, in interactions, denying another person's stance could be equivalent to a negation of their identity (Li and Ran 2012).

Identity as an image

Identity as an image concerns 'who I am' in other people's eyes, that is, the identity features manifested by interlocutors during interactions which might be consistent or inconsistent with the expectations of other people, such as 'polite' and 'literate'. According to Lakoff (1989), interlocutors not only exchange information during daily contact but also construct a self-image in the meantime, as they value the identity attributes they present in communication. In this sense, identity is similar to the concept of face raised by Goffman (1955), that is, an individual's self-image. Moreover, the 'personal identity' in Tracy's (2002) classification also concerns one's image (e.g. honesty, rationality, fairness and obsequiousness). C. T. Li (2008, 2010) translates 'identity' to '形象身份' (which literally means 'image-identity' in English), which proves that the sense of identity as an 'image' has already been acknowledged by scholars.

Identity as individuality

Identity as individuality refers to the uniqueness of an individual, such as their character and specialization, which is constructed by presenting one's unique self to others. Simon (2004), who raises the Self-Aspect Model of Identity from the perspective of social psychology, holds that identity can help people present their self-character, which to some extent is similar to the notion of individuality. Furthermore, in Tracy's (2002) classification, 'personal identity' also includes personality (e.g. character, manner of speaking, way of communicating), which also manifests the individuality aspect of identity.

Table 2.1 summarizes the subcategories or dimensions of identity, coupled with their definitions and connotations/illustrations.

Based on their studies of identity, Brewer and Gardner (1996: 84) propose three levels of representation of the self: the individual level, the interpersonal level and the group level. Identity can also be classified into three corresponding types, that is, 'individual identity', 'interpersonal identity' or 'relational identity', and 'group identity' (Tracy 2002) or 'collective identity' (Brewer and Gardner 1996; Spencer-Oatey 2008). 'Attributes', 'doer', 'image', 'individuality' and 'status' in Table 2.1 are forms of individual identity; 'identification', 'role' and 'stance' are forms of interpersonal or relational identity; and 'membership' is a form of group or collective identity. It should be noted that 'doer', as a dynamic and temporary individual identity, also possesses the features of relational identity. For example, when a person is a *questioner*, he/she could also construct his/her relational identity in the face of the *responder*.

It should also be noted that (i) the previous dimensions of identity might not be exhaustive – for example, the relationship presented by interlocutors in a certain situation, such as equal footing or social distance between the interlocutors, has not been included; (ii) instead of being constant, these dimensions of identity can be constructed or altered during the dynamic interaction; and (iii) studies from a pragmatic perspective focus on the construction, negotiation, deconstruction and even fabrication of these dimensions in interactional discourse. Take nationality for instance. A person can fabricate his nationality by using language. As for identification, the speaker can also strategically approach or keep his/her distance from the hearer(s) by choosing or constructing certain identities to achieve certain interpersonal effects, such as befriending or excluding others. It is hoped that the above exploration on the concept of identity could prompt research on the 'speaker' with respect to his/her diversified or dynamic identities.

Table 2.1 Subcategories, Definitions and Connotations/Illustrations of Identity

Subcategory	Definition	Connotations/Illustrations
attributes	Who am I, demographically?	Nationality, ethnicity, gender, height, etc.
membership	Who am I, in a group?	Family member, team member, group member, party member, etc.
identification	Who am I, emotionally?	Solidarity, camaraderie, affiliation, etc.
role	Who am I, in a social structure/relationship?	Teacher, student, husband, son, etc.
doer	Who am I, in an activity/task?	Introducer, timekeeper, Q&A organizer, questioner, commentator, etc.
status	Who am I, in a hierarchy?	Important, inferior, trivial, etc.
stance	Who am I, on an issue?	Ally, opponent, enemy, etc.
image	Who am I, in other people's eyes?	Polite, rude, responsible, capable, etc.
individuality	Who am I, unlike others?	Uniqueness, peculiarity, personality, etc.

2.2 Pragmatic identity

Contrary to the layman's view that identity is an abstract noun, here we embrace the idea that 'identity is a verb, something that a person *does* in situated social practices whilst pursuing practical goals (Antaki and Widdicombe 1998; Holmes 2007; Sarangi and Roberts 1999), i.e., identities are performative (Butler 1990)' (Donaghue 2018: 101). As stated in the introduction, this book is concerned with pragmatic identity, not the abstract notion of identity. By pragmatic identity, we refer to (i) a certain identity or identities that the addresser or the writer adopts when saying something to achieve certain interactional goals, which concerns 'who am I' when producing the current discourse in the current situation; or (ii) a certain identity or identities that the addressee or the reader adopts when interpreting a certain utterance or utterances for particular motives, which concerns 'who am I' when interpreting the current discourse in the current situation; or (iii) a certain identity or identities that the addresser or the writer constructs for the addressee or the third party to achieve certain interactional goals, which concerns 'who is the other person' being mentioned in the current utterance(s) in the current situation (see X. R. Chen 2013a, 2018a, but note that the definition in these two references does not involve the identity or identities constructed for the addressee(s) at that moment).[2] While the speaker could be the author, animator or utterer, principal, or figure, and the hearer could be the addressee, side participant, bystander or overhearer in terms of participation footing (see Culpeper and Haugh 2014: 127), in our case identity can be any dimension mentioned in Section 2.1 (i.e. attributes, membership, identification, role, doer, status, stance, image, individuality). For example:[3]

(1) Context: The following three utterances are spoken by the same dean to the same teacher in different situations.
   a. 我个人觉得你讲的很有道理，也非常支持你。
   b. 你讲的很有道理，虽然学院也有困难，但作为院长，我会支持你的。
   c. 我们都是同事，我会支持你的。
   a. ***I personally*** *feel that what you have just said is quite reasonable, and I will support you too.*
   b. *What you have just said is reasonable. Despite the difficulties in our school, I,* ***as the dean****, will support you.*
   c. ***We are colleagues****. I'll support you.*

In Example (1a), the speaker chooses the identity of an 'individual' (i.e. individuality) instead of his identity as the 'dean' (i.e. role); the speaker in Example (1b) adopts his identity as the 'dean'; he chooses the identity of 'colleague' (i.e. identification) in Example (1c) to express his support to the hearer. Consider Example (2):

(2) Context: On New Year's Eve, many Chinese people exchange New Year greetings by sending short text messages.
新春到来之际，我谨代表华阳公司以及我本人向您致以衷心的祝福，祝您及全家马年幸福、龙马精神、马到成功！

As Spring Festival is approaching, **on behalf of the Hua Yang Company and myself**, I want to extend our greetings to you, and wish you and your family happiness, health and success in the Year of the Horse!

The addresser in Example (2) adopts a dual identity: individuality ('myself'), and status (perhaps a leader in the 'Hua Yang Company'). Now consider Example (3):

(3) Context: The following dialogue takes place between a dean and his subordinate.
张院长：李老师，咱们都是同事，有什么话可以直接说的。
李老师：不敢，您是院长。有件事想汇报一下。

Dean Zhang: *Li, **we are all colleagues**. You can speak openly.*
Li (Teacher): *No, no, **you are the dean**. I have just got something to report.*

In Example (3), even though Dean Zhang considers the relationship between himself and Li to be that of 'colleagues' (i.e. identification), Li chooses to call him 'dean' (i.e. role). By doing so, Li selects a superior identity for Zhang and considers himself to be the dean's subordinate. Consider Example (4):

(4) Context: Director Chen is talking to Director Wang, who is from another university.
王主任，我认识你们单位的张明。他是我老乡。还请你多关照。

*Director Wang, I know Ming Zhang in your university. **He is my fellow townsman**. I'd appreciate it if you could look after him.*

In Example (4), Chen assigns an identity of identification to Wang's colleague, Ming Zhang. The speaker highlights that their relationship is one of 'fellow townsmen' (even though this might be a fake relationship and could thus be a fabricated identity), to achieve the interactional goal of persuading Wang to 'look after' Ming Zhang.

A chosen pragmatic identity can be a default or deviational identity relative to the interactional context concerned. For example, a member of an expert committee participating in a doctorial oral defence could construct various identities in his/her discourse sequences, within which the default identity is that of an expert, while the deviational identities might include a teacher, a researcher, a virtual advice-receiver, a layman and so on (Ren 2012).

Following Tracy (2002), Simon (2004) and Brewer and Gardner (1996), the pragmatic identities chosen by the interlocutors, that is, the identities which are presented or highlighted by the speaker and then perceived or inferred by the hearer(s) (or the identities chosen by the hearers after understanding the current discourse), can be further categorized into individual identity (e.g. gender, age, profession, title, race, personality, image, individuality), relational identity (e.g. friend, colleague, fellow officer, fellow townsman, comrade-in-arms, enemy) and collective identity (e.g. club member, committee member).

In terms of terminology, this book adopts 'pragmatic identity' (X. R. Chen 2013a, 2014, 2018a) rather than 'discourse identity' to avoid unnecessary misunderstanding, as the latter relates to discourse roles such as addressers, addressees, indirect participants, eavesdroppers, unexpected hearers and so on (Zimmerman 1998), and thus could not possibly cover all the chosen identities which have a consequence on interactional progress and which bear social or psychological attributes (such as Brewer and Gardner's (1996) categorization of individual identities, interpersonal identities and group identities, or Tracy's (2002) categorization of master identities, interactional identities, personal identities and relational identities). Furthermore, 'communicative identity' is not chosen because of its broad scope, ranging from linguistic to non-linguistic communication. 'Interactional identity' is also not chosen because this notion implies the speaker's spontaneous choice of roles in dynamic dialogues when faced with specific hearers (which we could call explicit interactional identities), and does not cover identities that are constructed in other interactions, such as monologic interactions (e.g. print advertisements, news reports, public notices) (which we could call implicit interactional identities), and thus does not cover individual identity and relational identity, or the aforementioned discourse identity. Certainly, there is a more important reason to use the notion of 'pragmatic identity': the 'identity' being considered in this study is pragmatic in nature, reflecting the choices made by interlocutors in realizing specific interactional purposes in the dynamic context; it manifests a pragmatic perspective and is pragmatic in nature.

Different levels of association between 'pragmatic identity' and 'identity' from a sociological perspective can be established from their definition: (i) the pragmatic identity chosen or constructed by speakers in the current discourse originates from their social identities, which could be one (or sometimes more than one) of several social identities; (ii) the pragmatic identity chosen by speakers in the current discourse is not the identity possessed by the speaker, but a social identity that is temporarily constructed or fabricated – for example, some fraudsters pretend to be friends of their victims, police officers or chief managers; and (iii) the pragmatic identity chosen by speakers in the current discourse might originate from the social identities of the speaker relative to some others being mentioned, as shown in Examples (3) and (4). As a certain type of contextualized identity, pragmatic identity can be one, or more than one, identity associated with a particular utterance. Therefore, the attributes and functions of identities in a sociological sense can influence the interaction and the interactional results through the process of language use.

The notion of pragmatic identity benefits from social constructionism, which can be roughly summarized as follows:

a. Identity is a process rather than a product or 'a fixed point' (Hall 1989: 15). It is an accomplishment, not a thing (Tracy 2002). Thus, identity is an 'emergent product rather than the pre-existing source of linguistic and other semiotic practices' (Bucholtz and Hall 2005: 588).
b. The attribute of identity is not stable but flowing and fragmented (see Antaki and Widdicombe 1998: 204).
c. Being intersubjectively rather than individually produced, it is interactionally accomplished or negotiated (Bucholtz and Hall 2005; De Fina 2010).
d. Identity is a social and relational phenomenon (Bucholtz and Hall 2005, 2010; Hall 1996a, 1996b; Hall and Bucholtz 2013).
e. We construct identities by using discursive practices. Being the primary locus by which distinctions between identity categories are negotiated, such as gender, ethnicity, race and immigration, discourse is fundamental to the understanding of identity (Bamberg, De Fina and Schiffrin 2011).
f. Being a process of transmission, identity should be studied within the context of information exchange (Hecht, Collier and Ribeau 1993).

Properties of pragmatic identity

On the basis of the above constructionist views of identity, it is better to consider pragmatic identity as a pragmatic notion than a sociological notion. As the contextualized or pragmaticalized production of certain identities, pragmatic identity possesses the following fundamental communicative attributes or pragmatic attributes (X. R. Chen 2013a):

a. Communicative dependency

Pragmatic identity is chosen or constructed during the course of communication when speakers or writers generate utterances, or when hearers or readers interpret utterances. It dissolves once the communication stops. Therefore, pragmatic identity is dependent on verbal communication, and is hence temporary and emerging. As a matter of fact, Bucholtz and Hall (2005: 585–6) argue in favour of approaching 'identity as a relational and socio-cultural phenomenon that emerges and circulates in local discourse contexts of interaction rather than as a stable structure located primarily in the individual psyche'.

As pragmatic identity is dependent on communication, it is contextually sensitive rather than contextually constrained, because the choice of pragmatic identity is not contextually fixed. Sometimes speakers choose inappropriate or indecent identities because of their insensitivity to the contextual elements if their pragmatic competence is insufficient. Sometimes speakers deliberately break away from contextual constraints and choose identities which do not conform to contextual norms, in order to achieve specific interactional goals or communicative effects.

b. Discursive construction

Inevitably, interlocutors should implement their selection of identities discursively (sometimes involving non-linguistic modalities), irrespective of the identities that are chosen. As a consequence, identity has been relocated from the private realms of cognition and experience to the public realms of discourse and other semiotic systems of meaning-making (Benwell and Stokoe 2006; Wetherell 2007).

c. Dynamic choice-making

At certain interactional stages, the pragmatic identity that is chosen or constructed can be a subjective decision. Such a decision is affected by current interactional contexts, interactional events, interactional goals, interactional targets and so forth. In keeping with the interactional context, events, goals, targets and so on, the choices made by interlocutors can be their default identities, non-default identities or even fabricated pragmatic identities which do not conform to their social roles. Therefore, pragmatic identities are chosen intentionally.

Interlocutors can alter or adjust their pragmatic identities according to changes in interactional goals, contexts, events, targets and so on. For example, one could start speaking by assuming one's professional identity, and then shift to using the identity of a family member or friend. Thus, pragmatic identities are chosen dynamically and variably.

d. Bilateral negotiability

During the course of an interaction, the pragmatic identities of the interlocutors are not unilaterally chosen but are sometimes negotiated with other interlocutors. The result of the negotiation could be a consensus, divergence or even conflict. Therefore, the dynamic choice of pragmatic identities is a bilateral process. Consider Example (5):

(5) Context: Ming Chen visits his supervisor Professor Wang, whose wife, Juan Wu, is a director of a public health bureau.
陈明：吴局，您做的菜真好吃。
吴娟：**陈教授**，您开玩笑了，可千万不要喊我"吴局"。叫我"吴老师"吧。
陈明：那您也不要叫我"陈教授"啊，我可是王老师的学生。

Ming Chen: **Director Wu**, these dishes are really delicious.

Juan Wu: **Professor Chen**, stop pulling my leg. Don't call me 'director'. 'Teacher Wu' will do.

Ming Chen: Please don't call me 'Professor Chen' either; after all, I am Professor Wang's student.

In Example (5), since Juan Wu has just been promoted to the post of director, Ming Chen chooses to use 'Director Wu' to address her, that is, the identity of a 'director', which is customary in Chinese society. However, Juan Wu declines the identity that has been chosen for her by Ming Chen, asking him to call her 'Teacher Wu' instead. In the meantime, Ming Chen also declines the 'professor' identity chosen by Juan Wu, and highlights his identity as being 'Professor Wang's student'.

e. Enabling resources

When identity becomes part of social intercourse, that is, pragmatic identity, various identity-related resources (power, status, allocated resources, etc.) help to boost the realization of interactional goals or influence interactional development. Such an attribute of pragmatic identity is called an enabling resource. Communicators with specific pragmatic identities frequently allocate identity-marked linguistic resources to satisfy their interactional needs in certain contexts. Consider Example (6):

(6)　Context: A (male) is on a business trip to the university where B (female) studies. Seeing that A has a suitcase, B offers to help.
甲：谢谢，不用的。
乙：您还是让我来拎吧。
甲：谢谢，我一个大男人，哪能让你一个小姑娘帮着拎箱子啊。
乙：您是客人啊。让我来吧。
甲：好吧，你真是太客气了。
A: *Thanks. Leave it to me.*
B: *Please, let me carry it.*
A: *Thank you.* **As a man**, *I can't allow* **a little girl** *to carry my case.*
B: **You [honorific form] are our guest**. *Please give me a chance.*
A: *Okay. That's so kind of you.*

In the above conversation, the interactional mode adopted by A and B undergoes a change. At the beginning, A declines the offer of help in a candid and straightforward manner. When the student insists on carrying his suitcase, A highlights his 'male' identity and B's identity as a 'little girl', which helps him to decline B's offer of help. In turn, B highlights A's 'guest' identity, making it easier for A to accept her assistance. Their pragmatic identities are chosen in line with the following context: (i) guest pick-up at the airport; (ii) A is the expert while B is the student welcoming A; and (iii) the expert has a suitcase. A chooses his pragmatic identity based on his explicit or implicit interactional needs: (i) to decline a female student's aid and (ii) to avoid embarrassing B when declining the offer of help. As the expression chosen at the beginning of the exchange does not achieve the goal of declining the offer, A adopts a more acceptable way of declining B's help (in Chinese culture, males are expected to shoulder burdens, and girls should be cared for). Similarly, B's utterance in the second turn also reflects her communicative need: allowing A to accept her assistance. Compared to her previous offer of help, her second attempt reflects her consideration of both A's refusal to accept her first offer and the need to make a greater effort to persuade A to accept her assistance. Thus, she also draws support from identity resources (in Chinese culture, it is the host's responsibility to help the guest). Appeals to identity resources are reflected in their discourse (both A and B use lexicons such as 'man', 'little girl' and 'guest' to manifest identities). Their identity discourse brings forth corresponding interactional effects, which are influenced by the other interlocutor's attitudes and responses, and thus is the result of bilateral negotiation. Although A does not achieve his desired effect despite his use of identity resources, B does achieve her desired effect and realizes her needs, because the rights and obligations associated with the identity resources that she uses are more compelling in the Chinese context. Compared with her first utterance, the identity work she performs in her second utterance makes quite a difference.

f. Communication strategy

Choosing a pragmatic identity during the course of an interaction is a choice-making process based on pragmatic considerations; interactional results vary according to the different pragmatic identities that are chosen. The choice of pragmatic identity cannot be separated from the context and the interlocutors' intentions, which influence the production or interpretation of certain discourses. To realize interactional goals, interlocutors with sufficient pragmatic competence choose or construct their pragmatic identity strategically; they choose the pragmatic identity which helps them to realize their interactional goals in the easiest way possible. Such strategies can be manifested by a dynamic shift in pragmatic identities during the interaction. Occasionally, interlocutors can make an inappropriate choice of identity because of insufficient pragmatic identity or for particular interactional goals, resulting in pragmatic failure or interactional conflicts. However, the efforts made by interlocutors to strategically choose pragmatic identities should not be ignored, even though their pragmatic identities are inappropriate from the perspective of interactional effect.

Evaluations based on pragmatic identity

Evaluations based on pragmatic identity involve the following dimensions:

a. Evaluation of the felicity of the discourse

According to the Speech Act Theory (Searle 1969), performing a speech act should satisfy a series of felicity conditions/rules, such as propositional content condition, sincerity condition, preparatory condition and essential condition. Felicity concerns the formation, legitimacy and effectiveness of the discourse. At the very least, identity should be regarded as one aspect of the preparatory conditions, if it cannot stand alone: to perform a certain speech act (such as announcing a sports meeting open or marrying a couple at a wedding), one should possess a relevant identity. If the speaker possesses a relevant identity and performs the act by assuming this identity, the act can be regarded as a felicitous one. For example:

(7) 5月22日，有媒体报道，国家发改委产业研究所所长助理黄汉权明确表态："三年之内免谈房产税。"

On 22 May, it was reported that Hanquan Huang, **the assistant director of the Industrial Institute for the National Development and Reform Commission (NDRC)**, declared that 'there is no need to discuss property tax within the next three years'.

In Example (7), the opinion of Hanquan Huang, a researcher in a subordinate organization of the NDRC, received extensive coverage. His opinion was represented as being the opinion of an NDRC officer and was regarded as the official opinion of the NDRC, which boosted the value of property stocks. On the day after the statement ('there is no need to discuss property tax within the next three years') was released, the relevant department of the NDRC remarked that it did not represent the NDRC's position because 'the content was largely inconsistent with the general housing policy at that time, causing a serious, baneful influence'. To enable the formulation of scientific policies, many central government departments have established subordinate research institutes, where researchers can publish academic opinions on social issues. However, the news media tend to deliberately neglect their identity as 'institute researchers/experts' and instead consider them to be 'officials'. Nevertheless, the relevant department of the NDRC provided clarification, adjusting the potential impact of the press coverage, which was therefore conducive to a proper public interpretation of Huang's words.

b. Evaluation of the appropriacy of the discourse

An evaluation of the appropriacy of the discourse concerns discourse properties from an interpersonal perspective, such as whether the discourse conforms to politeness norms. For a certain identity to be adopted at a particular moment, behaviour considered to be either impolite or overly polite would be regarded as being inappropriate. For example (*Obstetricians*, episode 37):

(8) Context: Jinming Qu and Yating Hu were married when they were younger, but broke up due to the involvement of a third party. Many years later, Yating Hu developed uterine cancer and sought treatment in the hospital in which Jinming Qu served as a vice president. Jinming Qu detailed his treatment plan, but Yating Hu insisted on a different plan.

胡亚婷：五年的存活率是两到三成。

曲晋明：理论上是这样，但是你也不要往坏处想啊。

胡亚婷：那又能怎么想啊？

曲晋明：如果手术彻底的话，至少会有一半的机会。我们可以按照常规的疗法，先做放疗。全子宫切除后在做放疗的同时，再做孕激素治疗。

胡亚婷：我想曾主任已经跟你说了，我不想切除子宫，更不想放疗。

曲晋明：亚婷啊，你别固执，难道生命对你那么不重要啊？

胡亚婷：曲院长，很高兴你能把病情如实地告诉我。谢谢，谢谢！

曲晋明：你干嘛这么客气。亚婷，作为老同学，我想就你的治疗方案再聊聊行吗？

Yating Hu: *The survival rate after five years is about 20 to 30 per cent.*

Jinming Qu: *Theoretically so. But don't think negatively.*

Yating Hu: *What else can I think?*

Jinming Qu: *If the operation is successful, the rate will rise to at least 50 per cent. You can undergo a traditional form of treatment, that is, have radiation therapy first. After the hysterectomy, you would then have progestogen treatment together with radiation therapy.*

Yating Hu: *I think Director Zeng has already told you that I don't want to remove my uterus, and no radiation therapy either.*

Jinming Qu: *Yating, don't be so stubborn. Is your life not important to you?*

Yating Hu: **President Qu**, *thank you for your honesty in telling me about my condition. Thank you, thank you!*

Jinming Qu: *Don't be so courteous. Yating,* **as your classmate**, *I want to have a further discussion about your treatment, okay?*

In Example (8), Jinming Qu's use of 'Yating' as a familiar form of address in his third turn indicates that she is still someone he remembers fondly. However, she uses 'President Qu' rather than 'Jinming' in her next turn, which indicates that she does not have the same memories of Jinming Qu, nor does she treat him as her former husband. Jinming Qu's use of 'don't be so courteous' reflects his bewilderment at her attitude. Even though he still uses 'Yating' when addressing her, he repositions their relationship from another angle, highlighting his identity as being her 'classmate' to avoid embarrassment when discussing her treatment.

c. Evaluation of the (im)politeness of the speaker

The pragmatic identity adopted by speakers when expressing themselves, or adopted by hearers when interpreting the speaker's discourse, can affect or even evoke an evaluation of politeness by others. Garcés-Conejos Blitvich, Lorenzo-Dus and Bou-Franch (2010), Garcés-Conejos Blitvich, Bou-Franch and Lorenzo-Dus (2013) and Bou-Franch and Garcés-Conejos Blitvich (2014) empirically demonstrate the close interconnections between (im)politeness and identity construction (see also Culpeper, Haugh and Kádár 2017; Graham 2007; Haugh 2010; Li and Ran 2012; Lorenzo-Dus 2009). They argue that the identities of the participants, as they are co-constructed in discourse, are closely linked to assessments of (im)politeness. Garcés-Conejos Blitvich (2009, 2013) argues that politeness evaluations can ensue as a result of (i) identity verification and/ or (ii) an implicit/explicit recognition of the authenticity/self-worth/self-efficacy attributes associated with one's identity; in contrast, impoliteness evaluations can ensue as a result of (i) partial or non-verified identity and/or (ii) a threat to the authenticity/self-worth/self-efficacy attributes associated with one's identity. Garcés-Conejos Blitvich (2013) also argues that face is closely related to identity, and is indeed embedded in identity. Chaemsaithong (2011: 247) states that face and identity are reflexive, indexed and constructed through the discursive accomplishment of the interactants' communication. Consider the following example:

(9) Context: Emily is discussing the arrangements for an academic conference with her friend Carl. Carl is the president of a national association, while Emily is one of the leaders of both the hosting university and the association.
Carl：辛苦啦！
Emily: 应该的！是个很好的锻炼机会。谢谢会长信任。您真是太信任我们了。我们一定努力。
Carl: 哪里啊，你太给力了。不要用"您"，好么？太疏远了。
Emily: 您就别客气了。

Carl: *Thank you for your hard work!*

Emily: *It's my responsibility! This is a really good chance to improve ourselves. Thank you, **President**, for your great trust. **You** [honorific form] trust us so much. We will definitely do our utmost.*

Carl: *Don't say that. You did an outstanding job. Don't use 'nin', ok? It's too estranging.*

Emily: *You are too courteous.*

In Example (9), Emily uses '会长' ('President') and '您' ('nin', the honorific form of 'you') to address Carl, and regards the opportunity to host the conference to be indicative of Carl's 'trust'; thus she chooses her subordinate identity (in the association) and regards Carl as her superordinate. Her choice of identity invokes Carl's evaluation ('too estranging') (in Chinese culture this appraisal is not negative but is used as a form of negotiation to shorten the emotional distance between them). The reason why Carl evaluates her in this way is that he positions their identity relationship as 'friends', which then calls upon Emily's further evaluation, that is, Carl is 'too courteous', which is a manifestation of politeness in China.

d. Evaluation of speaker (im)partiality

Speaker (im)partiality is concerned with whether certain targets have been understood or presented by the speaker in an objective and impartial way. From this perspective, people can determine whether or not speakers have stereotypes or discriminate against certain groups or individuals. Consider the following examples:

(10) Context: A daughter is recalling, along with her brothers and sisters, her memories of her father, who died a few years ago.

我说：爸，人家都说您"土"，不会当干部，一看就是农民出身。父亲听了一愣。他说，农民怕什么？本来就是农民，谁不是农民…？

*I said: Dad, people all say that you are 'countrified' and not cadre-like; at first sight, everyone can tell you are from a peasant household. He paused and then said, what is wrong with being a peasant? **I'm a peasant.** Who is not a peasant?*

(11) Context: Hui Xu and Zi Hua are classmates. They are having a graduation dinner with a group of friends, where they discuss their ideas about the most important things in life. Each of them must give his/her own answer.

许辉：我认为生活中最重要的东西是钱。
华子：错！农民！罚酒一杯！

Hui Xu: *In my opinion, the most important thing in our life is money.*
Zi Hua: *Wrong!* **You peasant!** *Drink as a punishment!*

In Example (10), 'peasant' is interpreted as 'countrified'; in Example (11), 'peasant' appears to imply a tasteless thought, such as the idea that money is the only important thing in life.

e. Evaluation of the truthfulness of the discourse

Discourse authenticity involves whether the current discourse truthfully and objectively reflects a certain situation, condition or state. From the perspective of pragmatic identity, the truthfulness of the discourse hinges on the authenticity of the speaker's current pragmatic identity. Zhong (2013) discloses the way in which fraudsters can fabricate identities through their use of discourse to cheat people out of money.

f. Evaluation of the legitimacy of the discourse

Discourse legitimacy involves the speaker's qualification or right to speak when uttering a certain discourse (content) or adopting a certain way of speaking. During the course of an interaction, people can make an intuitive judgement about the speaker's legitimacy to speak using specific identities. Consider Example (12) taken from the urban fiction romance *Love You More than Words* (《爱你何须言语》):

(12) Context: Yanshen Lin and Wei Shen are classmates. They were once in love with one another, but have since broken up.
眼看林彦深拄着拐杖就要下楼，沈唯忍不住了，"喂！"
林彦深扭头冷冷看着她，是真的很冷，眼睛里一点温度都没有。
沈唯心里有点凉，但还是好心提醒他，"楼梯上有雪水可能会滑，你去坐电梯比较安全。"
这是多么平常的一句话，真的是出于好心的关怀，沈唯不知道她这样说究竟有什么问题，林彦深竟然发脾气了。
"你管得着我吗？你以为你是我什么人？我的事，用得着你来操心？"

Seeing that Yanshen Lin is about to go downstairs with the cane, Wei Shen couldn't stand it anymore and shouts, 'Hey!'

Yanshen Lin turns around indifferently without any love in his eyes.

With a bitter heart, Wei Shen kindly reminds him, 'The stairs are full of snow-broth and might be quite slippery; or you can take the elevator. It will be much safer.'

Wei Shen feels that she has just said some common words with a kind heart; she can't see anything inappropriate in her words. But to her surprise, Yanshen Lin loses his temper.

'Why do you bother about me? **Who do you think you are to me?** It's my own business! Is it necessary for you to meddle in it?'

Before the scene depicted in Example (12), a conflict has been raging between Yanshen Lin and Wei Shen. Wei Shen witnesses Yanshen Lin using his cane to go downstairs and wants to remind him of the slippery stairs, advising him to take the elevator instead. It surprises her that Yanshen Lin regards, rather ungratefully, her care as being 'bother'. By using the words 'who do you think you are', he challenges their relational identity and refuses to accept her 'concern'.

It is worth noting that evaluating speakers in discourse from the perspective of pragmatic identity may include other dimensions, which will not be discussed here. Such an evaluation from the emic perspective of the discourse participants can be seen in Examples (3), (5), (6), (8) and (9). In this way, evaluation is a sound objective.

Evaluating the choice of pragmatic identity concerns the issue of deviation. From the perspective of moral order (Garfinkel 1967; Haugh 2015; Spencer-Oatey and Kádár 2016), deviation in the choice of pragmatic identity can be either a positive or a negative deviation. Correspondingly, we can choose to conduct either a positive or a negative critical pragmatic analysis (X. R. Chen 2020b) of identity deviation in discourse.

Positive deviation is generally manifested as a positive pragmatic strategy, which can prove beneficial for interlocutors when attempting to perform certain interactional functions, such as realizing communicative goals or promoting interpersonal relationships. Consider Example (13):

(13) 亲！今年征兵开始啦！如你具备高中以上学历，22周岁以下（本科毕业24周岁），请在8月1日前去兵役机关报名哦。详询80933162.

Dear! Conscription begins now! If you possess a minimum of a high school degree and are aged under twenty-two (or under twenty-four if you are a university graduate), please sign up at the military service office before 1 August. For more information, please call 80933162.

Example (13) is a conscription notice. It differs from other traditional forms of notice by adopting the address form ('亲', meaning 'dear').[4] As the discourse addresser, office staff deviate from their traditional identity norm, which would normally be '同志' ('comrade'). When used in conjunction with other interpersonal expressions like the second-person pronoun '你' ('you') and the modal particle '啦' (no equivalent is found in English), this helps to alleviate the impersonal tone of a traditional notice, thereby adding a refreshing and caring tone to it.

The negative deviation of a pragmatic identity refers to a situation where interlocutors make inappropriate choices for the pragmatic identities of self, other or a third party, and thus commit pragmatic failure. In Chinese, '亲自' (qīn zì, which literally means 'personally/in person') is a social deixis, manifesting hierarchical information about the identity relations of the interlocutors. Generally speaking, when a subordinate wants to ask a favour of a superordinate, the subordinate can use '亲自' to embellish the superordinate's acts. However, sometimes a superordinate can also use this word to describe his/her own acts. Consider the following examples:

(14)   局长，这种小事您以后不必亲自做的，让我们去做就可以了。
       *Chief, you don't have to do such trivial things **in person**; please leave them to us.*
(15)   小明，你放心好了，我会亲自过问此事的。
       *Xiaoming, don't worry. I will take up the matter **in person**.*

However, in the following example, '亲自' is used improperly:

(16)   学生：刘老师，我的作业已经完成，不知你明后天是否来仙林上课？要不我亲自送到鼓楼校区去？
       Student: *Mr. Liu, I've finished my homework. I wonder if you have any classes in Xianlin Campus these next two days. Or do I need to go to Gulou Campus and submit my work **in person**?*

There are numerous discourse phenomena which are worthy of negative critical pragmatic analysis. For instance, sometimes we hear indecent address forms being used. In hospitals, doctors and nurses might choose to use the bed number or the name of the illness to address their patients, an indication that they are being disrespectful to them. Due to space limitations, no further discussion will be offered here.

2.3 Identity work

By the term 'identity work', Tracy and Robles refer to 'the process through which talk makes available to participants and observers who the people doing the talking must be' (2013: 7). In their eyes, talk reflects who people are and is also the instrument through which people build who they want to be. Their definition incorporates two sides of identity work:

1. Talk does identity-work. Through a person's choices about how to talk, identity-work is accomplished. That is, people's ways of talking construct pictures of who people must be.

2. Identities shape talk. That is, people are embedded in various communities (e.g., by nationality, ethnicity, age, professional, recreational), and this results in their learning and using distinctive expressive styles. These community-shaped styles become markers of identity categories.

(Tracy and Robles 2013: 7)

Thus, identity work is 'the glue linking identity with ways of talking' (Tracy and Robles 2013: 20). However, as they correctly admit, although talk performs identity work and in turn identities shape talk, 'the process is by no means straightforward and certain (if a person says X, it means that he or she is a Y kind of person; or Y kinds of people will always talk in an X kind of way)'.

Even though the idea that 'talk performs identity work' reflects a constructionist view of identity, the claim that 'identity shapes discourse' appears to be a determinist view of identity, that is, one would speak in a way which is bound by one's identity. The definition neglects the agency and purposefulness of the speaker, the potential of identity as an interactional resource and the dynamics of identity construction. In the meantime, the definition also neglects the interactional feature of identity work; that is, bilateral or multilateral parties of communication can perform identity work together (identity construction can achieve the desired effect when the other side also acknowledges it. However, the opposite might challenge or overturn the identity of self or other that is constructed by the speaker). Therefore, identity work should be redefined and characterized within the scope of pragmatic identity.

As shown by the definition in Section 2.2, pragmatic identity is a certain (one, or more than one) identity adopted by the speaker or writer when generating certain discourse in a particular context, or a certain identity adopted by the hearer or reader when interpreting related discourse in a particular context, or a certain identity chosen by the speaker or writer for the addressee or a third party when generating certain discourse in a particular context. By considering all the aforementioned dimensions of identity, pragmatic identity can be any dimension of identity (attributes, membership, identification, roles, doers, status, stances, images, individuality, etc.). We can redefine identity work as follows: identity work refers to the discursive efforts of communicators, as the hearer perceives or assumes, to manage or operate the pragmatic identities of self, other or a third party in a particular context with a view to achieving specific interactional goals; it can be realized by constructing, highlighting, negotiating, challenging or even deconstructing certain dimensions of identity. In the following chapters, we will discuss the identity work performed in linguistic communication in Chinese society, with a view to describing and explaining how and why the dynamic management of the communicator's self- or other-identity has an impact on communicative outcomes.

It should be emphasized here that although the descriptions of identity work are primarily from the speaker's perspective, identity work is conducted by both sides in the communication, which is particularly obvious in interactional contexts. In monologues, identity work appears to be accomplished by only the addressers, but the potential addressees also have an influence, explicit or implicit, weak or strong, on the identity work of the addressers.

3

Generative mechanism of identity work

This chapter outlines the generative mechanism of identity work. Specifically, on the basis of appropriate data, it illustrates how communicators are contextually motivated and constrained to perform identity work at a point in time by choosing to construct, highlight, challenge or deconstruct a certain identity, or sometimes identities, primarily through their linguistic choices. Thus, it will demonstrate that identity work, which is generally perceivable, is essentially situated, purposeful and dynamic.

3.1 A general framework

By using an analogy of Verschueren's (2012) representation of the structure of a pragmatic theory (i.e. pragmatics as a theory of linguistic adaptation, Adaptation Theory for short), the performance of identity work in a situated context is characterized here as a motivated, dynamic and salient discursive process, as illustrated in the framework shown in Figure 3.1.

Identity work, as captured in this book, is motivated and discursively constructed[1] because it is generally driven by the desire to satisfy some communicative need and realized by means of discursive choices that correspond to identity choices. Such choices, both of identity and of discourse, with a view to fulfilling communicative needs, constitute the locus of identity work.

Identity work is dynamic in the sense that as communicative needs and the context change, the choice of identity can also change. The shift in identity then entails the mapping of discursive choices. Such a shift is evidence of the dynamic process of identity work.

Identity work is salient because it is generally indicated by the active or perceptible discursive choices of the communicators (which is particularly

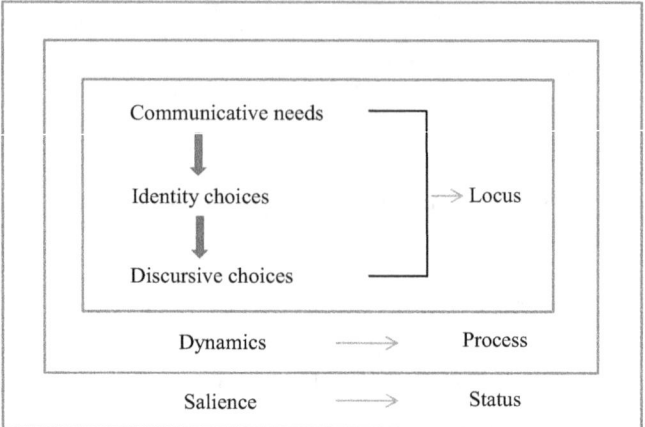

Figure 3.1 Performing identity work in context

true when using identity markers, as detailed later). In other words, doers are generally more or less aware of their identity choices. Such an awareness at either the pragmatic or metapragmatic level (Bublitz and Hübler 2007; Caffi 1984, 1994, 2006; X. R. Chen 2020c; Hübler and Bublitz 2007; Verschueren 1995, 2000) reveals the mental state of the doers regarding their identity work.

The next sections will provide a detailed account of how identity work is performed in a situated context with respect to its locus, process and salience.

3.2 Locus of identity work

Communicative needs

Verbal communication arises out of specific communicative needs in certain communicative contexts, such as asking somebody to close the door, inviting somebody to a party and asking others a question. However, factors that influence verbal communication involve not only specific and spontaneous communicative needs but also some implicit and constant needs such as emotions, face, interests and economy of effort,[2] which also exert considerable influence on the means, process and even the results of communication. Not only do speakers have communicative needs, but so too do listeners. As communication occurs in certain spatial and temporal spaces, different communicative needs can arise at different stages of communication, which can influence one another. We will discuss this in relation to identity selection in the following section.

Identity choices in identity work

Once a communicative need arises, communicators need to make an effort to satisfy it. Here, the various efforts made by communicators to satisfy their communicative needs are termed pragmatic efforts (X. R. Chen 2004a), and these can be divided into two main categories – namely, linguistic and paralinguistic. These two categories generally appear at the same time (which we can see in cases like making a phone call or engaging in non-face-to-face conversations when obstacles are located in between the communicators). A proper pragmatic effort generally requires harmonious coordination between the two categories. For example, when we apologize to somebody, not only do we say words like 'sorry', 'excuse me' and so on but, at the same time, we provide an apologetic gesture (such as bowing with folded hands and looking into the other person's eyes) to demonstrate our sincerity. More often than not, a pragmatic effort is manifested by our use of pragmatic resources.

The term 'pragmatic resources' (X. R. Chen 2004a) refers to the various resources that are deployed to serve specific communicative needs, including (i) linguistic resources (pronunciation and intonation, morphology, vocabulary, grammar, sentences, textual features, genre features, etc.); (ii) paralinguistic resources, including facial expressions (cry, smile, sadness, sympathy, etc.), hand gestures (clapping hands, beckoning with hands, waving hands, shaking hands, etc.), body gestures (shaking one's head, kneeling down, bowing with folded hands, leaning one's body forward or leaning on one's back, etc.) and emojis and emoticons; and (iii) contextual resources, including material world ingredients (a third party and objects that are present and perceptible at that moment, the physical distance between the two interacting parties, emerging incidents or occasions, weather conditions, geographic situations, etc.), social world ingredients (power, equality, institutional setting, kinship, qualifications, profession, age relationship, economic situation, etc.), mental world ingredients (beliefs, values, outlooks on life, encyclopedic knowledge, preferences, emotions, etc.) and co-texts (such as the previously uttered words of communicators, and, in a broad sense, this also includes the communication history of the communicators). In addition, the identities of the two parties involved in the communication process, and even that of a third party, are also a type of resource, but one which is stored in the mental world of the communicators as relevant assumptions. These assumptions will then be activated through mental processing, influencing communication.

The employment of the aforementioned resources by the speaker in linguistic or paralinguistic ways can result in a particular influence or force, which we will call a pragmatic force (X. R. Chen 2004a). In terms of pragmatic force, some factors are considered to be default, such as the power one party has over the other party (arising from the power endowed by an institutional system, qualification, profession, etc.) if the interpersonal relationship between the two parties involved in the communication process is stable. Whether the force invoked by these factors is strong or weak depends on sociocultural attributes. For example, while differences in age, qualifications, or generational gaps do not create any obvious power relationships in Western societies, it is generally the case that such differences will trigger power relationships in Chinese society. In general, the more powerful party does not need to intentionally employ this force but rather, by default, assumes that it is recognized and accepted by the other party. Therefore, the way in which these communicators speak takes the existence of this default force to be a prerequisite and reference. In other words, it does not mean that no deliberate employment of this pragmatic force amounts to the same thing as no employment at all. In fact, on some occasions, the more powerful party might mention their powerful identity on purpose to remind the other party to respect the power relationship.

A specific communicative need in the current context forces the speaker to select a certain type of identity (or identities) to perform identity work, in order to generate the relevant pragmatic force to satisfy his/her communicative needs. For example:

(1)　Context: A school is organizing an activity to visit the New Village of Plum Garden. Ping Li is the party secretary and Cun Yang is a young party member of the school.
杨存：书记，明天的活动我可以不可以不参加？
李平：最好参加啊。
杨存：我明天要出去开个会。
李平：你是个党员，这样的活动你应积极参与才是。
杨存：好吧。

Cun Yang: *Secretary, may I not attend the activity tomorrow?*

Ping Li: *You'd better go.*

Cun Yang: *Tomorrow I have to go to a meeting.*

Ping Li: ***You are a party member****, and you should take an active part in such activities.*

Cun Yang: *All right.*

In Example (1), Cun Yang wants to be excused from the Party Day activity the following day. Li first employs a suggestion ('You'd better') as a way of refusing Ping Li's request. Then, when Yang proposes a concrete reason ('go to a meeting') for his absence to increase his chances of having his request granted, Ping Li, in an attempt to enhance the force of his persuasion, not only demands that Yang take part in the activity but also tries to make him reflect on the conduct expected of a party member by highlighting his party member identity, which is implicated by the use of the word 'should'. It can be seen from Cun Yang's subsequent positive response that Ping Li's emphasis on Cun Yang's party member identity has indeed fulfilled his communicative needs.

While the identity work in Example (1) is oriented towards the transactional needs of communication, the exchange below is more oriented towards the interpersonal needs of communication.

(2) Context: Wang is the office director, while Zhang is a temporary employee of the school who helps in the office by doing some trivial and routine work.
王主任：张总，去把这封信寄一下。
张师傅：哈哈，主任拿我开心了。我这就去。
Director Wang: **General Manager Zhang**, *go and mail this letter.*
Master Zhang: *Ha ha, Director, you're making fun of me. I will do it right now.*

In Example (2), Director Wang addresses Master Zhang by using 'General Manager Zhang' and thus constructs Master Zhang's identity as the general manager. This form of virtually constructed identity for the purpose of teasing satisfies his interpersonal need to construct an approachable image and promotes affiliation between the two parties, which leads to Master Zhang happily accepting the task, namely mailing the letter. As a matter of fact, Master Zhang is aware that Director Wang is trying to amuse him, and is therefore able to experience the friendly attitude (at least at that moment) of his superior.

In comparison to the identity work illustrated in Examples (1) and (2), which demonstrate how speakers construct particular identities for the other party in order to fulfil certain transactional or interpersonal needs, Example (3) is concerned with how the speaker constructs or emphasizes a specific identity for him/herself to satisfy his/her own communicative needs:

(3) Context: A husband has just returned home from work.
丈夫：你老公累了一天，今晚就有劳你忙饭了。
妻子：理解理解。没有问题。

> Husband: *Since **your husband** is exhausted from working all day, will you please prepare the dinner tonight?*
>
> Wife: *I understand, I understand. No problem.*

In Example (3), the husband uses the address form 'your husband' rather than the more common self-referential pronoun 'I', with the purpose of satisfying his transactional need to get his wife to do something, namely cooking dinner, based on their close husband–wife relationship. The wife immediately consents to the request, perhaps due in part to the effect created by her husband's identity work.

From the above example, we can see that identity is an important pragmatic resource that can be employed by communicators to satisfy their communicative needs. Identity information can be presented as rhetorical resources, rather than only being factual background information. The identity constructed or highlighted by the language user in the ongoing context can have a considerable impact on the effect created by his/her utterance.

Generally speaking, the selection of a specific pragmatic identity depends on (i) the pragmatic force of the relevant social identity that is generated in the current context; (ii) the perception and assessment of the communicative needs that communicators are faced with in the current context; and (iii) the pragmatic force generated by the employment of other means (such as linguistic choices and paralinguistic features). For people with normal pragmatic competence, the selection and construction of pragmatic identity is subject to the constraints of pragmatic balance between the communicative need and the pragmatic force generated (X. R. Chen 2004a). In other words, the more/less difficult it is to fulfil a communicative need, the more/less pragmatic force needs to be generated.

Under normal circumstances, the identity that a speaker constructs for him/herself, the hearer or a third party can accomplish pragmatic balance in communication (reflected in the positive and supportive reaction of the hearer), as shown in the aforementioned examples. However, at times, depending on the particular communicative need, the speaker's selection of pragmatic identity may not be appropriate, thus leading to pragmatic imbalance and, hence, some negative communicative effects. This so-called pragmatic imbalance refers to the imbalance between the communicative need and the pragmatic force. Two situations exist: in one case, the communicative need is large but the pragmatic force is small (as a result of insufficient pragmatic effort); in the other case, the communicative need is small but the pragmatic force is large (as a result of too much pragmatic effort). In terms of communicative needs, there are also many different situations, such as the speaker failing to appropriately consider the hearer's communicative needs, or inappropriately considering one specific need out of many communicative needs. For example, some powerful speakers can weaken or conceal the power relationship they have with their interlocutors to demonstrate affinity and equality, positioning each interlocutor on the basis of equality. However, they may resort to using the power relationship again if there is a need to do so.

The identity selected by a speaker for certain communicative needs in the current context will influence the communicative value of the discourse and determine its appropriateness, validity, importance, degree of politeness and so on. Different choices of identity produce different communicative values, resulting in different communicative effects. If pragmatic balance can be maintained, identity selection and construction can facilitate the achievement of one's intended communicative effect; otherwise it may hinder the fulfilment of one's communicative goal. Let us now consider the following example:

(4) Context: Qiang Ren and Gang Wang are colleagues. They have just played a few games of table tennis. Qiang Ren wants to play some more games, but Gang Wang does not want to.
任强：我们再玩一局吧。
王岗：（向门口看）校长来了。
任强：那就算了吧。
Ren: *Let's play another game.*
Wang: *(looking towards the entrance gate)* **The headmaster** *is coming.*
Ren: *Then forget it.*

In Example (4), if Gang Wang had refused the request too directly, Qiang Ren would probably have been unhappy, or might have asked Gang Wang again to play another game. The appearance of the headmaster in the communicative context rescues Gang Wang from a difficult situation. He immediately uses the headmaster as a cover, appropriately and successfully declining Qiang Ren's request. Obviously, Wang assumes the identity of a third party, namely the headmaster, as a type of pragmatic resource, which he uses for the purpose of refusing the request.

Therefore, it is clear that the fulfilment of communicative needs sometimes entails identity choices. Communicators involved in social interactions, who more often than not have multiple social identities, are 'polymers' with a variety of social identities. Yet, at a specific moment in the interaction, and particularly in the case of a specific utterance, they generally only choose one type of identity (however, occasionally more than one type of identity is chosen) to fulfil their communicative needs in the current communicative context. At this particular moment, other social identities still exist, but they are in a state of inertia or are 'being filtered', and only the chosen identity is turned into a pragmatic resource.

Discursive choices in identity work

The identity selected by language users to satisfy a specific communicative need in a certain context is realized by means of various linguistic and/or paralinguistic devices. Generally speaking, from the way one is speaking, the identity being assumed by the speaker can be judged. In other words, the way in which one speaks constructs one's pragmatic identity (of course, the prerequisite is that he/she has adequate pragmatic competence and speaks in accordance with the Maxim of Identity, which will be elaborated upon in Section 3.4 below). The most typical and definite way of constructing a pragmatic identity is by the use of address forms, such as 'General Manager Zhang' in Example (2). Now consider another example:

(5) 　　　　　　　　　　　告市民书
尊敬的市民朋友：
　您好！
　为全面了解当前南京城乡居民的幸福感受，市委市政府委托国家统计局江苏调查总队于12月15日、16日（周六、周日）组织"幸福都市"民意调查。本次调查不记名，以随机抽选形式进行（入户调查、随机问卷、电话访谈）。希望广大居民群众积极配合，共同推导南京幸福城市建设，衷心感谢您的支持与合作！

　　　　　　　　　　　　　　　　　　　　　　　　　　XX街道

A Letter to Citizens

Respectable ***citizen friends***:
　How are you?
　*To gain a comprehensive understanding of the sense of happiness of both urban and rural residents in Nanjing, the Municipal Party Committee and the Municipal Government has entrusted the Jiangsu Survey Team of the National Bureau of Statistics to conduct the 'Happy City' poll on 15 and 16 December (Saturday and Sunday). It will be conducted on randomly selected individuals in an anonymous way (including a door-to-door survey, a questionnaire and an interview via a phone call). It is hoped that **all residents** will actively cooperate, and promote Nanjing's construction of a happy city together. Thank you for your support and cooperation!*

　　　　　　　　　　　　　　　　　　　　XX Neighbourhood Committee Office

In general, the normal address form used in this type of letter to citizens is '(Respectable) citizens', but in Example (5), the administrators in the XX Neighbourhood Committee Office use 'Respectable citizen friends', taking the citizens to be 'friends'. The construction of a friend identity assists with the formation of a more approachable image for the administrators.

Another means by which identity can be constructed is the mode of reference. Reference includes speaker reference, such as 'your husband' in Example (3); hearer reference, such as 'all residents' in Example (5); and also a third-party reference, such as the 'headmaster' in Example (4). Here is another example:

(6) 祥龙辞岁，金蛇迎新！在过去的一年里，我成长了许多。而这一切都离不开老师您的教诲、鼓励和帮助！我深表感激！在蛇年来临之际，真心恭祝您阖家幸福，身体健康，万事如意！学生XXX敬上。

*The auspicious dragon bids farewell to the outgoing year and the golden snake welcomes the incoming new year! In the past year, I have grown up a lot, which would not have been possible without the edification, encouragement and help from you, **my teacher**! I appreciate it greatly! At this time of the incoming Year of the Snake, I sincerely wish you and your whole family happiness, good health and good luck in everything you do! Respectfully yours, **Your student** XXX.*

In Example (6), the person sending the blessing (i.e. performing an expressive speech act) first addresses the recipient with the word 'teacher', then signs the letter with the self-reference 'your student'. Both of these two forms of reference explicitly identify the sender's own identity as the recipient's student and, at the same time, position the recipient's identity as a teacher.

Another common and important form of identity construction is the use of a direct statement or positioning, such as Li's remarks in Example (1), namely 'you are a party member'. In this example, the speaker directly selects an identity for the hearer, but a speaker can also select an identity for him/herself by means of a direct statement. For example (Ren 2014):

(7) Context: Teacher A has to go to his university's office for a business meeting with the party secretary. However, he does not know the exact location of the party secretary's office, so he asks B, who is on duty at the porter's lodge, for some information.
甲：你好！我想问一下林书记办公室在哪？
乙：那你要登记一下。
甲：我是咱们学校老师。
乙：哦，那你到三楼301问一下。
甲：好的。谢谢啊。

A: *Hello! Could you tell me how I can find Party Secretary Lin's office?*
B: *You need to register here.*
A: **I'm a teacher here.**
B: *Oh, you can go to office No. 301 on the second floor. They will give you the information.*
A: *Okay. Thanks.*

In Example (7), A asks B for the room number of Party Secretary Lin's office. As a rule, B has to ask visitors to register before entering the building, and so asks A to do so. In response, A states his identity as being that of a teacher at the university. B's response demonstrates that A's identity claim is effective and his communicative need has been satisfied (i.e. obtaining information about the location of Secretary Lin's office without having to register).

As we will present a fully fledged discussion on the discursive choices that are available to construct pragmatic identity in Chapter 4, we now turn to the process of identity work.

3.3 Process of identity work

Choosing an identity is not a one-shot job. As communication unfolds, interactants can shift from one identity to another in order to fulfil their dynamically changing communicative needs. Such a process of identity shifting is readily observed when a speaker makes an immediate change in his/her identity claim or attribution. Consider Example (8):

(8) Context: A mother has called her son to come out and eat his meal, but he has stayed in his room playing and won't come out. His mother then utters the following:
儿子 …… 明明 …… 晓明 …… 陈晓明，快出来吃饭！
Son … Mingming … Xiaoming … Xiaoming Chen, come out and eat!

In Example (8), the mother continuously changes the way in which she addresses her son ('Son', 'Mingming', 'Xiaoming', 'Xiaoming Chen'). By using these different address forms, she constructs different stance-related identities (from being intimate, to close, then to friendly and then finally to distant) to indicate the change in her emotions to a final state of dissatisfaction. The identity shift process she presents happens over a very short period of time, clearly reflecting the dynamics of identity construction, which is closely related to changes in her communicative needs. At the beginning of the exchange, the mother is just routinely (and very intimately) conveying the transactional need of asking her son to come for his meal. However, due to her son's non-cooperation, her need to express her emotions intensifies, which is directly reflected in her choice of address forms.

Although Example (8) demonstrates the way in which identities can shift over a very short period of time, the dynamics of identity selection can also be evident at different stages during the same interaction. For example:

(9) Context: Professor Kunrong Han and Professor Renliang Xiao work in different universities but share similar interests in closely related research fields, and they have met each other many times at academic conferences. Professor Xiao has edited a textbook, which Professor Han thinks is particularly good, and he intends to choose it as the textbook for his own teaching. The following is a series of short text messages between the two professors.

韩坤荣：仁亮教授，我下学期上修辞学课，我看到你编的一本修辞学教材，觉得教程后面的练习很好，打算把它当教材。不知有没有可供参考的练习答案？若有电子版，能否发给我一份？谢谢！韩坤荣

肖仁亮：韩教授你好，答案只做了八个单元。我发给你，供参考。仁亮

韩坤荣：太好了。谢谢仁亮老弟。

Kunrong Han: **Professor Renliang**, *I am going to teach rhetoric next term, and I've noticed your newly edited textbook on rhetoric, and I find the exercises following the lectures to be particularly good, so I intend to use it as a textbook. I wonder, are there answers to the exercises for my reference? If there is an electronic version, could you send it to me? Thank you! Kunrong Han*

Renliang Xiao: *Professor Han, how are you? The answers to the exercises only cover eight units and I will send them to you for your reference. Renliang*

Kunrong Han: *Great! Thanks,* **brother Renliang**.

At the beginning of Example (9), Professor Han makes a request of Renliang Xiao, that is, he asks him for an electronic version of the textbook answers, by addressing Renliang Xiao as 'Professor Renliang' and giving his full name at the end of the message. This indicates that the emotional distance between the two professors is neither too distant nor too close (according to Chinese address practices, 'Professor Xiao' is relatively distant, and 'Professor Xiao Renliang' and 'Xiao Renliang' both sound too serious, 'Renliang' is relatively close and 'Professor Renliang' is somewhere in between in terms of emotional distance). Renliang Xiao not only agrees to Kunrong Han's request but also uses his own given name rather than his full name at the end of the message (the use of the address form 'Professor Han' is appropriate, after all, because the party being addressed is much older than the addressing party. If Renliang Xiao had addressed Kunrong Han as 'Professor Kunrong' in the same way as Kunrong Han had addressed him, it would have been viewed as being insufficiently respectful). Professor Han immediately shifts the address form to 'Brother Renliang', which immediately reduces the emotional distance between the two professors, and positions them as close friends.

The dynamics of identity selection can also be examined from a diachronic perspective. Specifically, the pragmatic identities that the two parties select at different stages in the communication process can change. For example:

(10)　Context: Hongyun Zhang has written to Zhigang Wang, the organizer of a conference, to inquire about a hotel room reservation. They have met each other several times before and are thus very familiar with one another. However, they have not seen each other recently. Zhigang Wang is slightly older than Hongyun Zhang, and therefore enjoys a small level of seniority.

邮件一：

王老师：您好！

刚才接到会务有关宾馆预定邮件，第1条提示似乎与我们团队订房有关，特来信问一下--我们是否需要将四月份-您帮助登记华达宾馆3个双人标间及个人信息反馈到elt2014信箱？我想应该是一回事，但以防万一。我将4月份我们之间的交流邮件附下面了，请王老师指示:-)

谢谢帮助！

张红云

Email One:

Teacher Wang: How are you?

I have just received an email from the conference organization team about our hotel room reservation, in which the first item appears relevant to our team reservation. That's why I'm sending you this email to inquire about this: Do we need to send to the email address elt2014 the information that you used to reserve three double rooms in the Huada Hotel in April? I assume that these are the same thing, but just in case, I've attached below the emails that we exchanged in April. Please advise, Teacher Wang.:-)

Thanks for your help!

Hongyun Zhang

邮件二：

张老师您好！

谢谢！已经为您及团队订好房间，勿念。

该邮件的主要目的是了解有哪些代表没有通过会议组自己订房了，以便掌握房源取向并及时调配。叨扰了。

祝好！

志刚

Email Two:

Teacher Zhang: How are you?

Thanks! I have successfully reserved rooms for you and your team, and please don't worry about it. And the purpose of that email was to know how many conference delegates have booked hotel rooms without the assistance of the conference organization team, so that we know more about their hotel booking preferences to be able to coordinate them in time. Sorry for bothering you.

Best wishes!

Zhigang

邮件三：

谢谢志刚这么快回复！你们工作做得很细，辛苦了，向你们致敬！

红云

Email Three:

*Thanks, **Zhigang**, for replying so quickly! You have done your work really considerately and carefully. You work really hard and I pay my respects to you!*

Hongyun

At the beginning of Example (10), when Teacher Zhang sends an email to inquire about a hotel room reservation for the conference (Email One), she uses the address form 'Teacher Wang' and ends the email with her full name 'Hongyun Zhang', which demonstrates that she has constructed relational identities with a large emotional distance. By using the last sentence 'Please advise, Teacher Wang', she further elevates the recipient's identity, increasing the interpersonal distance between them. However, in the reply email, when she observes that Zhigang Wang (Email Two) constructs an identity with an even higher social status than the one she had previously constructed (reflected in the use of '您' ('nin', meaning 'you') and '叨扰' ('bothering'), and the fact that Wang has used his given name rather than his full name at the end of the email), she changes her address form in her reply (Email Three) by using her given name and not her full name, which indicates a shorter distance between the two parties. The self-reference at the end of the email has also been shifted into her given name rather than her full name, and she thus constructs a more intimate relational identity than the one created in Email One.

3.4 Salience of identity work

The above examples illustrate that, most likely, communicators consciously construct identities for themselves, hearers or third parties in order to perform identity work. We can assume that a person with normal pragmatic competence generally has a sufficiently high level of identity awareness to be able to select an appropriate identity, according to the specific communicative context, to satisfy his/her communicative needs. In fact, in the field of pragmatics, our use of the words 'choose' and 'choice' is not new. For example, Verschueren (1999) points out that 'using language must consist of *the continuous making of linguistic choices*' (p. 55; italics in original); 'a theory of language use should, therefore, be able to make sense of this "making of choices"' (p. 56). In his eyes, 'a language user has no freedom of choice between choosing and not choosing, except at the level where he or she can decide either to use language or to remain silent' (p. 57). As long as language is used, choice-making is unavoidable, regardless of whether or not there are adequate choices or room to satisfy communicative needs.

We maintain that the same is true for identity choice; that is, as long as a person speaks, he/she has chosen some identity with which to speak. Actually, when no one speaks, there is no new discourse; and when no one speaks, there is no identity to speak of. No matter who says what, the identity chosen is based on existing identities, or perhaps on virtually constructed identities (e.g. fraudsters often pretend to be telecommunications or public security personnel, see Zhong and Zeng 2020).

The dynamic process of identity choice-making can be highly conscious or totally unconscious. Even in the latter case, we still believe that communicators have made a choice. Tracy, a well-known communication studies scholar, points out that the use of membership categorization devices might not always be conscious or highly strategic behaviour when she discusses identity selection (2002: 58).[3] At this time (and in the majority of cases), pragmatic identity selection is a form of default behaviour without a high degree of salience, and, therefore, the speaker's awareness of identity selection is relatively low.

The selection of a pragmatic identity can reflect the **pragmatic awareness** of communicators and also their **metapragmatic awareness**. In the former case, the identity a communicator chooses is in accordance with the default identity in the current context. His/her linguistic choice of both discourse content and the way of speaking (which refers primarily to address forms and reference, etc.) follows the Maxim of Identity.

Maxim of Identity: Communicate with the identity that is appropriate in the current communicative context.

As an example, let us consider a teacher named Qiang Zhang. When he teaches in class, his pragmatic identity is positioned as, or expected to be, a teacher by other people; when he is at home and communicates with his child, his pragmatic identity changes to that of a father, as positioned, or expected, by other people; when he is at home and talks with his wife, at that moment his pragmatic identity is positioned as, or expected to be, a husband by other people; when he is in his office and talks with colleagues, his pragmatic identity in his utterances is positioned as, or expected to be, a colleague by other people; when he talks to his superior, his pragmatic identity is positioned as, or expected to be, an inferior by other people; when he takes part in an academic conference by hosting a session, during his talk his pragmatic identity is positioned as, or expected to be, a host by other people. If, on the aforementioned occasions, the pragmatic identities that Zhang adopts are in accordance with people's expectations, or positioning, of his pragmatic identity, then he has followed the Maxim of Identity. On the contrary, if on some occasion he communicates without meeting these expectations – for example, if he considers himself to be the students' friend when teaching in class or treats his superior as his colleague when talking to him – then he is violating the Maxim of Identity, deliberately or unconsciously.

The Maxim of Identity emphasizes the appropriateness of discursive interaction, particularly the default correspondence between pragmatic identity and communicative context. As a result of this, the selection of pragmatic identity is more often than not default, as far as communicative behaviour in a specific communicative context is concerned. For the pragmatic identity that communicators choose, based on the Maxim of Identity, in certain communicative situations or for certain activity types to satisfy their communicative needs, we can refer to Richards's (2006) study and call this pragmatic identity a default identity. Returning to the above example, it can be seen that Qiang Zhang's default identity when teaching in class is a teacher; when talking to his office colleagues, a colleague; when talking to his superior at work, an inferior; and when hosting an academic conference session, a host. The opposite of a default (pragmatic) identity is, of course, a non-default identity, or deviational identity.[4] In the case of the aforementioned Teacher Zhang, if he positions his identity as his students' friend in class, then he is speaking with a deviational identity. By adopting this identity, and in order to highlight his attempts to become the students' friend, he would tend to use a different way of speaking (e.g. 'as your friend') from that adopted if he assumed the identity of a teacher. When a speaker deliberately and overtly communicates without adopting the default identity that has been assigned to him/her by each of the other parties in the conventional social relationship, thus violating the Maxim of Identity, he/she most likely has some particular purpose in mind. The speaker's intention might be to satisfy some unusual communicative need (such as to establish an equal, close or hostile interpersonal relationship), which will exert either a positive or a negative influence on social relations. We will discuss this in later chapters.

At the very least, the functioning of the Maxim of Identity presupposes the existence of the following factors:

a. Identity schema: the identity or identity relationship in accordance with the performance of certain behaviours in a certain communicative context, which are reflected in a series of assumptions, expectations, beliefs and so on of certain behavioural norms related to a certain identity. For example, in PhD dissertation proposal meetings, people expect experts to provide professional suggestions on the proposals submitted by PhD students. As an indication of the knowledge gap, the identity relationship between experts and PhD students is unequal and asymmetric. As members of the academic community, experts should follow various academic norms, rules and regulations. They are supposed to give information to PhD students that they will find helpful for completing their dissertations and the like.
b. Identity discourse: the default or unmarked discursive devices used to perform certain actions in accordance with certain identities or identity relationships. Again, take PhD dissertation proposal meetings as an example. Experts tend to adopt relatively formal ways of questioning when asking questions, and are relatively direct when providing suggestions. They tend to address PhD students by using their full names, whereas they address other experts by using 'Professor XXX', 'Teacher XXX' or 'Expert' and so forth.

If we say that the maxims of the Cooperative Principle are concerned with default assumptions regarding truth, quantity, relevance and means of expression when communicating information, and the maxims of the Politeness Principle involve assumptions about certain aspects of the appropriateness of communication, then we can say that the Maxim of Identity touches upon the various types of identity that communicators adopt when they are speaking. By referring to the situations where the maxims of the Cooperative Principle are deliberately and overtly violated, we can analyse the conversational implicature conveyed by speakers, and by referring to the situations where the maxims of the Politeness Principle are violated, we can evaluate the performance of the speaker's discourse from the perspective of politeness. Now, by referring to the situations where the Maxim of Identity is violated, we can perform a contextual analysis of the socio-psychological effects (X. R. Chen 2004b) that speakers try to convey, for example, whether or not the interpersonal distance is shortened. We can also analyse if the speaker's discourse is valid or appropriate. We will discuss this further in later chapters (Chapters 7, 8 and 9).

It is considered to be a reflection of the communicator's rational thinking when he/she selects an appropriate identity for communication purposes in a certain context and uses appropriate discursive devices (primarily forms of address and reference, etc.) to satisfy his/her communicative needs. It is also a reflection of the communicator's pragmatic awareness, demonstrating that he/she has normal pragmatic competence.

In the latter case, from the perspective of identity selection, the metapragmatic competence of communicators is also reflected in their metapragmatic awareness. This so-called metapragmatic awareness, simply speaking, refers to the reflective awareness that communicators have of each other's use of language.

> Language users are self-aware: we are aware not only of the choices we make when using language, but also the choices of others. … In other words, in using language to interact or communicate with others, participants must inevitably think about what others are thinking, as well as very often thinking about what others think they are thinking, and so on. And not only do participants engage in such reflexive thinking in using language, they are also aware of this reflexivity in their thinking, albeit to varying degrees. (Culpeper and Haugh 2014: 235, 237)

The degree of metapragmatic awareness that communicators have reflects their level of pragmatic competence. According to Culpeper and Haugh (2014), metapragmatic awareness or reflexive awareness (see also Lucy 2000) includes three main types – namely, (i) metacognitive awareness, concerning the reflective presentations of the cognitive status of information, such as whether it is known, new, expected, easily accessible (and so on) information for participants, as indicated by the use of 'I mean', 'that is' and so on; (ii) metarepresentational awareness, involving the reflexive representations of the intentional states of self and others in their beliefs, thoughts, desires, attitudes, intentions and so on, such as irony and echoic instances of language use; and (iii) metacommunicative awareness, concerning the reflexive interpretations and evaluations of talk, which arises as a consequence of our awareness of self and others as social beings, and includes interactional awareness and interpersonal awareness, such as the use of 'to be frank' and 'you know'.

In terms of metapragmatic awareness, X. Chen (2020) proposes a new categorization based on the key aspects of a speech event, as shown in Table 3.1.

Of these, the metapragmatic awareness of identity construction is primarily concerned with the metapragmatic awareness of the addresser, addressee and contact (two or multiple parties). Let us consider the following examples taken from the Modern Chinese Corpus at the Center for Chinese Linguistics (CCL) at Peking University:[5]

(11) Context: A mother is recalling her memories of sending her daughter to school.
但我不想看见她哭，我们在学校的门口分手。我把书包交给了她，我说：妈妈会给你写信，会给你打电话 … 我看见她的眼泪就那么一串串顺着脸颊无声地流了下来，我心疼极了。

But I didn't want to see her crying, so we separated at the school gate. I handed the school bag to her, and said: **Mom** *will write to you, call you … I saw her tears silently flowing down her cheeks and my heart was broken.*

(12) Context: A student expressed his resentment in his composition that Jinghua Huang, his teacher, paid little attention to him.
黄静华在这名同学的作文簿上写下这样的话："老师会关心你的，再也不会让你感到孤独了。"

*Jinghua Huang wrote this in the student's notebook: '****Your teacher*** *will take care of you and will never let you feel lonely again.'*

In Example (11), the speaker not only uses 'I' but also the definite self-reference form 'Mom' to address herself. The latter clearly highlights the speaker's identity in her utterance, which reflects the mother's metapragmatic awareness of her self-identity. Similarly, in Example (12), when leaving a message in the student's notebook, Huang does not use the usual 'I', but rather 'Your teacher', when referring to herself, to emphasize the teacher–student relationship. This use of identity markers demonstrates the teacher's metapragmatic awareness, and in comparison with the word 'I', this type of identity work enables the student to fully experience the teacher's care.

Above all, the awareness or salience of the pragmatic identity that is selected in verbal communication is a continuum. Identity selection occurs everywhere, no matter where the speaker is located. Relatively speaking, identity selection with a low degree of awareness is not rhetorical, whereas identity selection

Table 3.1 Categorization of Metapragmatic Awareness

Dimension of awareness	Gloss
Metapragmatic awareness of context	The addresser has reflexive knowledge about the temporal, spatial and situational aspects of the communicative event.
Metapragmatic awareness of addresser	The addresser has reflexive knowledge about the presence, roles, beliefs, intentions, expectations, desires, thoughts, feelings, attitudes, knowledge, abilities, etc. of self.
Metapragmatic awareness of addressee	The addresser has reflexive knowledge about the presence, roles, beliefs, intentions, expectations, desires, thoughts, feelings, attitudes, knowledge, abilities, etc. of others, including the addressee and a third party.
Metapragmatic awareness of contact (be it two or multiple parties)	The addresser has reflexive knowledge about (each other's expectations about) relations (such as relation types and closeness) between self and others.
Metapragmatic awareness of message	The addresser has reflexive knowledge about the nature, purpose, goals, importance, values, difficulties, credibility, etc. of the event going on at that moment, or the status of the information as being known, new, (un)expected, etc.
Metapragmatic awareness of text	The addresser has reflexive knowledge about formats, logic, clarity, conventions, etc. of conversation participation and text organization.
Metapragmatic awareness of code	The addresser has reflexive knowledge about linguistic (including style), dialectal and non-linguistic resources (including hand gestures, eye contact, facial expressions, emojis, emoticons, etc.) used at that moment.

with a high degree of awareness is rhetorical. The latter can be termed identity rhetoric (Yuan 2020) or interpersonal rhetoric (Leech 1983).

3.5 Contextual assessment

Communicators perform identity work in context. By this, we mean the following:

a. The communicative needs, particularly the transactional needs, which motivate identity work, arise in context;
b. The identity choices that are driven by the communicative needs are made, negotiated or even challenged in context;
c. The discursive choices used to construct, negotiate or challenge the chosen identity or identities are also made in context;
d. The dynamic process of identity work unfolds in context; and
e. Identity becomes perceptible to the communicators in context.

There are numerous definitions of context. However, it is beyond the scope of this book to review them all. Primarily, we wish to distinguish between a social approach and a cognitive approach at the risk of overgeneralization and oversimplification. Whereas Verschueren's (1999) context characterization is social, Sperber and Wilson's (1986) model is cognitive. Essentially, they are complementary rather than contradictory. After all, those aspects of the context that exist socially are cognitively represented and processed.

According to Verschueren (1999), the term 'context' denotes everything with which utterances are interadaptable or within which utterances are processed. Specifically, the contextual correlates of utterances can be represented as shown in Figure 3.2.

The physical world involves the dimensions of communication time and location, and they both have a bearing on linguistic choices, such as in the use of greetings (e.g. 'Good evening' is different from 'Goodnight'), and time and space deixis (e.g. 'here' vs 'there', 'today' vs 'yesterday', 'come' vs 'go'). Moreover, the speaker's and/or hearer's position in the physical world, such as their bodily posture, influences both the production and interpretation of utterances.

The social world involves primarily the various features of social settings or institutions. It covers factors such as the relations of dependence and authority, moral order in terms of rights and obligations, or power and solidarity, not only between the speaker and the hearer, but also between the speaker and/or the

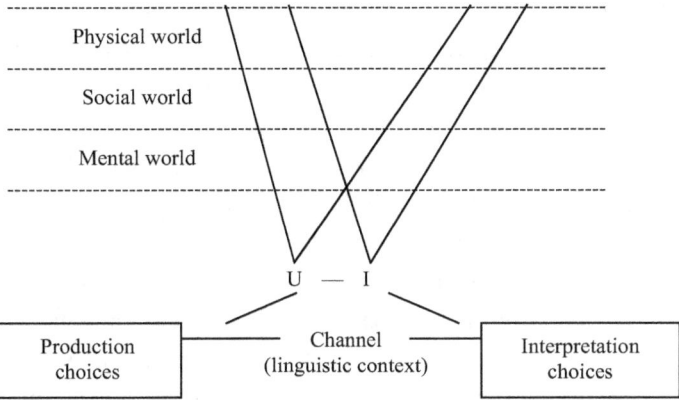

Figure 3.2 Contextual correlates (based on Verschueren 1999: 76)
Note: The broken horizontal lines are used to indicate that the three worlds do not have strict boundaries between them. U and I represent 'Utterer' and 'Interpreter', respectively.

hearer and what is being talked about. It also provides information about the degree of formality and expectancy of the current communicative event. Since relations like power and solidarity or dependence and authority do not exist or work on a single person, it is necessary to introduce the term 'relative social status'. Generally speaking, it is this relative social status rather than absolute social status that counts. Thus, the president of one company does not necessarily command verbal compliments or obedience from another company's clerk, even though the former appears to be on a higher social level than the latter.

The mental world involves both the speaker's and the hearer's psychological or mental states. It covers their world knowledge, expertise, expectations, ideologies, emotions, beliefs, desires or wishes, face wants, motivations, communicative intentions and suchlike.

As part of the communicative context, the number of speakers and/or hearers also affects how we talk. For instance, we use a hinting strategy more often in a multiparty situation than in a two-party situation (X. R. Chen 1998). Also, we are not supposed to criticize a child in the presence of some people.

Finally, the linguistic channel we communicate with, as well as the co-text of the utterances, also plays an important role in the production and comprehension of the current utterances. In conversation, the sequential context shapes our social actions via the use of language.

It is worth noting that context is not 'something out there' (Verschueren 1999: 109). Far from being static or given, context is generated during the course of language use. Although, in principle, every possible ingredient of the three 'worlds' can turn out to be a contextually relevant element, not all ingredients are simultaneously activated or mobilized during every moment of each occasion. Thus, contexts are created from a virtually infinite range of possibilities by the dynamics of the interaction between utterers and interpreters in relation to what is (or is thought to be) 'out there'. In other words, there are boundaries to the relevant context, even if they are unstable and permanently negotiable. It becomes necessary to discover these context boundaries in specific instances of language use, rather than impose a pre-conceived theoretical model on the context (Verschueren 1999: 109). That explains why Verschueren uses slanted lines in the diagram (Figure 3.2), which converge at Utterer (U) and Interpreter (I). The lines can be regarded as forming lines of vision for the interlocutors. Each aspect of the three worlds that fall within these lines of vision is seen to be activated or mobilized as a correlate of linguistic adaptability.

The cognitive context proposed by Sperber and Wilson (1986) conceives context as a mental or cognitive construct. It comprises a set of assumptions that are constructed under the guidance of the presumption of optimal relevance, and these assumptions are then used to interpret the current utterance. These assumptions come from a variety of sources, such as those activated background assumptions that are stored in our cognitive environment, those derived from the comprehension of preceding utterances, those obtained from processing the literal meaning of the current utterance and those retrieved from perceiving the situational context. As the ongoing interaction evolves, these assumptions will also change. Thus, context formation is open to choice and revision throughout the comprehension process (Sperber and Wilson 1986: 137).

Identity work is context-adaptive (X. R. Chen 2013a, 2018a; Yuan and Chen 2013). Communicators make a constant assessment of context and make adaptive identity choices.

First, identity work is interadaptable with the three 'worlds'. For example, in Example (4), Gang Wang avails himself of the sudden appearance of the school headmaster in the physical world, using his headmaster identity as a reason to refuse playing table tennis any longer.

Second, identity work is interadaptable with the linguistic channel and the co-text. Regarding the former, communicators sometimes change their identity when switching from one language to another or from the standard form of a language to a dialect. Regarding the latter, we need to consider Example (9) again.

We find that Professor Han adjusts his identity choice to adapt to the fact that Renliang Xiao uses his first name to address himself in the preceding turn.

In essence, identity work is a process of pragmatic cognition. During the process of verbal communication, the two parties involved need to identify and assess the other party's cognitive concepts, emotional states, sociocultural attributes, interests, linguistic competence, motives, contextual resources, intentions, personality, habits and so on to determine their own and the other party's communicative needs, which is what we call pragmatic cognition. Sperber and Wilson (1986/1995) also believe that the way of communicating reflects the relationship between the two parties involved, and communicators make an assessment about the other party's contextual resources and linguistic competence. We hold that the scope of pragmatic cognition reaches far beyond this, because it also covers the identities of two, or multiple, parties in communication. Whether or not the pragmatic identity selected by the speaker is appropriate depends on the psychological assessment conducted by the communicators on the discourse produced in the current context, and the content of this assessment includes various factors from the three worlds, namely those factors pertaining to the communicators, linguistic channels and co-texts.

4

Discursive practices of identity work

As stated in Chapter 2, pragmatic identity is the type of identity that communicators (speakers and hearers) choose to construct when they speak or understand a particular utterance or discourse, or the type of identity that speakers choose to construct for the other party or a third party. Essentially, communicators construct their pragmatic identity discursively. Since not every discursive effort is relevant to the construction of the speaker's identity, only discursive practices situated in verbal communication that are used to construct the speaker's pragmatic identity will be considered. In addition to focusing on verbal strategies, the role of non-verbal strategies in the process of indexing pragmatic identity will also be discussed.

4.1 Previous explorations

Although we can communicate our identity through our clothing or other means (such as a policeman's uniform, a construction worker's helmet or a nurse's white gown), the identity we intentionally or unintentionally adopt while speaking or understanding a specific utterance is constructed primarily through our discourse.

Scholars have conducted fruitful research on the ways in which communicators discursively construct their (pragmatic) identities. Some studies, for instance, have found that discursive practices and identities have a reciprocal relationship (as shown in Figure 4.1). The identity that one brings to an interaction influences the way of communicating; at the same time, the specific discursive practices that one chooses will correspondingly 'shape' who the person is taken to be (Tracy 2002; Tracy and Robles 2013).

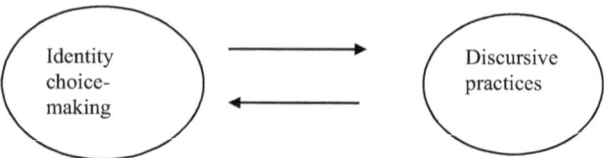

Figure 4.1 The reciprocal relationship between discursive practices and identities (based on Tracy 2002: 23)

In accordance with the research conducted by Tracy (2002: 22) and her collaborators, a speaker's discursive practices for the purpose of identity construction include person-referencing practices (words used to address others and to refer to self/others), speech acts (social acts performed through talk including criticizing, informing, praising, directing), sound of speech (dialect, ways of using one's voice, e.g. rate, pitch, quality), language selection (e.g. Chinese, English, Spanish, Vietnamese) and other simple building blocks, as well as more complex practices such as interactional structures (expected ways to pair utterances, rules about taking turns), style (degree of (in)directness characterizing how speakers talk), narrative (structure, content and style of stories), including interactive structure (the expected way to combine words, rules of turn conversion), directness (the directness or indirectness of the speaker's expression) and stance marking (linguistic, vocal and gestural means that convey an attitude towards a topic or conversational partner). Through her discussion and summary of the relationship between discourse and identity, Tracy (2002) integrates identities with discursive practices in a coordinated way and provides a helpful framework for analysing the construction of pragmatic identities in verbal communication. However, the framework can be further improved upon in terms of its descriptive adequacy (see X. R. Chen 2013a, 2018a).

Generally speaking, using language involves making constant linguistic choices, consciously or unconsciously, for language-internal (i.e. structural) and/or language-external reasons (Verschueren 1999). These choices can be made at every possible level of the linguistic structure: from macro to micro level, channel of communication, code, style, speech event (also called activity type), text or discourse, speech acts, propositional content, sentences, words and sounds. Any pragmatic theory should be capable of offering explanations for these choices. On the basis of Verschueren's (1999) proposal on the levels of the linguistic structure where linguistic choice-making occurs, X. R. Chen (2013a,

2018a) modifies Tracy's (2002) classification of discursive practices that are used to index identity (see Table 4.1).

The above classification of discursive practices based on the levels of discourse organization might comprehensively capture the discursive choices made by communicators during identity construction. However, it also has some shortcomings. There appear to be, for example, inevitable overlaps between the different levels – the construction of an expert identity involves strategies at the discoursal level (e.g. reference to certain topics, display of professional knowledge and opinions), the speech act level (e.g. performing the speech act of advising) and the lexical level (e.g. the use of jargon). Thus, analyses at different levels should not be taken as mutually exclusive. In addition, this classification based on different levels of the linguistic structure is only loosely associated with identity construction. Therefore, we have attempted to remodify it by drawing on Spencer-Oatey's (2008: 21) approach, which she uses to classify the discursive practices used in relational work (although her taxonomy revolves around rapport management, it can be adapted to categorize identity due to the inherent relationship between identity and rapport management, cf. Spencer-Oatey 2007). Taking into account the discursive characteristics of identity construction as well as the under-explored metapragmatics, I extend my earlier classification presented above (X. R. Chen 2013a, 2018a) and propose a new one, as shown in Table 4.2.

Next, I will discuss each of the domains listed above in which the discursive practices of pragmatic identity construction take place. However, I wish to highlight this caveat: by proposing such a framework, it is not my intention to confine the speaker's discursive efforts during pragmatic identity construction to a single domain. Instead, I wish to indicate that the speaker can make discursive choices in each of the domains for the purpose of constructing his/her chosen pragmatic identity.

4.2 Identity work in the address and referential domain

Address forms and referential expressions for self and others are two types of linguistic resources used for the explicit identity construction of the speaker, the hearer or a third party. The former are generally used vocatively, whereas the latter are used descriptively. Since both make a direct and explicit reference to the communicator's identity, we will consider them as forming one domain.

Table 4.1 Discursive Practices of Identity Construction

Discursive practice	Illustrations
Code	Languages (e.g. English, Chinese), dialects (e.g. north-eastern Mandarin), specific language codes, argot, etc. that suggest one's own or the other party's identity.
Style	Styles (e.g. a formal style, a casual style) that suggest one's own or the other party's identity.
Discoursal features	Discoursal or conversational organizational characteristics (e.g. turn-taking behaviour) that suggest one's own or the other party's identity.
Discourse content	Propositional content (e.g. topics, information, opinions, presuppositions) that suggest one's own or the other party's identity.
Ways of communicating	Ways of speaking (e.g. degree of directness and degree of engagement when expressing thoughts) that suggest one's own or the other party's identity.
Speech acts	Speech acts (e.g. criticizing, praising, advising, declaring) that suggest one's own or the other party's identity.
Address forms	Address forms that suggest one's own or the other party's identity.
Grammar	Grammatical features (e.g. personal pronouns, tag questions) that suggest one's own or the other party's identity.
Lexical features	Vocabularies (e.g. discourse markers, jargon, modal particles) that suggest one's own or the other party's identity.
Phonetic features	Phonetic features (e.g. pitch, rate, quality, accent, received pronunciation) that suggest one's own or the other party's identity.
Paralinguistic features	Gestures, distance, eye contact and other paralinguistic resources that suggest one's own or the other party's identity.

Table 4.2 Domains of Identity Work

Domain of identity work	Means of identity work
Address and referential domain	self-address terms; other-address terms; self-referential expressions; other-referential expressions; third-party-referential expressions; etc.
Illocutionary domain	self-identity claims; other-identity attributions; advice; commands; etc.
Stylistic domain	language, dialect; formality; indirectness; social deixis; jargon; identity markers; attitudinal or emotional particles; etc.
Participation domain	format of the discourse; turn-taking; participating footing; etc.
Non-verbal domain	gesture; speech rate; speech quality; accent; standard pronunciation; etc.

Note: Spencer-Oatey's (2008: 21) framework also includes 'discourse domain', which 'concerns the discourse content and discourse structure of an interchange', such as 'topic choice and topic management' and 'the organization and sequencing of information'. I exclude this domain from the above classification because it partly overlaps with some of the domains that I have included, such as illocutionary and participation domains. 'Address and referential domain' is partly extracted from Spencer-Oatey's (2008) original stylistic domain (which includes 'genre-appropriate terms of address or use of honorifics'), because it is of particular relevance to identity work in Chinese communication. Referential expressions used by communicators are considered at the same time because they are also highly relevant to identity work in Chinese communication.

An address form is perhaps the most direct discursive approach that is employed in the relational construction of speaker and listener identities. It includes forms of self-address, other-party-address and third-party-address. For example:

(1) Context: The following is an email written by a teacher to his former mentor (the content has been modified slightly).

X老师好！
学生这次写信又是要麻烦老师您了。☺
有个文件需要请老师您写个简要的评语。具体请见附件。这个 是我校MTI硕士论文的写作要求。前两天学校开学委会，要求这个文件需要提供相应专家的评议意见。
辛苦老师您了。谢谢老师！

学生：吴XX

Dear Teacher X [the family name of the mentor],
  Your student is writing at this time to trouble **you** *[honorific form],* **my teacher***, again.* ☺
  There is a file I need to request of **you** *[honorific form],* **my teacher***, to write a brief comment on. Please see the attachment for details. It is a requirement of our school's MTI master thesis. Two days ago, the school held a meeting, demanding that comments from corresponding experts should be provided.*
  Thank you [honorific form] for your help!
  Your student*,*

XX Wu

When writing letters, including emails, the use of address terms can often directly point to the relational identities of the two parties involved in the communicative process. In Example (1), student XX Wu not only uses 'Teacher X' but also 'my teacher' and 'you' (honorific form) several times to refer to the addressee. This method of referring to the teacher foregrounds the other party's identity as the teacher of the author of the email. In addition, the author also uses 'student' instead of the common self-mention device 'I' to refer to himself in the body of the email. Once again he uses 'your student', rather than simply writing down his name, in the signature at the bottom of the email to highlight his identity in relation to the other party.

Sometimes the address forms or referential expressions used by the communicator do not necessarily point to the true identities of the two interlocutors or a third party. For instance:

(2) Context: Li and Chen are chatting online. Li is younger than Chen.
李：陈哥，你用的手机是HTC吗？HTC可以双开双待。
陈：不是，是三星。
李：哦。三星酷。我刚换了个HTC，挺不错。华刚兄弟也买了，所以向陈哥推荐。
陈：谢谢李兄哦

Li: *Hi, **Bro Chen**, is your cell phone a HTC? HTC now produces dual-mode mobile phones.*

Chen: *No, it is a Samsung.*

Li: *Oh. Samsung, that's cool. I've just bought a HTC and it's pretty good. Our **buddy [brother] Huagang** has also bought one, so I recommend it to you, **Bro Chen**.*

Chen: *Thank you, **Bro Li**.*

In Example (2), Li refers to Chen as 'Bro [elder brother] Chen' and then uses 'our buddy [brother] Huagang' to refer to a third party; in return, Chen refers to Li using 'Bro [elder brother] Li' (note that in Chinese, a man may use 'elder brother' to address a male friend regardless of which one is older). However, they are not actually siblings. This constitutes an instance of the so-called kinship term generalization (Chen and Ren 2020; Ren and Chen 2019). In Chinese society, the address form surname/first name + 'brother' (or 'elder brother', 'younger brother') is often used by the speaker, not to refer to actual siblings, but to good (male) friends, in order to build an intimate relationship with the other party.

Some address forms fall into the scope of social deixis, encoding the social status of, as well as the relationship between, communicators. These address forms include endearments (e.g. (my) darling, love, sweetie), family/kinship terms (e.g. mum(my), dad(dy), grandma, granny), familiarizers (e.g. guys, mate, folks, bro), first names, titles and surnames, honorifics and so on. Communicators can construct self- and/or other-identities by selecting different social deixis.[1] Consider the following example:

(3) Context: In a WeChat group of old classmates, George gives out a bundle of online red packets.[2] His classmates who have received them express their gratitude to George one after another.
George: (在微信群里发了红包)
JGM: 谢谢！
ZXP: 谢谢老同学的红包！恭祝鼠年大吉！
ZDL: 谢谢永强! 新年快乐！

Dawn: 谢谢老同学的红包！

George: *(gives out red packets in the WeChat group)*

JGM: *Thank you!*

ZXP: *Thanks for the red packet, **my old classmate**! Wish you good luck in the Year of the Rat!*

ZDL: *Thank you, **Yongqiang**! Happy New Year!*

Dawn: *Thanks for the red packet, **my old classmate**!*

In Example (3), when expressing gratitude to George for giving out a red packet, both ZXP and Dawn use 'old classmate' to address him, whereas ZDL uses his first name. The former highlights their identity as classmates, while the latter only denotes the close social distance between himself and George.

4.3 Identity work in the illocutionary domain

According to Spencer-Oatey (2008: 21), the 'illocutionary domain' associated with rapport management concerns 'the rapport-threatening/rapport-enhancing implications of performing speech acts' like apologies and thanks. In our case, it concerns how certain speech acts are performed in the service of identity work. For example, communicators can construct self- or other-identity by performing identity-indexing using assertives, directives or declarations.

Assertives and identity construction

(4) 各位游客，大家下午好：
欢迎大家来到美丽的九寨沟。我是黄艳，来自XX旅游公司，是大家今天的导游，大家可以叫我小黄，也可以叫我黄导。很荣幸成为你们的导游，期待我的服务让您满意。

Dear Tourists, good afternoon:

*Welcome to the beautiful Jiuzhai Valley. I'm Yan Huang, from XX Travel Company. **I'm your tour guide today**. You can call me Huang or Guide Huang. I'm very honoured to be your guide. I am looking forward to making you feel satisfied with my service.*

In Example (4), the speaker Yan Huang makes a straightforward self-identity claim, not only telling visitors her own name and affiliation but also directly stating that she is their 'tour guide today'. Now, consider the following series of real estate advertisements (X. R. Chen 2018c):

(5) a. 您将成为东方高层人士
 You will be **a VIP of the Orient**
 b. XXX为每个成功的广州人建造一间别墅！
 XXX builds a villa for every **successful Cantonese**!
 c. 爱家的男人住百合
 The man who loves his family lives in Baihe

The statements in Example (5) involve attributing an identity to the recipient of the discourse. Real estate advertisers, through the employment of assertives, have constructed the identities of their potential buyers as 'a VIP of the Orient', a 'successful Cantonese' and 'the man who loves his family'. Specifically, while identity construction is achieved in Example (5a) through a complete statement, it is achieved in Example (5b) (in fact, this can also be taken as a commissive) and Example (5c) through a presupposition.

Directives and identity construction

(6) Context: During a doctoral viva, Professor Z gives his advice (Ren 2012).
 Z教授：XXX。
 学生：嗯。
 Z教授：我我还是接着W教授的讲，W教授讲的这两个方法呢确实就是说非常非常典型的。你要学会把专家的观点把它揉在一起。刚才W教授给你也说了，这个Y教授也讲了，(完了以后你可以)把他两个，一个就是刚才W教授讲的这个基于语料的这种方法，你可以用事件，就是按人工的，用 Leech 的方法去标注，还有一种是大量的，基于大量的语料库，用50到100万的，你广泛地去搜集，不跟事件相关，那个你就分析词频，搭配，就是你感兴趣的一些转述的词，比如说 report。
 学生：嗯。
 Z教授：还有according to，像这些，你把它挑出来，你做几个典型词。
 学生：嗯。
 Professor Z: *XXX [name of the student].*
 Student: *Mm.*

Professor Z: *I would like to continue with what Professor W has just said. The two methods Professor W has just mentioned are indeed very, very typical.* **You need to learn to put together the views of different experts.** *Just now, Professor Y told you about what Professor W had suggested. Then you can combine the two. One is the method based on data mentioned just now by Professor W. And according to this method,* **you can perform manual tagging based on the events and by adopting the method proposed by Leech. Another method is to use a corpus containing numerous words. You can collect some materials and build a corpus of about half to one million words. You only have to analyse word frequency, collocation and the reporting verbs that you are interested in instead of events,** *for example, 'report'.*

Student: *Mm.*

Professor Z: *And 'according to', like these words.* **You can single them out and analyse several typical ones.**

Student: *Mm.*

In Example (6), Professor Z makes a number of suggestions (such as 'You need to learn to put together the views of different experts', 'you can perform manual tagging based on the events and by adopting the method proposed by Leech', 'You only have to analyse word frequency, collocation and the reporting verbs that you are interested in instead of events', and 'You can single them out and analyse several typical ones'). In this context, giving advice is a typical speech act that is unique to experts. The implementation of such a speech act directly constructs the professor's expert identity. Consider another example:

(7) Context: Interacting with his students in the classroom, Mr Zhang attempts to go over what he taught during the last session in order to inspire thinking.

老师：**Grice 的合作原则包括哪些准则？**

学生：Grice 的合作原则包括质准则、量准则、相关准则和方式准则。

老师：很好。你觉得 Grice 的这四条准则如何？

学生：我个人觉得这四条准则好像不是在同一个层面上。

老师：**具体说呢？**

学生：质准则与讲真话有关系，量准则与讲多讲少有关系，相关准则与话题连贯有关系，而方式准则与说话方式有关系。讲真话好像是一个道德要求，而其他的几条与道德无关。

老师：说得太好了。也确实有学者这样批评Grice的。后来的学者在提出改进模式时就放弃了第一条准则。

Teacher: **What maxims are included in Grice's Cooperative Principle?**

Student: *Grice's Cooperative Principle includes the Maxim of Quality, the Maxim of Quantity, the Maxim of Relation and the Maxim of Manner.*

Teacher: *Very good.* **What do you think of Grice's four maxims?**

Student: *I personally feel that these four maxims do not seem to operate on the same level.*

Teacher: **Specifically?**

Student: *The Maxim of Quality is related to telling the truth, the Maxim of Quantity concerns the amount of information given, the Maxim of Relation is associated with topic coherence and the Maxim of Manner has something to do with the way of speaking. While telling the truth seems to be a moral requirement, the others have nothing to do with morality.*

Teacher: *Bravo. Indeed, some scholars have criticized Grice in this way. Later scholars gave up the first maxim when they proposed improved models.*

As shown in Example (7), questioning is a common method used by teachers in the classroom setting. The questions asked can be display questions or referential questions. While the former refers to questions whose answers are determined, the latter refers to those that have no definite answers and accommodate various opinions that can be freely expressed by students. All of Mr Zhang's questioning speech acts construct his identity as a teacher. In addition, providing positive feedback ('Very good' and 'Bravo') is a form of speech act that is often implemented by teachers in the classroom, and thereby marks their identity as a teacher.

Declarations and identity construction

(8) Context: The following are the opening remarks given by the chairman of a PhD dissertation defence committee.

博士论文答辩现在开始。首先我把答辩专家委员会组成向大家介绍一下。这位是XX大学博士生导师XXX教授。(鼓掌声) 这位是XXX大学博士生导师XX教授 … 我是来自XXX大学的XXX。(鼓掌声)下面我简要讲一下答辩的流程。

Now the PhD dissertation defence begins. First, I'd like to introduce the dissertation defence committee to you. *This is Professor XXX, PhD supervisor from XX University. (applause) This is Professor XX, PhD supervisor from XXX University … I'm XXX from XXX University. (applause) Next, let me briefly introduce the procedure undertaken during the defence.*

In Example (8), the speaker's utterance 'Now the PhD dissertation defence begins' is taken to be a declaration that constructs his identity as the chair of the defence committee. This identity is further confirmed when he introduces the other members of the committee. In accordance with university regulations, it is the responsibility of the chair of the defence committee to implement such presentations. Consider another example:

(9) Context: The following is an announcement given by an emcee at the start of a wedding ceremony.
现在我宣布，新郎XX、新娘XX的新婚典礼正式开始！
Now I announce that the wedding ceremony of Groom XX and Bride XX has officially started!

According to our world knowledge, we can infer that the speaker's identity in Example (9) is the emcee of the wedding ceremony – in Chinese weddings, it is generally the emcee who announces the beginning of the wedding ceremony.

Many other types of speech acts used in identity construction have not been exemplified or discussed here. Although it has been observed that, in a specific context, appropriately employed speech acts can perform the function of indexing identities, it should be noted that not every type of speech act – for example, requesting, complaining, criticizing – can do so. Thus, it is advisable to integrate speech act performance with other discursive practices (e.g. address forms) when accounting for the process of identity construction, even if a specific speech act is closely associated with the construction of a certain type of identity.

4.4 Identity work in the stylistic domain

According to Spencer-Oatey (2008: 21), the 'stylistic domain' in relation to rapport management concerns 'the stylistic aspects of an interchange, such as choice of tone (for example, serious or joking), choice of genre-appropriate lexis and syntax and choice of genre-appropriate terms of address or use of honorifics'. Similarly, in the stylistic domain in relation to identity work, there are also a great many discursive practices that can be used to construct a pragmatic identity. Here, we will only focus on some common types: (i) code, (ii) style, (iii) social deixis, (iv) jargon, (v) identity markers, (vi) (im)politeness, and (vii) modal words. Moreover, we subsume the choice-making of address forms mentioned by Spencer-Oatey (2008) into the address and referential domain (see Section 4.1) together with referential expressions. It should be noted that code switching in dynamic communication also constitutes a type of stylistic choice. In addition, the choice between accent and standard pronunciation also counts.

Code-choice and identity construction

The code-choice that we are discussing here refers to the communicator's choice of a specific type of language (e.g. English, Chinese), dialect (e.g. Mandarin, north-eastern Mandarin) or argot to construct salient self or other identities.

When we speak, we cannot avoid using a language or dialect. However, for the majority of the time, we do not intentionally choose a language or dialect, let alone relying on such choice-making to suggest a specific identity. We might say that when a Chinese person who can speak Chinese actually speaks in Chinese, we obtain one piece of information about his/her identity: being able to speak Chinese. Of course, it is not correct to infer that he/she is Chinese simply because he/she speaks Chinese.

In this section, we focus on those interlocutors who have the ability to communicate (more or less) in two or more languages or dialects. They often conduct code switching in their communication, that is, switching from one language to another. Consider the following example:

(10) Context: Two trainees are chatting in a Nanjing driving school.
 学员$_1$: 你是老师？
 学员$_2$: 是的。教英语。
 学员$_1$: **Really? I just returned from Canada. 我是学管理的。**
 Trainee $_1$: *Are you a teacher?*
 Trainee $_2$: *Yes. [I] teach English.*
 Trainee $_1$: ***Really? I just returned from Canada. I major in management.***

In Example (10), when Trainee$_1$ hears that Trainee$_2$ is an English teacher, he immediately switches to English, thereby constructing his own identity as an English speaker. Constructing a common identity between the two trainees (for an English teacher is supposed to be able to speak English) is objectively conducive to reducing the psychological distance between the two parties. Later in the same turn, Trainee$_1$ switches to Chinese since this context is a Chinese-speaking environment. Therefore, he finally makes salient his default identity as a Chinese person, an identity which he has in common with the other party.

In addition, we consider another type of code switching, that is, from Mandarin to a dialect or from a dialect to Mandarin. This also brings about the transition of current pragmatic identities. Consider the following example:

(11) Context: Teacher Zhang is chatting with his student Li.
张老师：你是姜堰人？
李同学：是啊。
张老师：（用姜堰话口音）那我们是正宗的老乡啊！
李同学：（用姜堰话口音）您是姜堰哪儿的？
张老师：（用姜堰话口音）溱潼的。
李同学：难怪听到老师说话就觉得很亲切呢！

Teacher Zhang: *Are you from Jiangyan District?*

Student Li: *Yes.*

Teacher Zhang: **(in a Jiangyan accent)** *Then we are indeed fellow townsmen!*

Student Li: **(in a Jiangyan accent)** *Which town in Jiangyan District do you come from?*

Teacher Zhang: **(in a Jiangyan accent)** *Qintong Town.*

Student Li: *It's no wonder then that when I first heard your voice, I felt like being friends with you, my teacher!*

Prior to the events in Example (11), the conversation between the two individuals was in Mandarin Chinese. Teacher Zhang then realizes that Student Li's accent is rather like that of his hometown, so he asks the other party for confirmation. When the student confirms that he is indeed from Jiangyan District, Teacher Zhang not only indirectly states that he is also from Jiangyan District ('we are indeed fellow townsmen') but also uses Jiangyan dialect to construct his own identity as a Jiangyan inhabitant. Li then immediately makes a speech accommodation by using Jiangyan dialect when asking Teacher Zhang which town in Jiangyan District he comes from. It can be seen that the code switching performed by the two parties from Mandarin to their hometown dialect jointly builds their relational identity as fellow townsmen. Besides, such an additional identity (for their current relational identities are primarily teacher and student) emotionally bridges the psychological distance between them. Student Li's response provides indirect evidence of this.

It should be noted that not all instances of code switching are related to the construction of pragmatic identities. For example, in foreign language teaching, teachers often switch between two languages. However, under such circumstances, this is done not to construct a specific pragmatic identity but to achieve specific teaching goals, such as broadening language knowledge and suchlike.

Style and identity construction

Our concern here is the communicators' selection of certain styles (formal style, casual style, etc.) to indicate their own or others' identities. Generally, while a formal style is manifested in the frequent use of formal vocabularies, low-frequency vocabularies, long and complex sentences, sentences with impersonal elements as subjects, sentences with nominalized elements and a complete structure, an informal style is characterized by a more frequent use of particles, high-frequency words, short sentences with relatively simple structure, nouns and pronouns that refer to subjects, abbreviated forms, elliptical sentences and little nominalization.

The communicators' choice of style is influenced by many factors including the relationship between the two parties, amongst others. For example, the closer the two parties are to each other, the less formal their manner of speaking. If topics and situations are both taken into consideration, we can make even more accurate judgements. Let us compare the following two invitation letters:

(12) a. Context: Mr Ping Wang, manager of a company, invites Mr Yu Li, manager of another company, to come to Nanjing for the International Horticultural Exhibition. They have not met each other before.

尊敬的李经理：
　　下一届园博会将于2019年10月15日至10月22日在南京举行，特邀请贵方参加此次交易会，本公司总经理和销售代表将在那里与贵方会晤。本公司的一些新产品也将在摊位上展出。园博会后我方将安排贵方参观本公司的基地。
　　如果贵方决定来访，我方将寄去正式邀请函。
　　XX公司销售部经理
　　　　　　　　　　　　　　　　　　　　　　　　王平敬上

Distinguished Manager Li:
　　Hope this email finds **you [honorific form]** well.
　　The next International Horticultural Exhibition will be held in Nanjing between 15 and 22 October 2019. The attendance of **your honour** at the fair is highly anticipated. There the general manager and sales representatives of **our company** will have a meeting with **your honour**. Some of **the company's** new products will also be displayed at our booth as scheduled. After the Expo, **our side** will arrange for your honor to visit our base.
　　If **your honour** decides to come to visit, **our company** will send you an official invitation letter.
　　Yours respectfully,
　　Ping Wang
　　Sales manager of XX Company

b. Context: Mr Ping Wang, manager of a company, invites Mr Yu Li, manager of another company, to come to Nanjing for the International Horticultural Exhibition. The two have been friends for many years.

李兄好！
　　下一届园博会将于2019年10月15日至10月22日在南京举行，欢迎李兄来参加此次交易会。到时我们的总经理和销售代表会给老兄安排好。我们会有一些新产品展出。园博会后我们将安排参观基地。
　　确定后别忘告知我一下哦，我让人给你寄正式邀请函。
　　　　　　　　　　　　　　　　　　　　　　　　王平

Dear **Bro [elder brother] Li**,
　　The next International Horticultural Exhibition will be held in Nanjing between 15 and 22, October, 2019. **Brother Li** is welcome to participate in this fair. Our general manager and sales representatives will arrange this for you, my bro! We will display some new products at that time. After the Expo, we will arrange for you to visit our base.
　　Don't forget to let me know if you decide to come. I will ask someone to send you an official invitation letter.
　　Ping Wang

The two distinct writing styles used in the above invitation letters mirror the different social relationships between the inviter (Ping Wang) and the invitee (Yu Li). In Example (12a), Ping Wang uses a rather formal style (honorifics 'distinguished' and 'yours respectfully', the address form 'Manager Li', self-references 'our side' and 'our company', the other-reference 'your honour', formal words 'have a meeting' and 'anticipated', etc.) to construct his self-identity as the sales manager of XX Company and Yu Li's other-identity as the manager of another company. In contrast, in Example (12b), Ping Wang employs a rather informal style (the other-reference 'Bro [elder brother] Li', informal words 'at that time', 'arrange' and 'don't forget', etc.) to construct their relational identities as friends.

In daily routines, an individual often switches between styles[3] during the course of an interaction. The term 'style switching' refers to the switching that occurs between different styles of communication. In keeping with the phenomenon of code switching discussed above, style switching generally tends to be identity-sensitive. Consider the following example:

(13)　　Context: The two interlocutors are having an academic discussion during a seminar.
　　　　张: 谢谢您的发言，听了您的报告后我很受启发。
　　　　王: 谢谢，您客气了。欢迎您多提宝贵意见。
　　　　张: **不敢**。我就是想问下您用的语料是从什么地方来的。
　　　　王: 我用的是一个现成的语料库，在网上可以直接免费使用的。

张: 哦，太好了。可以跟咱分享一下网址么？
王: 没问题，我回头写给你.
张: **太好了**，谢谢。
王: 不谢。咱们做研究都不容易的。
张: 谢王兄。

Zhang: *Thanks for **your [honorific form] report**. After listening, I am very much inspired.*

Wang: *Thank you, **you [honorific form] are very welcome**. Any of your [honorific form] opinions are welcomed and **valued**.*

Zhang: **You flatter me**. *I just want to ask where **you [honorific form]** collected the data from.*

Wang: *I used a ready-made corpus, which can be used for free online.*

Zhang: **Wow, great**. *Can you share the website with **me [intimate form]**?*

Wang: *No problem. I will write it down for **you** later.*

Zhang: **Great**. *Thank you.*

Wang: *Not at all. It is not easy for all of **us [intimate form]** to do research.*

Zhang: **Thanks, elder bro Wang**.

In Example (13), both parties have shifted their use of style, that is, from initially using a formal style to subsequently using a more casual one. More specifically, at the beginning of the interaction, Zhang and Wang use a variety of pragmalinguistic features that are characteristic of a formal style, demonstrated by the use of the honorific 'your ("nin")', flattering the other party by taking his speech to be a 'report' (this word is associated with something delivered by an official or a senior researcher), saying that the other party's 'opinions' are 'valued', providing a polite response to the other party's praise ('You are very welcome'), and using a self-depreciatory expression 'You flatter me'. At that moment, the two parties interactionally construct their identities as conference delegates. However, in the second half of the interaction, the style used by the two has undergone a significant change, which can be reflected in the following pragmalinguistic features: exclamations ('Great'), the use of 'you' that suggests a closer social relationship and is in marked contrast to 'nin', the use of the intimate forms for 'me' and 'us', the use of an elliptical form of 'thank you' ('thanks') and so on. It can be observed that the above instance of style switching has an effect on the relational identities of the two parties and temporarily shortens the social distance between them. This style shift can help the interlocutors to achieve their communicative goals (Zhang's wish to obtain from Wang the website address for the free corpus, enhancing the emotional states of both parties, etc.).

Jargon and identity construction

Jargon is another type of expression that can clearly convey information about a speaker's identity. Consider Example (14) (adapted from Chen et al. 2013):

(14) Context: A patient with a cerebral haemorrhage is asking a consultant about a related condition.

咨询顾问：严重在哪儿呢？大小便失禁那块儿？

咨询人：嗯嗯嗯。

咨询顾问：没什么太大的事，啊，他就是，什么，脑部神经受压迫，啊，压迫了咱们肢体神经，语言神经，导致你卧床。大脑意识没有消退的话呢，证明脑细胞受损还不是很严重，… 明白吧？

咨询人：啊，明白。

Consultant: *Where do you think it is serious?* **Incontinence?**

Patient: *Mm.*

Consultant: *Nothing serious, ah. It is, what, that* **the brain nerves are oppressed**, *ah, our* **limb nerves** *are oppressed,* **language nerves** *are oppressed, causing you to be bedridden. If* **your brain consciousness has not degraded**, *it suggests that the damage to the brain cells has not been very serious, … understand?*

Patient: *Ah, yes.*

In Example (14), the consultant uses a series of medical terms such as 'incontinence', 'the brain nerves are oppressed', 'limb nerves', 'language nerves', 'brain consciousness has not degraded' and suchlike in a very short utterance and thereby constructs his identity as an expert in pathology.

Sometimes, speakers directly mention terms in a foreign language to highlight their professional background. Consider Example (15) (adapted from Chen et al. 2013):

(15) Context: A student and a professor are participating in a PhD dissertation proposal meeting. (The words highlighted in bold were originally expressed in English.)

学生：嗯，Jackendoff 2005 年应该是，他这篇文章里面，他是发在 *Cognition* 上面的。

教授：对，对对。

学生：他说他的 parallel structure 跟 processing 是 compatible，然后他说 processing 也可以成为一个 component 当时 …

教授：哦，对，他是说他的 parallel architecture 可以和 processing，他认为这是他这个系统的一个长处、优点。

学生：对。

教授：但是这并不是说，还要和这个语言知识和语言使用，因为Jackendoff 是 Chomsky这一派的，他也，虽然也说了语言知识和语言使用呢，这个这个，不是特别分得开。但是呢，有时候，你还得总体上得分一下，不然，要不你有时候就没法操作，因为什么东西储存在头脑之中的，什么东西实际是使用的过程，这两者是两个领域，一个 linguistic theory 研究的，一个是 psycholinguistics 研究的。

Student: *Mm.* **Jackendoff** *2005, it should be this. In his article, he published it on* **Cognition***.*

Professor: *Yes, right.*

Student: *He said that his* **parallel structure** *and* **processing** *are* **compatible***, and then he said that* **processing** *can also become a* **component***. At that time …*

Professor: *Ah, yes. He said that his* **parallel architecture** *can go together with* **processing***. He thinks this is the strength and advantage of his system.*

Student: *Yes.*

Professor: *But this is not to say that this should be integrated with language knowledge and language use because* **Jackendoff** *is with* **Chomsky***. Although he also said something about language knowledge and language use, this – this – this can hardly be separated. But sometimes, you still have to distinguish between them; otherwise, sometimes you will not be able to operate on them. Because what is stored in the mind and what is actually used are two separate fields. While one is researched under* **linguistic theory***, the other is researched within the scope of* **psycholinguistics***.*

In Example (15), both parties adopt the names of foreign linguists ('Jackendoff' and 'Chomsky') and some linguistic terms (such as 'parallel structure', 'processing', 'compatible', 'component', 'parallel architecture', 'linguistic theory' and 'psycholinguistics'). In addition to some specialized knowledge given in Chinese by the two, the use of these English names and terms fully constructs their academic identities. Of course, we still need additional information to determine which one is the professor/student. After all, as far as the current information itself is concerned, it is difficult to make a decision.

Identity markers and identity construction

The implementation of identity work can also involve what we term 'identity markers', a type of discursive resource that directly manifests and highlights the speaker's pragmatic identity, such as 'as …', 'personally', 'on behalf of'. Consider the following examples extracted from the Contemporary Chinese Language Corpus:

(16) Context: Gang Wang has had a fight with his cousin. His father is very sad about the situation and exhorts his son to behave himself.

我们作为你的父母不可能不管，如果你以后自己有孩子了，你就会明白我们现在的心情，我们对你负有责任。

As your parents, we cannot ignore this. If you were to have your own children in the future, you would understand what we are feeling at this moment. We are responsible for you.

(17) Context: Liren Shan, a senior police officer, lives in the same hotel as a young couple. During the night, the wife was raped by an unknown person. The couple accuse Shan because she had gone into his room by mistake. A deputy director of the local police station is conducting the investigation and wants to take Shan to hospital for a test.

"我实在不愿采取这种对您身心健康极为不利的步骤，但问题很复杂，很棘手，我们又不得不如此，这几乎是我们唯一的选择。就我个人而言，我想做的第一件事就是立刻解除您的嫌疑！"

'I really don't want to take such steps that are extremely harmful to your physical and mental health. However, since the problem is rather complicated and tough, we have to do so. This is our only choice. **Personally speaking,** the first thing that I want to do is to immediately prove your innocence!'

In Example (16), the father uses 'as your parents' to highlight his own identity (i.e. the other party's parent), hoping that the other party can understand his reasons for speaking; the deputy director in Example (17) employs 'personally speaking' to indicate that he himself, rather than his group or affiliation, is accountable for his words.

(Im)politeness and identity construction

When engaged in an interaction, communicators can choose to use (im)politeness formulae (characterized by a degree of (in)directness, involvement, tentativeness, implicitness, etc.) in relation to their thoughts or emotions. Therefore, under certain circumstances, these discursive features can, to some extent, construct a prominent self- and/or other-identity. Consider the following example:

(18) Context: At the front of a ticket vending machine at a subway station.
    a. 丈夫（对妻子）：有没有零钱？
    b. 陌生人：不好意思，我没零钱了，不知方便不方便帮我换一下？谢谢。

a.   Husband (to wife): *Is there any change?*

b.   Stranger: *Sorry, I don't have any change. If it's not too much trouble, could you change it for me? Thank you.*

The above two utterances occur in similar situations in the sense that both speakers need change to buy tickets from a vending machine at a subway station. However, at the same time, the two situations are quite different in the sense that while the speaker in Example (18a) asks his wife for some change, the speaker in Example (18b) has to ask a nearby stranger for help. Directness is a feature of the first utterance, indicating the speaker's attempt to construct the relational identity (i.e. husband and wife) of people who are close and familiar with each other. In comparison, the second utterance features indirectness, tentativeness and indeterminacy, which reflects the speaker's attempt to construct the relational identity (i.e. strangers) of people with a significant social distance between them.

Modal particles and identity construction

Some modal particles can also serve to show identities (e.g. Ogi 2014). Consider the following example:

(19)   Context: Chen is Zhong's mentor and enquires about how Zhong is progressing with her writing through WeChat.
陈：你好！请问话语标记语与外语教学是你负责的吗？进展如何？
钟：是的，还没有完成。是最近就要提交吗？
陈：寒假里完成即可。
钟：好滴！

Chen: *Hello! Are you responsible for the chapter about discourse markers and foreign language teaching? How are you progressing?*

Zhong: *Yes, it has not yet been completed. Do I need to submit it soon?*

Chen: *It's fine if you complete it during the winter vacation.*

Zhong: **Okey-doke!** *('haodi')*

In Example (19), Zhong employs a variant of 'okay' ('haode'), that is, 'okey-doke' ('haodi'), that is generally used by females, particularly female students. Compared with the employment of 'okay' ('haode'), the use of 'okey-doke' ('haodi') not only expresses the speaker's 'compliance' and 'deference' but also conveys additional emotional information, such as cheerfulness, decisiveness and so on. In this sense, the speaker constructs her identity as a female and, at the same time, constructs a close relationship between the two parties.

4.5 Identity work in the participation domain

In the rapport management framework, the participation domain concerns primarily 'the procedural aspects of an interchange, such as turn-taking (overlaps and inter-turn pauses, turn-taking rights and obligations), the inclusion/exclusion of people present, and the use/non-use of listener responses (verbal and non-verbal)' (Spencer-Oatey 2008: 21). When it comes to identity construction, discursive resources in this domain also play a role. For instance, interruptions occur more frequently in the speech delivered by a superior to his subordinate, and a subordinate tends to use minimal feedback when talking to his superior relative to the reverse situation. Also, in some typical communicative situations, particular textual or conversational features also serve the function of claiming self- and/or other-identities. It should be highlighted that people with different identities sometimes have distinct conversational organizations when engaged in interactions. Consider the following example:

(20) Context: Two participants are involved in a trial.
审：XXX人民法院刑事审判庭现在开庭。提被告人XXX到庭。
审：被告人XXX。
被：到。
审：你是否还有别的姓名？
被：没有
审：你的出生年月日？
被：1965年10月8日。
审：你的出生地？
被：江苏省XX县。
审：你是什么民族的？
被：汉族。
审：你的文化程度是？
被：小学。

Presiding judge: *The Criminal Trial Division of XXX People's Court is now in session. Bring **Defendant** XXX to the court.*
Presiding judge: **Defendant** *XXX.*
Defendant: *Here.*

Presiding judge: *Do you have an alias?*
Defendant: *No.*
Presiding judge: *Your date of birth?*
Defendant: *8 October 1965.*
Presiding judge: *Your birthplace?*
Defendant: *XX County, Jiangsu Province.*
Presiding judge: *What nationality are you?*
Defendant: *Han.*
Presiding judge: *What is your highest educational level?*
Defendant: *Primary school.*

In Example (20), the presiding judge's mode of interrogation and the defendant's mode of response highlight the formulaic linguistic realizations of a trial. Such formulaicity is context-dependent and predictable – as long as it is a court trial, such interrogations and responses occur. If the defendant does not respond in accordance to conventional formulae (e.g. if he/she asks, 'Don't you know my name, why do you bother to ask for it again?'), he/she would immediately be ordered to respond in the expected manner (e.g. the presiding judge would say, 'Please answer my question,' or pose the same question until the expected answer is obtained). Therefore, such conversational formulae construct the questioner as a judge and the responder as a defendant.

Generally, the opening remarks of TV interviews also follow certain discursive formulae (such as the way in which the conversations are organized during the introductory stage) to convey information about the participants' identities. Consider the following interaction:

(21) Context: A host introduces his interviewee at the beginning of a talk show.
主持人：大家好！这里是新浪网传媒频道与傲视全球电视网共同组织的"制片人在线"。今天与我们在线对话的是一个给我们带来无数个开心的著名栏目的制片人，就是中央电视台《开心辞典》的当家人，一位出过一本小说，也出过一本散文的才女，她就是郑蔚。郑蔚你好，你好像也是新浪的老朋友了。
郑蔚：是的，跟新浪合作过很多次了。

Host: *Hello everyone!* **This is** **Face Producers,** **jointly organized by news.** **Sina.com and OurSilu.** *Today we are going to talk to the producer of a famous programme who has brought us countless happy moments, that is, the head of CCTV's* Happy Dictionary, *a talented girl who has published a novel and a prose. She is Zheng Wei. Hello, Zheng Wei,* **I can say you're an old friend of** **Sina.**

Wei Zheng: *Yes, I have joined hands with Sina many times.*

In Example (21), the host greets the audience by saying 'Hello everyone', indicating that he is actually speaking to the general public currently watching the program. After this greeting, his 'self-' introduction, initiated by 'This is …', makes salient his institutional identity as a member of staff at news.Sina.com. When he comes to saying, 'Today we are going to talk to …', he has more or less completed the construction of his situational identity as the host. The utterance 'Hello, Wei Zheng, I can say you're an old friend of Sina' not only conveys more information about the identity of the host but also constructs the other party's identity as a guest of the talk show, which is further confirmed by the other party's subsequent response.

4.6 Identity work in the non-verbal domain

In the rapport management framework, the non-verbal domain involves primarily 'the non-verbal aspects of an interchange, such as gestures and other body movements, eye contact and proxemics' (Spencer-Oatey 2008: 21). In a specific community or context, phonetic features (e.g. pitch, rate, quality, accent, pause) play a part in constructing the identities of the communicators. For instance, a linguistic anthropologist has discovered that members of a certain community adopt the phonological system of their language regardless of whether or not they are communicating with other members of the same group (cf. Verschueren 1999: 3). In other words, people can indicate their identity and achieve social identification through their phonological choices.

In daily face-to-face communication, some paralinguistic features (such as gestures, distance and eye contact), although rarely used to convey identity information alone, have a relatively explicit relationship with specific types of identities. Therefore, when analysing utterances, these paralinguistic features, when appropriated employed, can help us to more accurately pinpoint the pragmatic identity being constructed by the speaker. For example, while whispering in a person's ear suggests a close relationship between the communicators, glowering at each other can indicate a fallout, and crossed arms can suggest a conflict. In some interactions occurring on social media (such as interactions on WeChat), some emojis and emoticons, for example, can also contribute to the process of identity construction. Consider the following example:

In Example (22), when Sky gives out a red packet online, Zoe and Haizhi Zhaoxia immediately open it and express their gratitude. Both of them call Sky 'Boss Cai' and thereby foreground Sky's identity as a boss or a CEO (which is indeed in line with his social role as a boss). The last communicator posts a sticker with the textual description 'Thanks, boss', which also constructs Sky's identity as a boss. Of course, care should be taken when interpreting the use of similar stickers because they can also be used when the red packet giver is not actually a boss.

(22)   Context: In a WeChat group, a user named Sky gives out an online red packet; others who open the packet then express their gratitude.

Sky: (在微信群里发了红包)

Zoe: 谢谢蔡老板 🌷 🌷 🌷 新年快乐 🎉

Gatsby: @sky 新年快乐！

海之朝霞：谢谢蔡总！新年快乐！🎉 🙏

QYZ:

Sky: *(gives out red packets in the WeChat group)*

Zoe: *Thank you,* **Boss Cai** 🌷 🌷 🌷 *Happy New Year* 🎉

Gatsby: *@sky Happy New Year!*

Haizhi Zhaoxia: *Thank you,* **Boss Cai**! *Happy New Year* 🎉 🙏

QYZ:

As highlighted by X. R. Chen (2018a), different discursive practices can sometimes lead to the construction of the same identity. Moreover, the construction of the same pragmatic identity may involve simultaneous choice-making in different domains. In other words, choice-making in only one domain might be conducive to the construction of one particular pragmatic identity, but on its own might not be sufficient to construct the identity. Therefore, with the exception of a few cases (e.g. when explicit address terms are used), we need to take into consideration simultaneous choice-making in multiple domains before we decide on the exact pragmatic identity selected by the speaker.

It is worth mentioning that the choice and construction of a certain pragmatic identity can sometimes be implicit and do not necessitate an explicit or external discursive representation. Verschueren (1999: 79–80) discusses the following example:

(23) Context: Beatrice is a university student living in Manchester. She has applied for a three-month stay at the Universidad Autónoma de Madri. John is the department secretary there, and Ann is the chairperson of the department.

Beatrice: Do you know yet whether I can go?

John: I'll check with Ann. Can you come back tomorrow?

(Subsequently, John talks to the chairperson of the department, Ann.)

John: Can Beatrice go?

Ann: Sure she can!

(The next day, Beatrice sees John again and asks him.)

Beatrice: Can I go?

John: You sure can.

By examining the exchange in Example (23), it can be observed that although John is unmistakably the physical utterer of 'You sure can', he is not the source of the information being provided. In other words, he is actually speaking on behalf of the chairperson of the department.[4] Therefore, the utterer can have multiple voices that actually represent different identities.[5] In the above example, at times John speaks as the department secretary and at other times he speaks on behalf of his chairperson. This, although not fully represented at the discourse level, still reflects the communicators' different choices of pragmatic identity. Therefore, to accurately pinpoint the pragmatic identity that John chooses at a particular time, we need to consider broader background knowledge (e.g. John is a department secretary; he is authorized to convey various decisions on behalf of the chairperson of the department, etc.).

In addition, the context of the situation can also provide indispensable and direct support by which the particular type of discursively constructed identity can be judged. Consider the following example:

(24) Context: Both speakers attend a press conference given by the Ministry of Foreign Affairs.

a. 华春莹：中方曾与菲方就中菲南海争议进行过沟通，并取得了积极进展，双方达成了 " 循序渐进进行合作，最终谈判解决双方争议 " 的重要共识。中方与菲方也曾有过很好的合作，中国海洋石油总公司与菲律宾国家石油公司经两国政府批准，签署了 " 南海部分海域联合海洋地震工作协议 "，后扩大为中菲越三方协议，三方也进行过联合地震海上作业，为南海的稳定、合作与发展做出了积极贡献。

b. 刘为民：中方注意到阿基诺总统重视中菲关系的表态。中方同样重视发展中菲关系，希望菲方与中方共同努力，推动两国关系健康稳定发展。

a. Chunying Hua: **China** has communicated with **the Philippines** on the dispute between the two parties over the South China Sea, and positive progress has been made. The two parties have reached an important consensus of 'cooperating step by step and finally resolving disputes between the two parties through negotiation'. There has also been good cooperation between China and the Philippines. The China National Offshore Oil Corporation and the Philippine National Petroleum Corporation have signed the 'Joint Seismic Work Agreement for Parts of the South China Sea' after approval by the two governments, which later expanded to a tripartite agreement. The three parties have also carried out joint seismic offshore operations and made positive contributions to the stability, cooperation and development of the South China Sea.

b. Weimin Liu: **China** has taken note of President Aquino's emphasis on Sino-Philippine relations. China also attaches great importance to the development of Sino-Philippine relations and hopes that **the Philippines** and China will work together to promote the healthy and stable development of bilateral relations.

In both the above cases, the speakers, Chunying Hua and Weimin Liu, have constructed the identity of a spokesperson of the Ministry of Foreign Affairs. This is directly related to how they refer to their country and other countries ('China', 'the Philippines') and the content of the current discourse (the stance taken by the Chinese government on related issues). Although such content can also come directly from a leader's mouth, the current communicative context – the press conference of the Ministry of Foreign Affairs – precludes this possibility. In this sense, the content of the above speech points exclusively to the institutional identity of both speakers being that of a spokesperson of the Ministry of Foreign Affairs.

4.7 Summary

Identity work, in whatever form it takes place, is executed via discursive practices. While some pioneering explorations have been conducted into how identity is discursively constructed, this chapter has sought to propose a new framework for the detection of identity work, by both benefiting from and integrating Spencer-Oatey's (2008) ideas on the realization of rapport management. At the same time, it takes into consideration a number of ways in which identity is characteristically constructed in Chinese communication.

Five domains of discursive practices for performing identity work have been categorized: address and referential domain, illocutionary domain, stylistic domain, participation domain and non-verbal domain. While this categorization is neither exhaustive nor exclusive, it manages to capture the various types of identity work that are salient and observable in Chinese communication.

Meanwhile, it must be acknowledged that the discursive practices of identity work could, to a large extent, vary from culture to culture, and even from one social group to another within the same culture. As manifested in other areas of interactional practices and meanings, variations in the discursive practices of identity work are also 'inevitable' (Culpeper and Haugh 2014: 268). Thus, it may prove beneficial to compare how identity work is enacted in distinct ways across different social groups and cultures to inform intracultural and intercultural communication.

5
Taxonomies of identity work

Identity work takes place in a specific context to meet particular communicative needs. Due to differences in context and communicative needs, identity work also shows some variation. On the basis of collected data, this chapter categorizes identity work in Chinese communication from four perspectives: its direction, target, dimension and rapport orientation.

5.1 Directions of identity work

Broadly speaking, the directions of identity work in Chinese communicative contexts cover identity construction, identity questioning or challenging, and identity deconstruction. No matter what the identity work is, it points to a particular communicative need and is accomplished through some particular discursive practice. To ensure a clear understanding of how each category of identity work is obtained, this chapter only presents explicit identity work (i.e. the speaker uses explicit identity statements or markers), leaving aside the various forms of implicit identity work (such as the implementation of a specific speech act related to identity construction).

Identity construction

Identity construction includes the construction of different types of identity – namely, individual identity, relational identity and collective identity. Although these types of identities can be further explored with respect to the various dimensions of identity, due to space limitations, this chapter will not subdivide them further.

A. Constructing an individual identity. Consider Example (1):

(1) Context: ZTYF posted a photograph of the decorations in Tiananmen Square ahead of the National Day celebrations.

ZW:

HYP: 真漂亮
作为一个老兵，很想去看看。怀念阅兵的音乐。

HTYS: 谢谢ZTYF的分享

ZW:

HYP: *It's beautiful*
As a veteran*, I'm keen to go and have a look. I miss the music of the military parade.*

HTYS: *Thank you, ZTYF, for sharing the nice photo*

In Example (1), HYP (a female professor), upon seeing the beautiful photograph of Beijing that has been shared by ZTYF, a WeChat group friend, ahead of the National Day military parade, expresses her admiration. She constructs an individual identity of a senior soldier by using an identity marker ('as a veteran'). She is worthy of the name because she used to serve as a soldier and worked in a military academy for many years. The speaker's words also mean that she wants to witness the actual parade. Her construction and highlighting of her veteran status conveys her reasonable desire to watch the parade (after all, a soldier should be able to). Here is another example (http://ccl.pku.edu.cn/):

(2) Context: Junsheng, a village cadre, asks Shuchun Luo to employ a few villagers in his factory.

罗述春指着家里正忙于搞加工的热闹场面告诉俊生同志，他家办了个皮鞋厂，一年少说也要赚一、二万块钱，这点负担承受得了。

"你是大老板，负担得起。"俊生同志点点头，鼓励罗述春发展生产，多消化村里的劳动力。

Shuchun Luo pointed to the lively scene where his family was busy with processing and told Junsheng that his family had set up a leather shoe factory, and he would earn at least 10,000 to 20,000 yuan a year. So, the burden was affordable.

'**You are a big boss**, and you can afford it.' Junsheng nodded and encouraged Shuchun Luo to improve production and attract more labour in the village.

In Example (2), Junsheng directly constructs the individual identity of the hearer as a big boss ('you are a big boss') through an identity statement. Moreover, he agrees with Shuchun Luo's statement ('the burden was affordable') to encourage him to expand production and provide more employment opportunities for the villagers.

B. Constructing a relational identity. Consider Example (3) (http://ccl.pku.edu.cn/):

(3) Context: Qing Liu is Zhenzhen's mother. Liu is very strict with her daughter. She works out a tight study schedule for the little girl, which causes her great dissatisfaction.

（刘清）忽然想起珍珍这个周末要同几个好朋友到同学家过夜，"还有这个周末不能去琳琳家过夜了。"

"为什么？"珍珍大叫，愤怒和绝望像洪水一样扭曲了她的五官。"我要去，我就要去，你是一个坏妈妈。"

看着女儿那种狂怒的表情，刘清也有些不安了。她知道女儿是多么盼望着这个机会能与小伙伴一起过夜，但她的愤怒和自尊都阻止她收回这道"命令"。

(Qing Liu) suddenly remembered that Zhenzhen was going to spend the night with a few good friends at her classmate's house this weekend. She said: 'Besides, you can't go and stay with Linlin this weekend.'

*'Why?' Zhenzhen yelled, with anger and despair distorting her facial features. 'I want to go. I want to go. **You are a bad mother.**'*

Looking at her daughter's angry expression, Qing Liu was also a little disturbed. She knew how much her daughter looked forward to this opportunity to spend the night with her friends, but her anger and self-esteem prevented her from taking back this 'command'.

In Example (3), Qing Liu is a strict mother and, at times, she can be unreasonable. She prohibits her daughter Zhenzhen from spending the night at her female classmate's house the following weekend. Zhenzhen cannot accept her mother's 'prohibition', angrily saying that she must spend the night at her classmate's house. Meanwhile, she constructs Qing Liu's relational identity as that of a 'bad mother' to her. The following example also portrays the construction of a relational identity, taken from a *Legal Report* broadcast called 'Guess Who I Am':

(4)   Context: Mr Liu's phone rings, and a woman's voice comes over the microphone.

女：（带广东口音的普通话）猜猜我是谁？

刘：不知道啊。你是？

女：（用很熟稔的语调）老同学，这么久没见面，连我的声音你都听不出来了？

刘：（想了一会儿）是XX吗？你不是在加拿大吗？

女：是呀，我已经到厦门了，帮一个朋友买房子，但是现在手头缺钱，想向你借1万块钱……

Woman: *(Mandarin with a Cantonese accent) Guess who I am?*

Liu: *I do not know. Who are you?*

Woman: *(in a familiar tone)* **Old classmate**, *we have not seen each other for a long time, but can't you identify me from my voice?*

Liu: *(thinking for a while) Is it XX? Aren't you in Canada?*

Woman: *Yes, I have arrived in Xiamen to help a friend buy a house, but now I'm short of money and want to borrow 10,000 yuan from you …*

In Example (4), the woman constructs the relational identity of old classmates by using the address term 'old classmate'. The woman is making a fraudulent call, and her constructed identity is false. Her purpose is to deceive Mr Liu into sending her money.

C. Constructing a collective identity. Consider Example (5):

(5)   Context: As the New Year approaches, classmates who joined the Foreign Languages Department of Yangzhou Teachers' College in 1985 are sending New Year greetings in their WeChat group.

JGM: @所有人

鼠年即将到来，祝同学们鼠年吉祥，幸福安康，万事如意！

LZ: 鼠年即将到来，祝所有的**老师和同学**鼠年吉祥，幸福安康，万事如意！

LH: 祝**群里全体成员**新年快乐，让疾病远离你们！

JGM: *@ all*

*The Year of the Rat is approaching. I wish that all **my classmates** will have an auspicious Year of the Rat, happy, healthy and lucky in all ways!*

LZ: *The Year of the Rat is approaching. I wish that all **my teachers and classmates** will have an auspicious Year of the Rat. Be happy, healthy and lucky in all ways!*

LH: *I wish **all members of this WeChat group** a Happy New Year and all illness will shy away from you!*

In Example (5), several college students wish their former teachers and classmates a Happy New Year in a WeChat group chat, to which the college classmates and teachers all belong. In one post, LH uses the address term 'all members of this group chat' to construct a collective identity, which he/she also shares. Unlike LH, JGM uses the address term 'classmates' when wishing everyone a Happy New Year, constructing a collective identity with some of the addressees (his classmates). LZ constructs a relational identity (classmates) for those addressees. He also constructs a teacher–student relational identity with some of the addressees by using the other-address term 'teacher'.

Identity questioning or challenging

Like identity construction, this direction of identity work involves identity (individual identity, relational identity or collective identity) questioning or challenging. This section will discuss identity questioning or challenging with appropriate examples.

A. Questioning or challenging an individual identity. Consider Example (6) (http://ccl.pku.edu.cn/):

(6) Context: *A young man has gone to a community clinic to receive an intravenous drip. The young nurse was a little nervous and could not insert the needle into his blood vessel until the tenth attempt.*
小伙早急了，扎上了，才忍着说："美女，你是不是叫李十针（李时珍）？"
小护士尴尬的笑了笑，答到："这里的护士都去武汉了，我是西藏来实习的，名字叫扎死得勒！"
*The guy was a little angry and said: 'Beauty, **are you called Li Shizhen?**'*
The little nurse smiled awkwardly and replied: 'All the nurses here have gone to Wuhan. I'm an intern from Tibet, and my name is Zhasi Dele!'

In Example (6), seeing that the young nurse has not succeeded in inserting the needle until the tenth attempt, the young man deliberately uses homophonic sounds ('Li Shizhen', which literally means 'Li Ten-Needle', has the same pronunciation as the well-known sixteenth-century Chinese doctor 'Li Shizhen') and asks her sarcastically, 'Are you called Li Shizhen?' The purpose of these words is to question the identity of the nurse, for if she was really a nurse she would not have needed so many attempts. The following is another example, taken from *The Story of the Editorial Department*, a TV series.

(7) Context: Xiufen Liu is the wife of the writer Yihe Zhang. She has had an argument with her husband and asks her friend Sister Niu to help her judge who is right and who is wrong.

牛大姐：小刘啊，你也太不知足了！像老张这样有追求、有理想的人你都不能理解，那你还算是个女人吗？

Sister Niu: *Liu, you are so insatiable!* **Are you still a woman** *if you can't understand a person like Old Zhang, who has aspirations and ideals?*

In Example (7), Niu criticizes Xiufen Liu, believing that she cannot be satisfied. In her eyes, Yihe Zhang is a person with dreams and ideals. Therefore, she questions whether Xiufen Liu is a good woman for not seeing that her husband is a good person.

B. Questioning or challenging a relational identity. Consider Example (8):

(8) Context: Liang Wang and Ping Zhang are good friends. They have just dined together at a restaurant. After the dinner, Ping Zhang uploads a photograph of their social gathering onto their common WeChat group.

王亮：老张，你怎么可以把我在酒店吃饭的照片放到群里啊？！

张平：老哥，不就是发了一张照片吗？多大事？

王亮：我真不知道怎么说你好。你这样做可不像是兄弟。

张平：你也太顶真了吧？

Liang Wang: *Lao Zhang, how can you share the photos of me eating at the restaurant in the WeChat group?!*

Ping Zhang: *Brother, what's up? Isn't it just a photo?*

Liang Wang: *I don't know what to say.* **You are not doing what a brother should do**.

Ping Zhang: *Aren't you too serious?*

In Example (8), Liang Wang is annoyed when he sees that Ping Zhang has uploaded a photograph onto their WeChat group which shows him eating at a restaurant. According to some regulations, Chinese officials are not permitted to use public funds for private dining. Although Liang Wang has dined privately with his friends and he has spent his own money, such photographs showing him eating meals at a restaurant are likely to create misunderstanding and may even cause him trouble. Knowing that it was just a private party, Ping Zhang believes that this should not create any bother. His posting of the photograph makes Liang Wang very nervous and unhappy, leading him to question whether Ping Zhang treats him like a brother.

C. Questioning or challenging a collective identity. Consider Example (9):

(9) Context: Dong Li and Chun Wang, who are both university professors at two different universities, are former classmates.
李东：王春，我下周到南京一高校参加专业评估。
王春：你是专家组成员？太意外了！
李东：我怎么就不可以做专家组成员？你小看人了吧？
王春：那倒没有。只是没有想到专业评估专家组会包括纯专业的教授。

Dong Li: *Chun Wang, I am going to a university in Nanjing next week to participate in a programme evaluation.*

Chun Wang: ***So you're a member of the expert group?*** *What a surprise!*

Dong Li: *Why can't I be a member of the expert group? Are you underestimating me?*

Chun Wang: *Not really. I just didn't expect that an expert group participating in a programme evaluation would include mere professors.*

In Example (9), Chun Wang expresses surprise at the news that Dong Li, a classmate, is going to a university in Nanjing to participate in a programme evaluation. He believes that experts participating in such evaluations are generally professors in administrative positions. Yet Dong Li is a doctoral supervisor without a formal administrative position. Because of this, Chun Wang raises doubt about the suitability of Dong Li's identity as a member of the expert group. This questioning appears to have displeased Dong Li, and thus Chun Wang provides a hasty explanation to avoid any misunderstanding.

Identity deconstruction

In addition to identity construction and identity questioning or challenging, the direction of identity work can be further described and discussed from the perspective of identity deconstruction (with respect to individual identity, relational identity or collective identity).

A. Deconstructing an individual identity. Consider Example (10) (http://ccl.pku.edu.cn/):

(10) Context: Zhaoli Gao is from a large family of nine brothers and sisters. He has just returned to his hometown to be a cadre. His younger brothers and sisters are excited about this. With her four-year-old daughter living at her parents' home, his divorced sister has no job or income. She comes to ask Zhaoli Gao for a temporary job.
高招利说：" 妹，我不是官，只是一个普通干部。你生活有困难，可以在家里吃，家里住，但找工作的事我帮不了忙。"

*Zhaoli Gao said: 'Sister, **I'm not an official**, but an ordinary cadre. You can eat and live at home if you have difficulties in life, but I can't help you find a job.'*

In Example (10), faced with his sister's request to help her find a temporary job, Zhaoli Gao, a township cadre, says, 'I'm not an official.' He deconstructs himself as an official and then constructs himself as 'an ordinary cadre'. In the minds of many Chinese people, if one family member becomes an official, then all his/her family members will benefit. Zhaoli Gao's deconstruction of his identity as an official helps him to decline his sister's request without hurting her feelings too much.

B. Deconstructing a relational identity. Consider Example (11) (http://ccl.pku.edu.cn/):

(11) Context: Suosuo Zhu is chatting with his old friend Nansun. Nansun has suffered some emotional trauma, and to cheer her up, Suosuo Zhu changes topics frequently.
"南孙，告诉我关于你的新男友王永正。"
南孙说："他不是我的男朋友，我再也无暇搞男女关系。"
"老太太说他是。"
"她误会了。"

'Nansun, tell me about your new boyfriend, Yongzheng Wang.'

Nansun said: '**He's not my boyfriend**. I have no time to engage in romantic relationships.'
'But Granny said he is.'
'She misunderstood.'

In Example (11), Suosuo Zhu's request for Nansun to 'tell me about your new boyfriend, Yongzheng Wang', presupposes that Yongzheng Wang is Nansun's new boyfriend. However, Nansun deconstructs the relational identity between herself and Yongzheng Wang, saying that she has no time to hang out with a boyfriend.

C. Deconstructing a collective identity. Consider Example (12):

(12)   Context: A customer is at the checkout of a health store.
收银: 请出示会员卡。今天搞活动，八五折优惠。
顾客：我还不是会员。我现在补办还可以参加活动吗？
收银: 可以的。

Cashier: *Please show me your membership card. There's 15% off for all members today.*

Customer: *I'm not a member yet. Can I still take part in the event if I register now?*

Cashier: *Yes.*

In Example (12), the cashier's request 'Please show me your membership card' presupposes that the customer is a registered member of the health store and is therefore eligible to receive discounts. The customer's answer deconstructs this assumed collective identity. Interestingly, the customer deliberately uses 'yet' while deconstructing his/her identity, which implies that he/she wants to become a member. Indeed, he/she follows up this request by applying for membership.

5.2 Targets of identity work

From the perspective of the target of identity work, we can attempt distinctions based on the three types of identity work described above, that is, identity construction, identity questioning/challenging and identity deconstruction. Each of these types also involves individual identity, collective identity and relational identity, but due to space limitations and to avoid repetition, not all combinations will be presented here.

Speaker-oriented identity work

Consider Example (13):

(13) Context: Some classmates, who joined the Foreign Languages Department of Yangzhou Teachers' College in 1985, had a reunion a few days ago to celebrate the thirtieth anniversary of their university graduation. Jiang is teasing Edgar in their classmates' WeChat group.

Edgar: @Mr Jiang 病从口入不乱吃，祸从口出不胡说哈

Mr Jiang: 平常彼此都很忙，难得紧张里轻松

Edgar: @Mr Jiang 是哒

@Mr Jiang没有看到你哎

@Mr Jiang三十年啊 侬也太忙了

Mr Jiang: 俗人一个，穷忙

Edgar: @Mr Jiang *We don't eat blindly because diseases may enter our mouth, we don't talk blindly because disasters may also come out of our mouth*

Mr Jiang: *We're so busy when we're working that it's hard to find time for relaxation in the midst of stress*

Edgar: @Mr Jiang *Quite true*

@Mr Jiang *I didn't see you*

@Mr Jiang *It's been thirty years. You're always so busy*

Mr Jiang: **I'm just an ordinary guy**. *Busy for nothing*

In Example (13), Edgar, who attended the reunion party to celebrate the thirtieth anniversary of his class' university graduation, noticed that Mr Jiang had not attended the reunion party. When he sees that Mr Jiang is chatting on his class' WeChat group, he jokes with him. Unhappy about Mr Jiang's absence from the class reunion, Edgar says rather sarcastically, 'It's been thirty years. You're always so busy,' implying that Mr Jiang should have cherished this opportunity to meet his former classmates. In Chinese, when others are too busy with their lives, they tend to be euphemistically criticized or ridiculed. Hearing Edgar's evaluation, Mr Jiang constructs his own identity as 'an ordinary guy' who is 'busy for nothing'. By this, he means that although he has been busy, he has not made any significant achievements. In effect, his self-derogation can be regarded to be an excuse in response to Edgar's mild criticism.

Hearer-oriented identity work

Consider Example (14) (*Child Slave*, Episode 25):

(14) Context: Zhigao Liu and his wife, Li Lu, are quarrelling over the education of their son, Huanhuan.

卢丽：那你说，欢欢成绩成这样了，我该做什么？我除了给他补习之外我还能做什么？

刘志高：我真没办法理解你，人家孩子上学得到的是知识，是快乐。你看看欢欢得到的是什么？你作为一个母亲你非得追求快班慢班这种可笑的评级啊？

Li Lu: *Then, what should I do about Huanhuan's grades? What else can I do besides tutoring him?*

Zhigao Liu: *I really don't get your point. What other children have received from school is knowledge and happiness. Look at Huanhuan ... What has he got?* **As a mother**, *do you really have to worry about the ridiculous rating of the so-called 'fast classes' and 'slow classes'?*

In Example (14), faced with his wife's complaints and accusations, Zhigao Liu believes that her expectations of their son are too high, so even though their child has acquired knowledge, he is not happy. Literally, he constructs Li Lu as Huanhuan's mother, but he is indirectly questioning her role because he believes that a qualified mother should not 'worry about the ridiculous rating of the so-called "fast classes" and "slow classes"'.

Third-party-oriented identity work

Consider Example (15):

(15) Context: Zheng Wei, a celebrity, is invited to attend an interview organized by Sina Media Channel and OTV Global Television Network.

主持人：大家好！这里是新浪网传媒频道与傲视全球电视网共同组织的"制片人在线"。今天与我们在线对话的是一个给我们带来无数个开心的著名栏目的制片人，就是中央电视台《开心辞典》的当家人，一位出过一本小说，也出过一本散文的才女，她就是郑蔚。郑蔚你好，你好像也是新浪的老朋友了。

郑蔚：是的，跟新浪合作过很多次了。

Host: *Hello, everyone! This is* Face Producers *jointly organized by news.Sina.com and OurSilu. Today we are going to talk to **the producer of a famous programme** who has brought us countless happy moments, that is, **the head of CCTV's** Happy Dictionary, **a talented girl** who has published a novel and a prose. She is Wei Zheng. Hello, Zheng Wei, I can say you're an old friend of Sina.*

Wei Zheng: *Yes, yes, I have joined hands with Sina many times.*

In Example (15), the host uses identity statements to construct Wei Zheng's multiple identities in front of the online audience, including 'the producer of a famous column', 'head of CCTV's *Happy Dictionary*' and 'a talented woman'. When he speaks directly to Wei Zheng, he constructs her identity as 'an old friend of Sina'.

Identity work oriented towards the relationship between the speaker and the hearer

Consider Example (16):

(16) Context: Hua Wang and Yong Cai are good friends and often play cards together as partners.

王华：最近在忙啥？本周末有掼蛋双打比赛，有空参加吗？

蔡勇：没问题！咱们是黄金搭档嘛！期待继续合作。

王华：太好了，期待一场大胜！

蔡勇：同期待！

Hua Wang: *What're you up to these days? There will be a doubles match of Guandan this weekend. Will you be free to participate?*

Yong Cai: *No problem. **We're golden partners!** I'm looking forward to our next teaming-up.*

Hua Wang: *Great! I shall look forward to a big victory!*

Yong Cai: *Same expectation here!*

In Example (16), faced with an inquiry (as well as an invitation) from his friend Hua Wang, Yong Cai not only agrees to participate in the weekend's Guandan match but also constructs a relational identity for them as 'golden partners'. Such identity work not only strengthens their motivation for the competition but also enhances mutual rapport. The use of the particle '嘛' (no equivalent is found in English) can further enhance the interpersonal effect (C. T. Li 2008).

Identity work oriented towards the relationship between the speaker and a third party

Consider Example (17) (http://ccl.pku.edu.cn/):

(17) Context: Lu, an officer, has been injured and subsequently hospitalized. Hearing that his daughter has been kidnapped, he insists on saving her himself.

队长：局长，不行，你身体还没好，不能去。

陆警官：**萱萱是我女儿**，出了问题你要负责！

Captain: *Director, no, you're not in good health. You can't go.*

Officer Lu: ***Xuanxuan is my daughter***, *and you will be held accountable if anything goes wrong!*

In Example (17), when Lu expresses his strong desire to save his daughter himself despite his injury, the captain discourages him because he is not in good health. In response, Lu constructs a relational identity between himself and the third party, that is, the kidnapped person ('Xuanxuan is my daughter'), emphasizing his responsibility as her father for saving her life. Of course, his utterance is also likely to indirectly convey the importance of saving Xuanxuan.

Identity work oriented towards the relationship between the hearer and a third party

Consider Example (18) (*Child Slave*, Episode 25):

(18) Context: Li Lu and Zhigao Liu are a couple who have rather different views on how to educate their child, Huanhuan.

卢丽：你说我可笑吗？如果你是项立强的话我不会追求这种可笑的评级，我会从小把欢欢送到国外，让他享受快乐。如果你是吕坤的话，我也用不着这种可笑的评级 …… 就因为是你！你儿子才陷入这种什么都不是，什么都要追的尴尬境地。你这个当爹的现在来笑话我 ……

刘志高：好！从今天开始，你说什么，我回答都是"行""好"。你满意了吗？

Li Lu: *Do you think I'm being funny? If you were Liqiang Xiang, I would not have worried about this kind of ridiculous rating. I would have sent Huanhuan abroad at an early age and let him enjoy some happiness. If you were Kun Lv, I would also not have worried about such a ridiculous rating … just because you were not them!* **Your son** *has just fallen into this embarrassing situation of chasing everything meaningless.* **You, the father,** *come so far as to laugh at me now …*

Zhigao Liu: *Good! From today on, I will answer 'OK', 'fine' for whatever you say. Are you satisfied?*

In Example (18), Li Lu uses two ways to refer to her son: 'your son' and 'Huanhuan'. Unlike the latter, the former form of reference highlights the relationship between the child and Zhigao Liu, his father, suggesting that her husband is responsible for her son's embarrassing situation. Similarly, when referring to her husband, Li Lu not only uses 'you' but also 'you, the father'. In a sense, the latter makes Zhigao Liu feel guilty about the current 'embarrassing situation' of their child.

Identity work oriented towards the relationship between two third parties

Consider Example (19) (http://ccl.pku.edu.cn/):

(19) Context: Jin Jiang and Hong Wang are colleagues. They are chatting in a WeChat group and talking about Liu's failure to enter a talent show.

江瑾：听说老刘这次落选了，吴良反而上了。

王红：我也听说了。不过也不奇怪，据说有一个评委是吴良以前的老师。

江瑾：原来是这样。老刘也太背运了。

Jin Jiang: *I heard that Liu was not selected this time, but Liang Wu was instead.*

Hong Wang: *I also heard about it. But it's not surprising because* **one of the judges was said to be Liang Wu's former teacher.**

Jin Jiang: *I see. Liu was so unlucky.*

In Example (19), Hong Wang constructs a relational identity for one of the judges and the selected candidate, Liang Wu (the former is the latter's 'former teacher'), as a possible reason for Liu not being selected, whereas Wu Liang was.

5.3 Dimensions of identity work

Previously, in Section 2.1, we explored the various dimensions of identity, including social attributes, membership, identification, roles, doers, status, stances, images and individuality. From our data we found that identity work in the Chinese context addresses each of these dimensions. This section will present examples of identity work which involve the various dimensions of identity.

Attribute management

Attribute management involves explicit reference to the age, gender, occupation, nationality and suchlike of the participants. Consider Example (20) (http://ccl.pku.edu.cn/):

(20) Context: *When Yuanyuan gets better, Jiahua Xie, her father, wants to send her back to the kindergarten. Ting Lu, a nanny, does not agree with this idea.*
"那个幼儿园对孩子不负责任，要不然媛媛怎么会发烧？我来照顾她吧。"
谢嘉华不同意："就你？你自己还是个孩子呢！"
卢婷的脸一下红了："你小瞧人，我怎么说也是个女人，比你这个大男人强！"
俩人争了半天，最后卢婷还是不得不服从命令，跟他一起把媛媛送回了幼儿园。
'That kindergarten has been irresponsible for the child, or why else would Yuanyuan have a fever? I'll take care of her.'
Jiahua Xie disagreed: 'You? **You're still a child!**'
Ting Lu's face flushed: 'You look down upon me. **I am a woman**, better than **a big man like you!**'
The two argued for a long time, and finally, Ting Lu had to obey the order and she took Yuanyuan back to the kindergarten with him.

In Example (20), Jiahua Xie and Ting Lu disagree about whether or not to send Yuanyuan, who has a fever, to the kindergarten. Jiahua Xie disagrees with Ting Lu, who wants to take care of Yuanyuan herself, because he thinks she is 'still a child'. Faced with Jiahua Xie's construction of her as a child, Ting Lu retorts that Xie looks down upon her, emphasizing that she is a 'woman' who is better than the 'big man' Xie.

Consider Example (21) (http://ccl.pku.edu.cn/):

(21) Context: Xi Su and Weiming Tong are good friends. Weiming Tong suspects that Xi Su is having a secret affair.

"你刚才怎么没害怕啊?我觉得上一次你说你害怕坐摩托的。"
"不知道，好像忘了害怕。"
"你下午去哪儿了？" 童未明问。
"干吗突然问我这个？" 苏曦不高兴地说。
"你一个女人家都忘了害怕，肯定去了不同寻常的地方。"
"没去哪儿，就办了点私事。" 苏曦关上了内心的大门。
"我也不是非得知道。我想我们是同事，也算是好朋友。你有事我绝不能看着，但你有问题我也不能不说。今天下午差一点儿出事，你知道吗？"
苏曦没有回答。

'Why weren't you afraid just now? I think you said last time you were afraid of riding a motorcycle.'

'I don't know. It seems I forgot to be afraid.'

'Where were you this afternoon?' Weiming Tong asked.

'Why do you suddenly ask me about this?' Xi Su said, upset.

'**You, as a woman**, forgot to be afraid. You must have gone to an unusual place.'

'I didn't go anywhere. I did some personal affairs.' Xi Su closed the door to her heart.

'I don't have to know. I think we are colleagues and good friends. I can't leave you alone if you're in trouble, but I have to ask you if you're indeed in trouble. Some trouble almost happened this afternoon, do you know?'

Xi Su did not answer.

In Example (21), Weiming Tong is puzzled how Xi Su can sit on her motorcycle without feeling afraid because she has never been like this before. When Xi Su says that she has forgotten to be afraid, Weiming Tong is suspicious, believing that if she, as a woman, has forgotten to be afraid, then she must have 'gone to an unusual place', because her behaviour is incompatible with her identity as a woman (identity as an attribute in this case). Apart from working on the attribute dimension of identity, Weiming Tong also highlights the identification aspect of her relational identity with Xi Su ('we are colleagues and good friends').

Membership management

Membership management involves making explicit reference to one being a member of a particular organization, group or institution. Consider Example (22) (http://ccl.pku.edu.cn/):

(22) Context: Shuanquan Wang is a village cadre. Due to a new construction project, the homes in his village have to be moved, but the villagers are reluctant to leave their homes. Realizing that the demolition of his own family's home will have an impact not only on the whole village and town but also in the whole county, Shuanquan Wang decides to take the lead in moving his home, because thousands of eyes are watching him. So, he needs to convince his family first.

"定了拆就得拆，咱不拆别人更不拆，我是党员，不能因为咱一家影响了工程！"家里人看到一向不爱多言语的王拴全话说得这么坚决，都知道不能再阻拦了。

*'Since it's been decided that our house must be demolished, we have to demolish it. If we don't, others won't follow. **I'm a party member**, so we can't let the project be delayed just because of our family!' When the family saw Shuanquan Wang, who never really said very much, speak so firmly, they knew that they could not stop him any longer.*

In Example (22), facing the demolition order issued by his superiors, Shuanquan Wang realizes that, as a Communist Party member, he has the responsibility to take the lead in the demolition campaign, so he persuades his own family to allow their house to be demolished first. Seeing that he has highlighted his identity as a party member, his family understand that he is determined to follow through with his intentions, and so agree with him.

Identification management

Identification management involves making explicit reference to the cognitive or emotional consensus between the participants, which may have arisen from them being classmates, friends, partners, people from the same village, county or province and so on. Consider Example (23):

(23) Context: WAH has requested that members of the WeChat group formed by the alumni of the Yangzhou Teachers' College complete a questionnaire for her research.

WAH: @ WY 万分感谢 🙏🙏🙏

WY: @ WAH 不用客气 🌸 🌸

WAH: @ WY 谢谢您 🌸 🌸 🌸

WY: @ WAH 校友大家庭应该做的，我87的 😁 😁

WAH: @ WY 非常感谢，感激 🙏 🙏 🙏 ☺

WAH: @ WY Thanks a million 🙏 🙏 🙏

WY: @ WAH You're welcome 🌸 🌸

WAH: @ WY Thank you 🌸 🌸 🌸

WY: @ WAH We all come from the same **alumni family**. That's what I should do. I joined our Alma Mater in 1987 😁 😁

WAH: @ WY Thank you so much. I'm so grateful 🙏 🙏 🙏 ☺

In Example (23), WAH, who enrolled in the Yangzhou Teachers' College in 1992, sent a questionnaire to the alumni WeChat group, asking the alumni to complete it. WY immediately responded to WAH's request and completed the questionnaire. WAH is very grateful and thanks him for his assistance. In return, WY highlights that they attended the same university ('We all come from the same alumni family') and, in so doing, enhances their identification with one another. He believes that classmates should help each other, as indicated by his earlier response ('You're welcome'). Now consider Example (24) (http://ccl.pku.edu.cn/):

(24)   Context: Xue Ouyang plans to start a business in Beijing and needs some assistance. With the help of Yawen Xiao, Jing Zhang recommends Yang Xiao, who has been employed by her parents. Ouyang accepts her recommendation, which leads Zhang to thank her.

欧阳雪说："张小姐客气了，我们也是希望能找个知根知底的人，谈不上谁谢谁。咱们都得谢谢亚文，有她帮忙咱们才都合适了。"

肖亚文看了看表，说："都是朋友，不客气了。张姐，那边已经跟房东约好了10点半见面，没时间了，有话咱们以后再聊，今天就到这儿吧。"

张静说："好的，你们忙，我们先告辞了，有机会一定一起坐坐。"

Xue Ouyang said: 'Ms Zhang, you're welcome. We also hoped to find someone who we knew well. Don't thank me. We all need to thank Yawen for her help.'

Yawen Xiao looked at his watch and said: '**We're all friends**, and you're welcome. Sister Zhang, I've already arranged an appointment with the landlord for 10:30. Time is limited. We'll talk later. Let's call it a day now.'

Jing Zhang said: 'Okay, since you're busy, let's say goodbye. We'll sit down together again when we have the opportunity.'

In Example (24), Yawen Xiao sees that Jing Zhang was the first to thank Xue Ouyang, and then he thanks her himself, saying that 'we're all friends' and thus constructing emotional identification with one another. By saying 'you're welcome', Yawen Xiao implies that they should act as friends instead of strangers.

Role management

Role management involves making explicit reference to the position of the parties in a specific social organization, for example, a family. Consider Example (25) (http://ccl.pku.edu.cn/):

(25) Context: Xiuli goes shopping with her husband and asks him to buy her some jewellery.

"你还从来没有跟我买过首饰呢？就这一次吧，我知道你是天底下最好的丈夫，一定不会叫我失望的。"秀丽开始撒娇了，看来今天不买是难以下台的了。

'You've never bought me any jewellery. Why not just this time? I know that **you're the best husband in the world**, and you will not disappoint me.' Xiuli began to act coquettishly, and it seemed that he would not be able to leave without buying it today.

In Example (25), Xiuli constructs her husband's role as the 'best husband in the world'. Her 'acting coquettishly' makes it hard for her husband to refuse. Consider Example (26):

(26) Context: Some attendees at a pragmatics seminar are chatting in a temporary WeChat group.

LCY: 今天冬至，还想着赶回去给孩子包饺子

TT: 一看就是好妈妈

LCY: 那是努力的方向

LCY: *It's the winter solstice today. I'm thinking of going home and preparing jiaozi for my child*

TT: **What a good mom** 😊

LCY: *That's what I aspire to become* 😊

In Example (26), LCY sends a message in a WeChat group formed by the attendees at a pragmatics seminar, saying that today is the winter solstice and she must hurry back home to make *jiaozi* (dumpling) for her child. Seeing this, TT immediately constructs the role identity of a 'good mom' for her. In response to this compliment, LCY humbly states that being a good mother is 'what I aspire to become'.

Doer management

Doer management involves making explicit reference to the role of the participants in a specific situation, task, activity and so on. Consider Example (27):

(27) Context: Y has organized the panel at a national pragmatics conference. His academic brothers and sisters are discussing his performance as the chair.

Sally: 主持人Y师兄压轴 👏👏👏

Roger: 👏👏👏👏

Gavin: Y帅魅力四射 🌹🌹🌹

ZQW: 今天下午是南大语用学专场啊！向C老师和各位同仁致敬！

Gavin: Y帅总结发言，高屋建瓴！👍👍👍

Sally: *The chair of the panel, academic brother Y, is doing the finale* 👏👏👏

Roger: 👏👏👏👏

Gavin: *Marshall Y is full of charm* 🌹🌹🌹

ZQW: *It's the exclusive performance by pragmaticists from NJU today! Salute to Professor C and all others!*

Gavin: **Marshall Y's summary reaches a high level!** 👍👍👍

In Example (27), after the panellists have had their turn speaking, it is the chair Y's turn to summarize the presentations. His academic brother, Gavin, praises him for his 'charm' and concluding summary, which 'reaches a high level'. Gavin's compliment constructs Y's doer identity as an excellent host.

Status management

Status management involves making explicit reference to the power and role of the parties in specific organizations, departments, groups and so on. Consider Example (28) (X. R. Chen 2019a):

(28) Context: Lao Zhu goes to Dazhong New Village, where he previously worked. He meets Mr Zhang from Building Four, greeting him enthusiastically.
老朱：张老师好！
张老师：是老朱啊，很长时间不见了。今天来视察咱们小区啊？
老朱：张老师拿我老头子开心了，我哪里是视察，就是来转转。
Lao Zhu: *Hello, Mr Zhang!*
Mr Zhang: *Lao Zhu, long time no see. Are you **inspecting** our community today?*
Lao Zhu: *Mr Zhang, you're kidding me. I'm just walking around, not inspecting at all.*

In Example (28), seeing that Lao Zhu, a former community guard, has come to greet him, Mr Zhang immediately responds by, interestingly, describing Lao Zhu's visit as an inspection. In Chinese, an 'inspection' is generally used to refer to a formal visit by (senior) leaders for investigation purposes and to provide guidance. Therefore, Mr Zhang establishes Lao Zhu's identity as a leader, thereby promoting his status. Of course, he is just playing a joke, which he might have intended to contribute to the interpersonal bonds between them (Boxer and Cortés-Conde 1997). Lao Zhu is aware that Mr Zhang is joking, and directly denies that he is 'inspecting' but is 'just walking around' instead. Consider another example:

(29) Context: A friend sends the recipient a WeChat message, asking for help to find an expert from the latter's school to show him how to write a grant application.
不知是否方便，若有可能，烦请陈老师帮我邀请贵校外院一位专家，帮助我们指导一下课题申报书。实在不好意思，我人微言轻，怕请不动。
Mr Chen, I wonder if it's convenient for you to help me find an expert from your school to show me how to write a grant application. I'm embarrassed to say that **in my humble position my word does not carry much weight***, so I am afraid I won't succeed in finding an expert.*

In Example (29), the friend constructs his low status identity by using the phrase 'in my humble position my word does not carry much weight'. Of course, this is a form of modesty, and is said with the purpose of enhancing the recipient's willingness to help.

Stance management

Stance management involves making direct reference to the participants' emotional attitudes to specific events, people, behaviours and so on. Consider Example (30):

(30) Context: A post has been shared in a WeChat group which details how to write good academic papers.

JXM: 谢谢C老师推送好文 👍 👍 👍 👍 👍 👍

WYD: 好文章！深有同感！

RYX: 👍 👍 👍

JXM: *Thank you, Professor C, for sharing this good post* 👍 👍 👍 👍 👍

WYD: *A good post!* ***I couldn't agree more!***

RYX: 👍 👍 👍

In Example (30), Professor C has posted an article in a WeChat group on reviewer-guided paper writing. JXM, a former student of the professor, thanks him, saying that it is an excellent article. Another former student, WYD, also praises this article. In addition, he adds that 'I couldn't agree more' in support of the view given by JXM. In so doing, he can expect to enhance mutual harmony. Consider Example (31):

(31) Context: The Year of the Rat is approaching. Some friends exchange New Year greetings in their WeChat group. WHP has given out red packets to the group.

YP: 祝发红包的人 心想事成

LMC: 下次投票只投发红包的人

YP: 严重同意

LZ: 附议@ YP

YP: 祝发红包的人 心想事成

LMC: *Next time we'll only vote for the guy who gives out red packets*
YP: ***I seriously agree***
LZ: ***I agree with you*** @ YP

In Example (31), WHP gives out red packets to a WeChat group of college academic teachers, and YP immediately uses a package emoji (indicating that he 'wishes the person giving out the red packets every luck') to express his gratitude. Seeing this, LMC jokingly suggests that he would only vote next time for those people giving out red packets, which is an indirect way of thanking WHP. YP adopts an exaggerated manner (here 'seriously' is an intensifier meaning 'very strongly') to express the same view as LMC and to construct a supportive stance. LZ immediately follows suit (the person after the symbol @ is chosen as the addressee) and constructs a dual supportive stance with LMC and YP.

Image management

Image management involves making explicit reference to the appearance, charm, demeanour, temperament or other identity characteristics presented by the participants of a social interaction. Consider Example (32) (adapted from Feng 2020), in which a couple have been quarrelling. The young woman has called the police for help, saying that her boyfriend will not let her part with him.

(32)   Context: A young woman, who has been in love with her boyfriend for some time, decides to end their relationship. The man does not want to leave and quarrels with her, so the young woman calls the police.

民警：你们谈了多少时间了？谈朋友？

女：快一年了。

民警：快一年，那为什么现在不谈了？

女：反正就是不想谈了嘛！

民警：（对女）一年多也不是时间短了，总有感情的喽，突然说走就走，那他接受不了呀。

（对男）你出来，我跟你说两句话（并伸手拉男方）。

男：别！有什么你就在这里说好吗？！（情绪激动）

民警：强扭的瓜甜不啦。

男：我不想跟她分手！

民警：男子汉，有点出息行吗？好聚好散!

Policeman: *How long have you been dating? Dating each other?*

Woman: *Almost a year.*

Policeman: *Almost a year. Then why do you want to break up now?*

Woman: *I just want to break up!*

Policeman: *(to the woman) More than a year is a long time. There must be some affection between you two. Now you want to break up suddenly, and he can't accept it.*

(to the man) Come out. I will say a few words to you. (reaches out to the man)

Man: *Don't touch me! If there is anything to say you can say it right here?! (agitated)*

Policeman: *You can take a horse to water, but you can't make it drink.*

Man: *I don't want to break up with her!*

Policeman: **Man, is it that hard to be a bit manly?** *Merry meet, merry part!*

In Example (32), a young woman proposes ending the relationship with her boyfriend, but the boyfriend rejects this proposal and the two have an argument. The policeman, faced with the woman's sudden decision to break up, uses a Chinese proverb, 'You can take a horse to water, but you can't make it drink,' to persuade the man to give up. However, he does not agree to the ending of their relationship. The policeman is rather puzzled and even slightly dissatisfied. He uses 'man' to address the boyfriend. Apparently, he ostensibly constructs a responsible and 'favourable' image of the man, but, in fact, he implies that he is not 'manly' enough because a real man would respect a woman's wishes and 'merry meet, merry part'. Consider another example (X. R. Chen 2019a), in which Ruoxi Sun, a teacher, has fallen in love with Chunling, and Shuxian is trying to persuade Chunling to marry him.

(33) Context: Shuxian and Chunling are good friends. Shuxian thinks that Ruoxi Sun would be a good match for Chunling, who is still single.

淑娴摇着她的手，恳切地说："照我说，春玲啊，你就点头吧。孙老师文化高，长得也好，对你又那末贴心，你再打着灯笼也难找上这样的女婿啦！"

春玲依然发呆，无话。

Shuxian shook Chunling's hand and said earnestly: 'Chunling, trust me. Just say yes to Sun. **Teacher Sun is well educated and good-looking**. *What's more, he is so nice to you. It's hard to find a man like him!'*

Chunling remained silent.

In Example (33), in an attempt to persuade Chunling to marry Ruoxi Sun, Shuxian not only points out that Mr Sun cares for her but also constructs his image identity as 'well educated and good-looking'. In Chinese culture, being well educated is essential for men, while a good appearance is a universal attraction for the opposite sex.

Personality management

Personality management involves making explicit reference to the uniqueness or individuality of the interactant involved, for example, his/her personality or specialty. Consider Example (34) (X. R. Chen 2019a), in which Sangsang, who has been studying abroad, has just returned to visit her granny.

(34)   Context: Sangsang has just returned from abroad. She is paying her granny a visit. They have not seen each other for over three years.

"晚上睡得好吗？棉被会不会太厚或是太薄了？有没有关好窗子？夜里没做噩梦吧？我们早上有没有吵你？屋里没蚊子吧？有什么想要的东西吗？……"

"奶奶"她咽下一大口稀饭。"我什么都好，睡得又香又甜，梦里都是奶奶！"

"马屁精！"奶奶笑着用筷子打她的手腕，眼眶又湿了。"既然这么想奶奶，怎么三年多了才回来？"

"人家在念书嘛，在念那个鬼硕士嘛……"

'Did you sleep well? Is the quilt too thick or too thin? Did you forget to close the window? Did you have nightmares? Have we disturbed you this morning? Are there mosquitoes in your room? Is there anything you want? …'

'Granny, I'm fine in every way. I slept well and always meet Granny in my dreams!'

'Ass-kisser!' *Granny laughed and tapped Sangsang on the wrist with her chopsticks. Eyes wet, she said: 'Now that you miss Granny so much, why didn't you return until three years had passed?'*

'But you know, I had to read for my master's degree …'

In Example (34), after hearing Sangsang's words, the older woman uses the expression 'ass-kisser' to construct an apparently negative individuality-related identity for her. Of course, she is not serious because she laughs when uttering it. This explains why Sangsang does not take offence at her 'abusive' utterance, partly indicated by her use of the affectionate Chinese self-reference term '人家' (meaning 'other') instead of '我' (meaning 'I') and the final particle '嘛'

(indicating a little girl's cute-playing in front of the elderly) (not translated in the English version). Here is another example:

(35) Context: Gang Li and Yulu Tian are two strangers who have met each other unexpectedly.
"可以认识一下吗？"李刚来到田雨露身边坐下。
"我好像在哪儿见过你？"
"我也好像在哪儿见过你。"
"你叫什么名字？"
"田雨露。"
"真的？怪不得觉得你与众不同。"
'How do you do?' Gang Li sits down beside Yulu Tian.
'It seems I've seen you before?'
'It seems I've seen you somewhere too.'
'What's your name?'
'My name is Yulu Tian.'
'Really? **No wonder you are different from others.**'

In Example (35), both interlocutors feel that they have seen each other before. When Yulu Tian gives her name, Gang Li says that he feels she is 'different' and constructs her unique personality identity. He says, 'No wonder' because Tian's name 'Yulu' is actually one of the twenty-four Chinese solar terms (each term corresponds to a day marking one of the twenty-four divisions of the solar year in the traditional Chinese calendar). Of course, Tian's unique name is not the only reason that she is 'different', because Gang Li feels like this before knowing her name.

5.4 Rapport orientations of identity work

Spencer-Oatey (2008: 32) discusses four rapport orientations in interpersonal interactions:

a. Rapport enhancement orientation: a desire to strengthen or enhance harmonious relations between the interlocutors;
b. Rapport maintenance orientation: a desire to maintain or protect harmonious relations between the interlocutors;

c. Rapport neglect orientation: a lack of concern or interest in the quality of relations between the interlocutors (perhaps because of a focus on self); and
d. Rapport challenge orientation: a desire to challenge or impair harmonious relations between the interlocutors.

Considering that there is a substantial difference between challenge and impairment in the fourth orientation mentioned above in terms of their impact on relationships, X. R. Chen (2018b) has chosen to divide this category into two. In other words, he distinguishes five orientations for relationship management. Correspondingly, we will explore the different goals of identity work from these five orientations (of course, we will also examine them from the perspective of the effects created by identity work).

Rapport enhancement

This type of identity work aims to promote or meet specific communicative needs by commending each other's attributes, applauding each other's membership, elevating each other's role, praising each other's capability, strengthening mutual identification, enhancing each other's status, supporting or agreeing with each other's stance, beautifying or praising each other's image or beautifying or praising each other's personality. For example (X. R. Chen 2019a):

(36) Context: Wang is the office dean, while Zhang is a temporary employee of the school who helps in the office by doing some trivial and routine work.
王主任：张总，去把这封信寄一下。
张师傅：主任拿我开心了。我这就去。
Dean Wang: **General Manager Zhang**, *go and mail this letter.*
Master Zhang: *Ha ha, Dean, you're making fun of me. I will do it right now.*

In Example (36), Dean Wang addresses Zhang as 'General Manager Zhang', which is not his real identity. This joke can help improve mutual relations and allows Zhang to experience the friendliness of his boss. Here is another example:

(37) Context: A friend is having a WeChat talk with the author.
笔者：上课了没有？
友人：没，在家。赶国家社科书稿，6月份要结项。
笔者：祝顺利结项！

友人：我努力，等我结项后细细打磨论文时，再找您这位语用专家请教。

笔者：不客气，随时欢迎。

Author: *Are you in class yet?*

Friend: *No, I'm at home. I'm catching up with my manuscripts for my National Social Sciences grant because the project will end in June.*

Author: *I wish you a smooth end to your project!*

Friend: *I will work hard. When I finish the project, **could I consult you, a pragmatics expert?***

Author: *You're welcome. Any time is OK.*

In Example (37), the friend does not simply use the default deictic term 'you' in the last sentence, but also '语用学专家' ('a pragmatics expert') to construct a high academic status for the author. The use of '请教' ('consult') also has the same function. The use of the two expressions to show respect is in accordance with Gu's (1990) Address Maxim and Self-Denigration Maxim, and helps enhance the friendship between him and the author. This might explain why the author says to his friend, 'You're welcome' and 'Any time is OK'.

Rapport maintenance

This type of identity work aims to promote or meet specific communicative needs by communicating in accordance with usual or default identity relationships by recognizing each other's attributes, membership, roles, doers, status, stances, images, individuality or mutual identification. Consider Example (38):

(38) Context: The Year of the Rat is approaching. Some classmates exchange New Year greetings in their WeChat group. George (LYQ) has given out red packets in the group.

JGM：谢谢！

ZXP：谢谢老同学的红包'　！恭祝鼠年大吉！
ZDL：谢谢George! 新年快乐！
QSX：谢谢老同学的红包！
JGM: *Thanks!*

ZXP: *Thank you, **my old classmate**, for your red packet'* *! Wish you great luck in the Year of the Rat!*

ZDL: *Thank you, George! Happy New Year!*

QSX: *Thank you,* **my old classmate***, for your red packet!*

In Example (38), LYQ gives out Chinese New Year red packets in the university classmates WeChat group. Unlike JGM, who expresses gratitude, ZXP and QSX highlight the identity of LYQ as a classmate, which is aimed at maintaining their mutual relationships. ZDL refers to LYQ by his English name, which is also in line with their usual identity relationship (the two are in the same class and usually address each other by their English names), and this helps to maintain the harmonious relationship between the two. Of course, each of the participants acknowledges the receipt of LYQ's red packets, which also helps to maintain each of their mutual relationships. Consider Example (39):

(39) Context: Qiang Li, who used to be a non-administrative teacher in the math department, has just been appointed the deputy chair of another department.

秘书：主任好，发给您的邮件收到了没有啊？

李强：收到了。不要叫我主任，叫我老师就可以了。

秘书：您客气了，您本来就是主任啊。

Secretary: *Hello, Chair. Have you received my email?*

Li Qiang: *Yes, I have received it. Please don't call me Chair, just call me teacher.*

Secretary: *You're standing on courtesy.* **You are of course our chair***.*

In Example (39), the secretary addresses Qiang Li as 'Chair' when asking him whether he has received her email. Although Qiang Li is only a deputy chair, the secretary's use of the address form 'Chair' is seen as a way of elevating him (He and Ren 2016). Of course, since this addressing practice is 'normal' in Chinese social interactions, it is not considered to be flattering. Qiang Li is accustomed to addressing colleagues as 'teacher', and so he tells the secretary that he prefers colleagues to use this professional title. The secretary says that he is 'standing on courtesy' because she understands that he is, after all, 'our chair'. The identity constructed by the secretary by using Qiang Li's official title can help maintain a harmonious relationship between them.

Rapport neglect

This type of identity work aims to achieve the communicative goal of ignoring each other's relationships by neglecting each other's attributes, membership, roles, doers, status, stances, images, individuality or mutual identification. In the Chinese context, discursive practices such as ignoring the other's identity (occupation, title, high-level professional title, etc.), boasting one's own identity (status, image, etc.), calling the other person by his/her full name (when he/she is angry) and so on amount to the neglect of rapport. Consider Example (40) (*Child Slave*, Episode 6):

(40) Context: Zhigao Liu and Li Lu are a couple who disagree about how their child, Huanhuan, should be educated. For this reason, they often have arguments.

刘志高：人要那么成功干啥呀？

卢丽：你上不上进我不管，欢欢的使命就是上重点中学！我的使命就是让欢欢上重点中学，没有商量的余地！

刘志高：你啊，现在就像那个视频《虎妈战歌》里的虎妈了。

卢丽：虎妈怎么了？虎妈有什么不好啊？美国人就是大惊小怪，中国孩子都是这么长大的。

刘志高：行了，行了，别吵了，别生气啦。

卢丽：你都不知道我为什么是生气，我不是光气你没报上名，我是气你骗我，刘志高！

Zhigao Liu: *Why do people have to be so successful?*

Li Lu:: *I don't care if you aspire to this or not. Huanhuan's mission is to go to a top middle school! My mission is to let Huanhuan enrol in a top middle school. No negotiation!*

Zhigao Liu: *You're like the tiger mother in the video 'Battle Hymn of Tiger Mother'.*

Li Lu:: *What's wrong with Tiger Mom? What's bad about Tiger Mom? Americans are just making a fuss. Chinese children all grow up this way.*

Zhigao Liu: *OK, OK, don't shout. Don't be angry.*

Li Lu:: *You don't know why I am angry. I am not angry because you didn't register Huanhuan at school, but because you,* **Zhigao Liu,** *lied to me!*

In Example (40), Zhigao Liu disagrees with his wife, Li Lu, on whether their child should attend the Mathematical Olympiad class. He believes that Li Lu should not behave like a tiger mother and force their child to study too hard. Li Lu is very angry at Zhigao Liu's delay in enrolling her son in the Mathematical Olympiad class, particularly as Zhigao Liu has deliberately deceived her. Disappointed, she calls him by his full name and expresses her dissatisfaction. Under normal circumstances, Li Lu would address her husband as 'Zhigao', or '老公' (meaning 'husband'). Calling him by his full name in this context constructs her husband's identity as a general acquaintance or even a stranger, and reflects her neglect of his identity as her husband.

Rapport challenge

This type of identity work aims to achieve the communicative goal of challenging each other's relationship by questioning or challenging each other's attributes, membership, roles, doers, status, stances, images, individuality or mutual identification. Consider Example (41) (Guo 2020):

(41)   Context: Zhigao Liu and Li Lu are a couple who disagree about how their child, Huanhuan, should be educated. Li Lu has asked Zhigao Liu to register Huanhuan with a training class. But Zhigao Liu has not done so, and instead has taken the child to play. This leads Li Lu to believe that Zhigao Liu has lied to her.

刘志高：我为什么骗你？一点点小事你就揪在手里不放，无限扩大！

卢丽：孩子的事是小事吗？夫妻间的信任是小事吗？为什么我无限扩大，是因为对咱们的婚姻来说无限重要！这么多年了，我为这个家，为孩子，我付出了一切，你管过吗？你不仅不管还处处跟我作对！不仅跟我作对，还教育我说是我错了！说我忽略了你，忽略了我作妻子的角色！最可笑的是我还真去反思了。刘志高，经过了这么多事我告诉你，我反思的结果有了，那就是我对你太好了！你是不是觉得这一切都是应该的啊？我郑重告诉你，刘志高同志，你对这个家也是有责任的！你也应该多关心关心你的妻子，你的孩子！

Zhigao Liu: *Why should I lie to you? You always focus on the trivial things and stretch them infinitely!*

Li Lu: *Are children's matters trivial? Is trust between a husband and a wife a trivial matter? I stretch these things because they are infinitely important to our marriage! For so many years, I have given everything for this family, for this child. Have you ever cared about your child? You not only don't care, but you always act against me! You not only act against me but also tell me that I am wrong! You said that I ignore you and ignore my role as a wife! The ridiculous thing is that I have had a self-examination. Zhigao Liu, let me tell you, after so many incidents, the result of my self-examination is that I've been too kind to you! Do you think I'm solely responsible for all of this? I solemnly tell you, Comrade Zhigao Liu,* **you also have responsibility for this family! You should also care about your wife and child!**

Prior to the exchange in Example (41), Zhigao Liu has rented his female subordinate's room. This was subsequently discovered by Li Lu, which triggers a crisis in trust. Li Lu believes that her husband lacks trust in her and ignores her role as a wife. She also believes that Liu has never cared about their child. By saying 'You also have responsibility for this family', she conveys the presupposition that

Liu has not fulfilled his familial responsibilities, and by saying 'You should also care about your wife and child', she presupposes that Liu does not care about them. This type of identity work revolves around each other's obligations as family members, spouses and parents, and might challenge their husband–wife relationship (and even the father–son relationship between Zhigao Liu and his child), creating a significant negative impact on the harmonious relationship between the interlocutors.

Rapport impairment

This type of identity work aims to achieve the communicative goal of impairing or destroying each other's relationship by disapproving of the other's attributes, negating the other's membership, denying the other's role, denying or belittling the other's ability to act, refusing to identify with the other, disapproving or belittling the other's status, contradicting the other's stance or vilifying the other's image. Consider Example (42) (http://ccl.pku.edu.cn/):

(42) Context: The Chen and Xu families are related. Jiazhen Chen and the narrator are a young couple. The narrator has taken to gambling and loses all his family's money. This provokes his father-in-law.

我丈人朝我娘摆摆手，又转过身来对我喊：

"畜生，从今以后家珍和你一刀两断，我们陈家和你们徐家永不往来。"

我娘的身体弯下去求他："求你看在福贵他爹的份上，让家珍留下吧。"

My father-in-law waved his hand at my mother, then turned around and shouted at me:

'**Beast**, from now on, Jiazhen will turn her back on you. Our Chen family and your Xu family will never come together.'

My mother bent down and begged him: 'For the sake of Fugui's father, let Jiazhen stay.'

In Example (42), Fugui (the narrator) is called a 'beast' because he has offended his father-in-law. The abuse deconstructs Fugui's identity as a person. Such identity work is inherently harmful and directly harms the relationship between the speaker and the hearer. The following is another example (http://ccl.pku.edu.cn/):

(43) Context: A reporter is sitting in a car with several other people. The driver is stopped by the police because he has been speeding.

记者走到交警面前，说："他的确没超车。我们几个都可以证明。"

交警说："你是内行还是我是内行？你看得准还是我看得准？"

记者掏出记者证，说："我是电视台的。我们赶会议拍新闻，您今天就放他一马吧。"

交警说:"记者？我今天已经抓两了。"

The reporter walked up to the traffic policeman and said: 'He did not overtake. We can all prove it.'

*The traffic policeman said: '**Are you an expert or am I**? Are you correct or am I?'*

The reporter took out his press card and said, 'I'm from the TV station. We are in a rush to a meeting to film the news. Will you please let him go today?'

*The traffic policeman said: '**Reporter**? I have caught two of them today.'*

In Example (43), when the reporter testifies that the driver did not overtake, the traffic policeman asks him, 'Are you an expert or am I?' which indirectly constructs the hearer's layman identity and his own professional identity. The reporter takes out his press card and asks the traffic policeman to release the driver by constructing his identity as a reporter (reporters often enjoy privileges that are not available to ordinary people). However, unexpectedly, the traffic policeman challenges the identity of the 'reporter', implying that he is probably a fake. The traffic policeman's identity work harms the current rapport that exists between himself and the reporter.

5.5 Summary

By using collected data, this chapter has classified the identity work in Chinese communication from four perspectives: its direction, target, dimension and relationship orientation.

In terms of the direction of identity work, Chinese communicators can construct, question or challenge, or deconstruct the individual or collective identities of themselves, others or a third party according to their communicative needs in the contexts concerned. They can also construct, question or challenge, or deconstruct the relational identity between themselves, others or a third party.

In terms of targets, Chinese communicators can orient their identity work towards the addresser, the addressee, a third party, the relationship between the addresser and the addressee, the relationship between the addresser and a third party, the relationship between the addressee and a third party, and the relationships between three different parties.

In terms of dimensions, the identity work performed by Chinese communicators can involve the social attributes, membership, roles, doers, status, stances, images or individuality of the addresser, addressee and a third party. It can also involve identification between the two parties, or between one of the interlocutors and a third party.

In terms of rapport orientations, the identity work conducted by Chinese communicators can promote, maintain, ignore, challenge or impair the harmonious relationship of one or both of the communicators, or even that of a third party.

Communication in the real world is always much more complicated than the generalizations offered by researchers. Therefore, it must be admitted that this chapter could not have possibly covered all the categories of identity work under each classification and all the situations under each different category. However, the classification provided in this chapter demonstrates the diversity and complexity of identity work in Chinese communication and provides a reference for classifying identity work in specific communications.

6

Identity work strategies

As stated in Section 5.4, identity work is often motivated by the communicator's need to properly and tactfully achieve specific communicative goals by means of selecting appropriate rapport management orientations. In other words, the strategic manipulation of identity work involves what is termed 'identity rhetoric' (Yuan 2020). This chapter, by considering various sources and types of data, analyses some commonly observed identity work strategies, including those that manipulate the features of identity such as its salience, similarity, closeness and truthfulness. It must be admitted, though, that I do not intend to, nor could I possibly, exhaust all the possible strategies that are used to perform identity work, thus leaving room for these strategies to be explored in future studies. The same stipulation applies to the classification of identity work strategies because there could well be additional, or better, approaches to their classification.

6.1 Strategies that manipulate identity salience

Identity is one of a communicator's social attributes. However, once communicators have chosen an identity in a particular context, such an identity becomes pragmatic or communicative in nature, and will affect the process and outcome of the current communication. Generally speaking, interlocutors are able to understand what identity is being adopted even when it is not explicitly stated. As it is generally unnecessary to explicate the identity of any party, including that of the speaker, the addressee or a third party, in verbal communication, providing explicit identity information can be regarded as a **foregrounding strategy**. The data show that identity markers such as 'as' and 'on behalf of' or identity-related claims can be used to foreground the identity of the speaker or addressee (the particular dimension of identity that is highlighted may relate to one's attributes, roles, position, membership, image and personality). The foregrounding of one's identity helps the addressee to understand the speaker's identity positioning and its related rights and obligations, appropriateness and legitimacy, to further his/her communicative goals, eliminate possible misunderstanding and enhance, maintain, ignore, challenge or impair the rapport between them. Consider Example (1):

(1) Context: Jian Xiao, chairman of the board, has been challenged by a major client of the company. Xu Chen, Jian Xiao's friend, and also a member of the board, is talking to him.
   a. 老肖，我觉得你应该辞职了。
   b. 老肖，作为朋友，我觉得你应该辞职了。
   a. *Xiao, I think you should resign.*
   b. *Xiao, **as your friend**, I think you should resign.*

In Example (1a), the identity adopted by the speaker, Xu Chen (a member of the board), is not explicitly stated. In contrast, Example (1b) indicates explicitly the speaker's identity as a friend of the addressee, rather than as a member of the board, by including the identity marker 'as your friend'. Identity salience might help to highlight his agreement with the hearer and mitigate the face threat evoked by his suggestion to resign, thus enhancing their relationship. Accordingly, Jian Xiao will understand Xu Chen's utterance as being from the perspective of his friend rather than a member of the company's board.

Sometimes, communicators highlight their identities to provide reasons for their actions, thus fulfilling their communicative goals. Consider Example (2) (*The Land*, Episode 22):

(2) Context: Shortly after the founding of New China, Ran Lin, a municipal government leader, held a symposium with a number of intellectuals to publicize the party's attitude towards scientific and academic work. Professor Xianyu was invited. He quietly left the meeting room before Ran Lin's speech had finished. Seeing this, his friend Wenhua followed him out.
   文华：鲜于，你怎么走了？
   鲜于：我是做学问的 … 我对政治家的观点不感兴趣，有这点时间我不如回去看看书。
   林然：（突然出现在门口）鲜于教授怎么走了？是不是对我有什么意见哪？
   鲜于：我回去上课。

   Wenhua: *Xianyu, why are you leaving?*

Xianyu: ***I'm an academic person*** ... *I'm not interested in the views of politicians. I prefer to go back and do some reading.*

Lin Ran: *(suddenly appearing at the gate) Professor Xianyu, why are you leaving? Do you disagree with me?*

Xianyu: *I'm going back to give a class.*

In Example (2), Xianyu, faced with Wenhua's question about his early departure, answers by providing the reason why he has left the symposium (he is not interested in Ran Lin's speech). More importantly, he further explains the reason for his lack of interest, saying that he is 'an academic person'. Xianyu performs identity work to provide a reason for his hasty departure (researchers do not want to listen to politicians). Consider Example (3):

(3) Context: A driving school instructor rudely corrects his student's irregular driving.

学员: 教练，你的语气能不能温柔一些？我好歹是个医生！

教练: 医生？医生怎么啦？你们医生学车就是慢！告诉你，在这里学车，得听**教练**的。各行有各行的规矩！

Trainee: *Coach, can you be more gentle?* ***I'm a doctor anyway!***

Coach: *A **doctor**? So what? You, **doctors**, are slow learners! I tell you, if you are learning to drive here, you have to listen to **the instructor**. Each walk of life has its own rules!*

In Example (3), the trainee, unhappy with the instructor's rude behaviour, asks him to be more gentle by stating his identity ('I'm a doctor anyway'), which implies that he deserves the instructor's respect and expresses his dissatisfaction with the instructor's ignorance of his identity as a doctor and the underlying rapport. In response, the instructor highlights his own identity in another way, that is, by means of self-reference ('you have to listen to the instructor'). By doing so, he indicates that the trainee has neglected the rights and legitimacy associated with that particular identity. The coach's reason for performing this identity work is probably to remind the trainee of his instructor identity and to accept his instructions, even though this could have an impact on their harmonious relationship.

Not only do communicators foreground their own identity, as shown in Examples (1)–(3), but the addressee's identity can also be intentionally highlighted. Consider Example (4) (Xiao n.d., Chapter 5):

(4) Context: Xiuhua Liu, employed by Yulian Wu as a nanny, has left the door open after entering the room, which has caused Yulian Wu some annoyance, leading to an argument between them.

吴玉莲说，你做错了，还怪我？！

刘秀华也不示弱，说，明明是你做错了，咋还怪我呢？！

吴玉莲喊，你错了！！

刘秀华也喊，我没错！！

……

两个人都觉得自己有理，针尖对麦芒，谁也不让份。王保存在床上躺不住了，劝解说，你们俩就少说两句吧，有什么大不了的问题 …… 玉莲，**你是长辈**，你少说两句 …… 小刘，**你做晚辈**的要忍让一点……

可两人谁也不听劝，越吵越凶……

最后，吴玉莲高声说，小刘，你要不认错，现在你就给我走人！这世上三条腿的蛤蟆不好找，两条腿的女人遍地都是！！

刘秀华根本就不怕，也高声说，走就走！天底下用保姆的又不是你一家！给我算工钱！说着就去收拾包袱。

王保存在床上喊，小刘，你当保姆的气咋这么大，说走就走？这哪行啊？

Yulian Wu said, 'It's your fault. Don't blame it on me!'

Xiuhua Liu did not retreat but said, 'Obviously you did something wrong. Why are you blaming me?!'

Yulian Wu shouted, 'It's your fault!!'

Xiuhua Liu also shouted, 'It's not my fault!!'

…

*Both felt they were right. Neither would concede. Baocun Wang couldn't lie in bed any longer. He tried to persuade them to stop quarrelling. 'It's not a big deal. Yulian, **you are a senior**, so just say less … Liu, you have to be a little more tolerant **as a junior** …'*

But nobody listened to him and it got worse …

Finally, Yulian Wu shouted loudly, 'Liu, if you don't admit your fault, then go away! A three-legged toad is not easy to find, but a two-legged woman can be found everywhere!!'

Xiuhua Liu was not scared at all, and shouted loudly, 'Ok I am leaving! You are not the only person to employ nannies in the world! Pay me!' She packed up as she was speaking.

*Baocun Wang shouted from his bed, 'Liu, **as a nanny**, how bad-tempered you are! And so you really mean it? It's no good.'*

In Example (4), Baocun Wang tries to settle the argument between Xiuhua Liu and Yulian Wu. He first foregrounds Wu's identity ('you are a senior'), requesting her to complain less as seniors tend to be more magnanimous and forgiving than juniors. He then highlights Liu's identity ('as a junior'), which implies there is a discrepancy between her verbal behaviour ('how bad-tempered you are! And so you really mean it?') and her identity as a nanny.

In addition to highlighting the identity of the hearer, as in Example (4), communicators sometimes query or challenge the identity of the addressee. Consider Example (5) (CCL, Wang Shuo's novel):

(5) Context: Jing Yao has been cheated out of money and is asking Liren Shan to turn to Interpol for help.

"那你还来找我干吗？我不是法力无边，不能到国外抓人。"

"不是说，有个国际刑警组织？"

单立人诧异地望着姚京："你可真是敢想，你是什么大人物，你以为你是什么大人物？要想让国际刑警组织出面，你还得至少再让他骗去五百万，我看这事这样吧，你也不要找警察了，找个小报记者，哭诉一番，让他给你写一篇'她为什么痛不欲生'，利用舆论揭露一下，鞭挞一下，搞臭他，你出出气完了。"

"看来也只能这样了"

'Then why do you come to me? I am not powerful enough to arrest a suspect abroad.'

'There's Interpol, right?'

Liren Shan looked at Jing Yao in surprise: 'You really dare to think about it. **What a big man you are?** If you want to turn to Interpol for help, you'd have had to be swindled of at least five million. From my point of view, you don't have to resort to the police, but to a tabloid reporter, to whom you could complain. Finally, an article entitled 'Why She Is in Great Pain' could be used to get him exposed to the public. Then you would calm down.'

'It seems that's the only way out.'

In Example (5), faced with Jing Yao's unreasonable request, Liren Shan uses a rhetorical question involving the listener's identity ('What a big man you are?'). In so doing, he intends to challenge Yao's status and highlights his confusion over his request ('Liren Shan looked at Jing Yao in surprise'), implying his inability to satisfy this unreasonable request.

In addition to highlighting the speaker's or hearer's identity, the speaker sometimes foregrounds the relational identity between them. Consider Example (6) (J. Chen 2019):

(6) Context: A student advisor and a student are having a one-to-one talk in the office.
辅导员：那除了学习之外呢？
学生：生活方面吗？
辅导员：生活方面，你有没有什么困难啊？我们既是师生，更是朋友，你有困难不妨直接说。
学生：有啊，我觉得，嗯
辅导员：或者还有这个，社会工作啊，等等。
Student advisor: What else do you want to talk about apart from your studies?
Student: My daily life?
Student advisor: Do you have any problems in your daily life? **We're not only teacher and student, but also friends.** *Just let me know if you do.*
Student: Yes, I think, mm.
Student advisor: Or, how about your social work? And so on.

In Example (6), the advisor asks the student if he has any problems in his life. While performing a declarative speech act to state each other's relational identity, she emphasizes their relationship as friends ('We are not only teacher and student, but also friends'). Her strategic emphasis might serve to make the student more willing to tell his tutor about his troubles.

In addition to highlighting the speaker's or hearer's identity, the speaker sometimes foregrounds the identity of a third party. For example:

(7) Context: During the Covid-19 pandemic in Wuhan, medical staff and military personnel rushed to the city.
Pan: 昨晚朋友发的：家人即将前往武汉，在门口跟哭泣的女儿道别
Pan: 道别图片
Luo: @Pan 不去不行吗？
Zhang: 作为军人，能不听命令吗？开玩笑吧！
Pan: From a friend last night: A family member is going to Wuhan and bids farewell to his crying daughter at the gate
Pan: Farewell photo
Luo: @ Pan Is it okay if he does not go?
Zhang: **As a soldier,** *can he disobey orders? Are you kidding?*

In Example (7), Zhang employs an identity marker ('as a soldier') to foreground the identity of the soldier in the photograph and further activate assumptions about the obligations demanded of soldiers ('obey orders'). He implies that he is 'just kidding' in questioning whether a soldier can disobey orders.

The identities of the interlocutors or a third party can not only be foregrounded, but at times they can also be shadowed or obscured. The latter is a form of **de-identification** operation and can be conceptualized as a **shadowing strategy** or **backgrounding strategy**. Consider Example (8) (Jin and Chen 2020):

(8) Context: A boyfriend has posted a message on WeChat Moments to express his dissatisfaction with his girlfriend's habit of writing Weibo (Chinese microblog).
男友：早安必须说早点，晚安也可以说早点。按时吃饭，按时睡觉，只希望某人能早点晚安，不要熬夜追剧。
女友：哈哈哈，年轻人就是要熬夜，好吗？
Boyfriend: *Good morning must be said earlier. Goodnight could be said earlier, too. Take your meals on time, and go to your bed on time. I only wish **mouren** would go to sleep earlier; don't stay up watching TV.*
Girlfriend: *Hahaha. Young people can stay up late, right?*

In Example (8), the boyfriend deliberately uses the indefinite pronoun 'mouren' (meaning 'someone') to refer to his girlfriend. As he is expressing his dissatisfaction in an open forum (Weibo), the boyfriend does not directly indicate whom he is complaining about or specify the target's name, which might help to soften the complaint slightly and not harm the couple's dating relationship. The girlfriend's response of 'hahaha' also proves that the practice of shadowing the girlfriend's name and identity, as shown above, has not had an adverse interpersonal impact. Her use of 'young people' instead of 'I' in her response is, in a sense, adopting the same strategy.

Sometimes, the strategies of foregrounding and shadowing a third party's identity can be employed simultaneously in news headlines. Consider Example (9):

(9) Context: *Beijing Daily* reports on a press conference held by the State Council on the spread of the coronavirus.
中科院院士：新冠病毒不能透过皮肤进入人体
2月21日10时，国新办就科技创新支撑疫情防控有关情况举行发布会。中科院院士周琪介绍，病毒进入人体，通过粘膜，口、鼻、　　　眼，主要是通过口和鼻进入人体。研究证明，新冠病毒不能通过皮肤进入人体。（北京日报客户端记者 李如意）

An academician of the Chinese Academy of Sciences: *Coronavirus cannot enter the human body through the skin*

> At 10 on 21 February, the State Council Office held a press conference on technological innovations for epidemic prevention and control. Qi Zhou, an academician of the Chinese Academy of Sciences, said that the virus enters the human body through the mucosa, mouth, nose and eyes, particularly the mouth and nose. Research has proven that the coronavirus cannot enter the human body through the skin. (Beijing Daily *reporter Ruyi Li*)

In Example (9), the news reporter, on the one hand, highlights the professional identity of the person ('an academician of the Chinese Academy of Sciences') who has released the coronavirus-related information ('Coronavirus cannot enter the human body through the skin') and deliberately shadows his name. While the conventional way to disclose an identity is 'professional identity + name', the reporter highlights the former, but shadows the latter, to enhance the authority of the released information. Comparatively speaking, the name of the academician is not that important, and finds mention only in the body of the article rather than the headline. The same applies to the following online news report from *Sichuan Online–West China City Daily*.

(10) Context: An online news report of a child saving her mother when a fire broke out in a restaurant.
餐馆突发火灾，6岁女童冲进火海救妈妈
*A **six-year-old girl** rushed into the fire to save her mother, when a fire broke out in a restaurant.*

In Example (10), when making reference to the girl who rescued her mother in the headline of the online news report, the reporter deliberately highlights the girl's age, growth stage and gender ('a six-year-old girl') and relationship with the other party ('her mother') but shadows their names and other information such as the restaurant's location. This type of headline helps to attract the reader's attention. As a six-year-old girl generally cannot accomplish such an amazing feat (saving her mother from a fire) because of her age and gender, news readers would probably feel that the content of the news story is worth reading.

As Examples (8)–(10) have shown, the listener or reader is often able to uncover identity information that has been deliberately shadowed by the speaker or author. However, on some occasions, the listener is unable to do so because of an information gap or lack of a clear context. For example (*Divorce Lawyers*, Episode 32):

(11) Context: Li Luo's father went to the hospital for a medical examination and has since learned that he has some swellings in his abdominal cavity. Li Luo's father believed that he would die soon. In order not to burden his wife, he wants to get a divorce. He visits Haidong Chi's law firm and asks the lawyer to write him a divorce agreement.

罗鹂爸：我啊，有一老哥们，就是岁数跟我差不多，最近啊想跟老伴离婚，可是又不想弄得满城风雨，谁都知道。你看这事有什么办法没有？

池律师：这容易啊，那就离婚协议，两个人起草一份这个离婚协议，到民政局去办个证，这个只要自己不说，谁都不知道。

罗鹂爸：那这个协议怎么写啊？

池律师：写上离婚的理由，这个财产的分割，儿女这个到底跟谁过。

罗鹂爸：你这太复杂，这，这我表述不清楚回去。这么着，你看你能不能帮我写一个写个协议的样本，是吧，我让我那个哥们在上面填个名字，你看这样行不行？

池律师：那他这个具体离婚的？

罗鹂爸：他说了，所有的财产都归这女方，今后男方的生老病死与这女方没关系了。把这条写上就行。

Li Luo's father: *I have **an old pal** of my own age. Recently, he has decided that he wants to get a divorce, but does not want all the neighbourhood to know about it. Can you find any way of doing this?*

Lawyer Chi: *It's easy. A divorce agreement can do it. The divorce agreement is drafted, and then you have to go to the Civil Affairs Bureau to apply for a certificate. As long as they don't leak the details, no one will know.*

Luo Li's father: *What should the agreement include?*

Lawyer Chi: *It needs to include the reasons for the divorce, partitioning of the estate and arrangements for the children.*

Li Luo's father: *It is rather complex, er. I cannot express it clearly. So, can you please give me a ready-made agreement, and **my old pal** just signs his name on it, ok?*

Lawyer Chi: *But for those details?*

Li Luo's father: *He has emphasized that if it explicitly states that all his property belongs to his wife, and that the man's illness and death are not her responsibility, it would be enough.*

In Example (11), Li Luo's father asks the lawyer to keep a secret for him before stating his request. He then mentions the divorce after receiving confirmation from the other party, but what he fails to mention is that it is he himself who wants a divorce, not his 'old pal'. He further consults the lawyer, Chi, about the details of the divorce agreement, which appear quite complicated to him. Therefore, he asks the lawyer to provide a ready-made agreement so that all he has to do is sign the agreement. He still uses 'old pal' to refer to himself. In addition, 'He has emphasized that …' conveys the idea that what he wants to say has actually been spoken by his 'old pal'. If readers are unclear about the story's plot, they would not be able to tell from the above dialogue that Li Luo's father has deliberately shadowed his true identity.

6.2 Strategies that manipulate identity similarity

During daily communication, communicators sometimes choose to actively construct or strengthen the same or similar identity (attributes, affiliations, stances, agreements, roles, status, etc.) to the addressee (or the addressee to the speaker) in a situated context, by using identity-related statements and identity markers (such as fellow townsmen, fellow students, people with the same family name, comrades, peers, compatriots, colleagues, etc.), the purpose of which is to fulfil the communicative goal of enhancing rapport between the interlocutors. This strategy is called **identity alignment**. Consider Example (12):

(12) Context: Chen B has invited Chen A to give a lecture. Chen A has sent him the topic of his lecture.
陈甲：请本家查收。
陈乙：好的，收到了。本家，把你们打算乘坐的航班告诉我，以便订票。
陈甲：我自己订吧。
Chen A: *Please check,* **benjia**.
Chen B: *Ok, I've got it.* **Benjia**, *please tell me the flight you plan to take so that I can book a ticket.*
Chen A: *I can book it myself.*

In Example (12), after sending the topic of his lecture, Chen A reminds Chen B to check it by using the address term *benjia* (one who has the same family name), which is then employed again when Chen B asks Chen A for his flight details a few days after receiving the topic. Consider Example (13):

(13) Context: Zhao and Chen are fellow university students. Chen has organized an annual conference in which Zhao is also participating.
赵：老同学，17年外国语言学会年会的电子邀请函还有吗？最近报销，缺一份会议的邀请函。

陈：我在外地，回南京后找下发给你？
赵：好的谢谢啦！
陈：（发邀请函）美女同学，请查收！
赵：万分感谢哦！

Zhao: *My fellow student*, do you still have the electronic invitation letter for the Annual Conference of the Foreign Languages Association in 2017? I need the conference invitation letter for the reimbursement of my expenses.

Chen: I'm out of town. Can I send it to you when I return to Nanjing?

Zhao: OK. Thank you!

Chen: *(sending the invitation letter)* **My beautiful fellow student**, please check!

Zhao: *Thank you very much!*

In Example (13), Zhao's use of 'my fellow student' to address Chen clearly reflects their relational identity (as former fellow students). By doing so, she efficiently maintains their harmonious relationship while performing her request (asking Chen to send her the conference invitation letter). In response, Chen uses almost the same address term, except he adds 'beautiful' before 'fellow student' to highlight the addressee's female identity and image, which enhances the harmonious relationship between the two parties.

In addition to the use of identity address terms, communicators sometimes use identity statements to shorten the social distance between them. For example (CCL):

(14) Context: A doctor has asked Ennian Gong, president of the hospital, for assistance.

宫恩年严肃地说："你知道医院的院规吗？请你不要给我难堪。"
接着又耐心地解释："咱们都是医生，应该有更多的共同语言。"
这位医生既敬佩又惭愧地说："宫大夫不仅仅治好了我妻子的身病，也治好了我的心病。今天，我才真正懂得了应该怎样做人。"

Ennian Gong said seriously: 'Do you know the rules of the hospital? Please don't embarrass me.'

*Then he explained patiently: '**We are both doctors**. We should have more in common.'*

The doctor said with a mixture of admiration and shame: 'You not only cured my wife's illness, but also my mental problem. Today, I know how to behave myself.'

In Example (14), while responding to the unreasonable request made by another doctor, Gong replies that they share the same professional identity ('we are both doctors'), so they 'should have more in common'. He implies that the addressee should understand his own difficulty because the rules of the hospital cannot be violated.

Speakers (and probably hearers as well) may choose to actively seek and construct the same or similar identities, as indicated in the above examples. In contrast, speakers (and probably both parties) may also choose to construct, challenge or even deconstruct the specific identity (attribute, affiliation, stance, role, etc.) of the speaker, the listener or a third party, by performing identity-related speech acts, using identity markers and so on, to seek and construct different identities. By deliberately emphasizing differences in identity, the speaker might challenge or even harm rapport. We term this strategy **identity disalignment**, and it is frequently adopted in disputes or argumentative contexts. Consider Example (15) (Xiao n.d., Chapter 5):

(15) Context: Xiuhua Liu is from the countryside and works as a nanny for Yulian Wu, who lives in the city. Yulian Wu has a grudge against Xiuhua Liu because she always leaves the door open.
吴玉莲瞪起眼睛问，小刘，你咋到现在还不关门？
刘秀华看着关好的门，一时愣住了。
吴玉莲说，告诉你，这是城里，不是你们农村，到处都是小偷，办事毛手毛脚，丢三落四，家里丢了东西你能赔得起吗？
Yulian Wu stared and asked, 'Liu, why do you always leave the door open?'
Xiuhua Liu looked at the closed door and froze for a moment.
Yulian Wu said, 'Listen, **it is the city and not the countryside where you used to live***. There are thieves about. Can you afford the loss of stuff caused by your own carelessness?'*

In the Chinese countryside, people tend not to close or lock their doors during the daytime when they are at home, but do so at night. However, the situation in urban areas is rather different, where doors are normally closed, or locked, even when people are at home. Xiuhua Liu's experience of living in the countryside means that she fails to 'do as the Romans do' when working as a nanny for Yulian Wu. One day, she is wrongly accused of leaving the door open by Yulian Wu and they have an argument. Yulian Wu explains the reason for her anger, by saying 'it is the city and not the countryside where you used to live'. In China, a significant difference exists between urban and rural areas. Some city residents have stereotypical impressions of rural people. Quite a few city residents are not in favour of marrying rural people. Even if they do get married, conflicts are common. The story in Example (15) is actually a microcosm of these social problems. Yulian Wu's words that 'it is the city and not the countryside where you lived' actually highlight the difference in the communicators' identities, which is the root of the speaker's offense.

6.3 Strategies that manipulate identity closeness

Sometimes, as indicated by the data, communicators may choose to use generalized terms such as 'brother', 'sister', 'friend' and 'partner' to perform identity work, with a view to fostering social or emotional closeness between the interlocutors, constructing in-group membership (Brown and Levinson 1978, 1987) and enhancing mutual rapport. We might term this tactic of identity work as an **endearing strategy**. For example:

(16) Context: Professor Kunrong Han and Professor Renliang Xiao work in different universities but share similar interests in closely related research fields, and they have met each other many times at academic conferences. Professor Xiao has edited a textbook, which Professor Han thinks is particularly good, and he intends to choose it as the textbook for his own teaching. The following is a series of short text messages between the two professors.

韩坤荣：仁亮教授，我下学期上修辞学课，我看到你编的一本修辞学教材，觉得教程后面的练习很好，打算把它当教材。不知有没有可供参考的练习答案？若有电子版，能否发给我一份？谢谢！韩坤荣

肖仁亮：韩教授你好，答案只做了八个单元。我发给你，供参考。仁亮

韩坤荣：太好了。谢谢仁亮老弟。

Kunrong Han: *Professor Renliang, I am going to teach rhetoric next term, and I've noticed your newly edited textbook on rhetoric, and I find the exercises following the lectures to be particularly good, so I intend to use it as a textbook. I wonder, are there answers to the exercises for my reference? If there is an electronic version, could you send it to me? Thank you! Kunrong Han*

Renliang Xiao: *Professor Han, how are you? The answers to the exercises only cover eight units, and I will send them to you for your reference. Renliang*

Kunrong Han: *Great! Thanks,* **brother Renliang**.

In Example (16), Professor Kunrong Han first uses the expression 'Professor Renliang' to address Renliang Xiao, and then uses his full name as a self-reference at the end of his message. His choice of address forms reflects his perception that the emotional distance between the two is neither distant nor close. However, when Renliang Xiao employs his own first name as a self-reference in his reply instead of his full name, Professor Kunrong Han immediately switches to using 'brother Renliang', which suggests he has changed his perception of the emotional distance between them, and he is making an effort to treat Renliang Xiao as a friend. Consider Example (17) (J. Chen 2018):

(17) Context: A tutor and a student are having a one-to-one talk in the office.

辅导员：你现在大一哎。

学生：没有，但是我现在已经很大了。

辅导员：哦，但是问题是你现在还没有切实的做什么勤工助学什么的，你还没有设想别的，对吧？

学生：对对对。

辅导员：制定的还没有做，嗯，行啊，没问题。好像后面，但是做兼职要注意安全啊。**我们做家长的**，最担心的就是你们的安全了。

学生：嗯。

辅导员：第一个要注意安全，第二个，当然男生可能要稍微好一点，但是仍旧有人身安全的问题，第二就是那个，做兼职的话你可能要有一些取舍。就是不要什么都去做，第一价钱你肯定要考虑，千万不要充当廉价劳动力，第二要对自己今后发展有帮助的。

学生：对对。

Tutor: *You're a freshman.*

Student: *No, I'm older now.*

Tutor: *Oh, but the problem is that you haven't actually done any work placements or anything else. You haven't got any other plan, right?*

Student: *Yeah.*

Tutor: *What you had planned has not been carried out yet. En, ok, it doesn't matter. But pay attention to your safety when doing part-time jobs. This is what we, as **parents**, worry most about.*

Student: *OK.*

Tutor: *The first point you need to care about is safety, and the second also relates to personal safety issues, even though it may be slightly better for boys. Then you need to conduct some trade-offs when doing part-time jobs. Don't just do anything. You must first consider the salary, so as not to be treated as cheap labour, and secondly whether the experience will benefit your future development or not.*

Student: *Yes, yes.*

In Example (17), when the tutor reminds the student to be aware of his own safety when taking part-time jobs, he/she deliberately uses a marked form of self-reference ('parents') instead of the default identity ('tutor') (the referential expression used here is marked because the tutor is instructing students in the office, rather than communicating with his/her own child). Such self-reference enables the tutor to express his concerns about the student's safety, and it thus contributes to arousing the student's appreciation and builds trust between the two parties, thereby further enhancing their mutual harmonious rapport.

In addition to the use of generalized kinship terms, identity markers such as *zijiren* ('in-group member') can also be employed by interlocutors to perform identity work. For example (W. Li 1999, Chapter 7):

(18) Context: The government is collecting rates.
"请大家不要嚷了，布店王老板有困难，他家里有两个病人，这饷银俺替他交！"
说完以后，他又挤到那当官的面前，对他说道："请老爷息怒，还是听俺一句良言，把王老板的饷银拿去吧！"
那当官的只得见梯子下楼，也不再固执了，对李小芳说道："还是李老板爽快，俺这就走！"
他一边说，一边从李小芳手里抓过两只元宝，分开围观的人群溜走了。
那布店的王老板，立即来到李小芳面前，噗陋跪下，正要磕头。李小芳赶忙将他扶起，说道："快起来，王老板，都是自己人。谁能不遇困难呢！"

'Please don't shout. The boss of the cloth shop is in trouble as there are two patients in his family. So I'll pay it for him.' Then, he squeezed in front of the official and said to him: 'Please calm down, master, and take my advice. This is Boss Wang's rates. Take them, please!'

The official had no choice but to give up and was no longer being stubborn. He said to Xiaofang Li: 'What a straightforward person your Boss Li is! Ok, I am leaving!'

While saying so, he grabbed the two ingots from Xiaofang Li and slipped away from the crowd.

Boss Wang of the cloth shop came immediately to see Xiaofang Li and knelt down. When he was about to kowtow, Xiaofang Li hurriedly lifted him up and said, 'Get up quickly, Boss Wang, **we're of one side**. Everyone encounters difficulties some day!'

In Example (18), being afraid that Wang, the boss, would get into trouble if he failed to pay his rates to the government, Xiaofang Li quickly steps forward to mediate by promising to pay the money for him. His assistance leads Boss Wang to thank him sincerely, as can be seen when he kneels down. Xiaofang Li's use of 'we're of one side' clearly and directly constructs their in-group membership, which is reinforced by his additional remark that 'everyone will encounter difficulties some day!'

Unlike the above examples where the communicators have attempted to shorten the distance between themselves, sometimes Chinese communicators deliberately elevate the other person or denigrate themselves to show deference. This strategy, which might be termed as **elevating strategy**, is also used to enhance harmonious relations. Consider Example (19):

(19) Context: President Li and Professor Gu were postgraduate classmates. After graduating, they worked at different universities. President Li has phoned his former classmate about his upcoming visit to Zhenjiang the following weekend.

李校长：顾教授，最近在忙什么呢？有空来广州指导指导工作。

顾教授：校长拿我开心了。我哪敢到你那里去指导什么工作啊。让我学习学习倒是可以的。

李校长：好啊。你说个时间吧，好让我有思想准备。

顾教授：一定的。到时我再联系你。

李校长：对了，我下周末会来镇江一趟，也许我们可以见见面？

顾教授：好啊，热烈欢迎！

President Li: *Professor Gu, what have you been busy with recently?* ***Please come to Guangzhou to supervise our work if possible***.

Professor Gu: *President, you are kidding me. I wouldn't dare supervise your work. It's better for me to learn from you.*

President Li: *OK. You can fix a time so that I can make some preparations.*

Professor Gu: *Certainly. I'll contact you then.*

President Li: *Well, I'm coming to Zhenjiang next weekend. Maybe we can meet there?*

Professor Gu: *OK. A warm welcome awaits!*

In Example (19), in order to enhance the harmonious relationship between them, Li does not use Professor Gu's first name as an address form, which would signal an intimate relational identity, but instead chooses a professional title ('Professor Gu') to construct a deferential, but distant, identity for the addressee. Professor Gu interprets President Li's utterance as 'kidding', and replies that he would not dare 'supervise' work in his school, but it would be more appropriate to 'learn' from him. Accordingly, during the course of the conversation, it can be seen that the participants have a clear awareness of their own identity choices and understand what identity is both appropriate in the situated conversational interaction and will satisfy their communicative needs.

In contrast to the above identity manipulation, Chinese communicators may choose to deliberately defamiliarize the identities of self, others or a third party (I'm a *wairen* ('an out-group member')). The purpose of such an interactional practice is generally to construct out-group membership (Brown and Levinson 1978, 1987), challenge or deconstruct specific relational identities, and challenge or impair each other's rapport. This strategy can be termed **identity distancing**. For example (*Massage*, Episode II):

(20) Context: Hai Wang, Quan Wang's younger brother, who has been spoiled since a child, believes that his brother, Quan Wang, and his prospective sister-in-law, Jiayu Kong, have returned to Nanjing to rob the house and get free meals. What has caused Quan Wang even more pain is that his kinship with Hai Wang has broken down and there is nothing left between the two brothers except money. However, no matter how bad Quan Wang's situation has become, Hai Wang still asks him for money for business purposes.

王海：哥，能不能借我几万块钱啊？我广告费一到就还给你呢！

王泉：我没有钱。

王海：你不说给我结婚的那一万块礼钱啦！

孔佳玉：王海，你结婚的时候你哥不是已经寄了两万块钱了吗？你看啊，我们两个现在都没工作，也是需要钱的时候。

王海：哥，咱们兄弟俩说话的时候能不能别人不要插嘴啊！

王泉：你怎么跟我说话都可以，她是你嫂子啊！你伤她就是伤我。

王海：老婆随时都是可以换的啊，兄弟能换吗？

王泉：以后不要讲这种混账话，我不爱听！

Hai Wang: *Brother, can you lend me tens of thousands of Chinese yuan? I will pay you back as soon as I get the advertising fee!*

Quan Wang: *I have no money.*

Hai Wang: *But you promised that you would give me a gift of money, 10,000 yuan, for my marriage!*

Jiayu Kong: *Wang Hai, didn't your brother transfer 20,000 yuan to you when you got married? You see, neither of us is employed now, and we need money as well.*

Hai Wang: *Elder brother, when we brothers talk, don't let* **outsiders** *interrupt!*

Quan Wang: *You can talk to me in whatever way you like, but she is your sister-in-law! If you hurt her, you hurt me.*

Hai Wang: *We can change our wives any time, but can we change brothers?*

Quan Wang: *In future, don't say this kind of bullshit. It's annoying!*

In Example (20), when Hai Wang shamelessly proposes to borrow money from Quan Wang, Jiayu Kong, as his prospective sister-in-law, could not help but defend their interests. Her speech is considered an interruption by Hai Wang. It is worth noting that Hai Wang does not use 'sister-in-law' or even her name to refer to Jiayu Kong but a particularly alienating referential term ('outsiders'). The term shadows her family-member identity as if she had no relationship at all with their family. Quan Wang is extremely irritated by his younger brother's reaction, and explicitly corrects his words by foregrounding her identity as Hai Wang's 'sister-in-law' via a declarative statement related to her identity ('She is your sister-in-law').

6.4 Strategies that manipulate identity truthfulness

The dataset used in this study also shows that Chinese communicators sometimes manipulate identity truthfulness in a number of ways.

Firstly, Chinese communicators can make use of fictive identities (attributes, affiliations, roles, etc.) to enhance mutual rapport by making identity-related statements or using address terms. Such strategy may be termed a **fictionalizing strategy**. Consider Example (21):

(21) Context: Dean Li and Professor Wang are good friends. Dean Li has invited Professor Wang to give a lecture to the teachers of their college by sending a short text message on WeChat.

李院长：王博导，你什么时候方便，我们想请你来指导。

王教授：你下命令。

李院长：我们周三下午老师们更容易集中，本月底或下月初如何？主要看你时间方便。

王教授：周三可以。

李院长：好的，那我月底提前联系你，谢谢。

王教授：好的。悉听尊命。

Dean Li: *PhD Supervisor Wang, we would like to invite you to give us some guidance at your convenience.*

Professor Wang: ***You just issue an order.***

Dean Li: *It would be more convenient for our teachers to get together on Wednesday afternoons. How about the end of this month or the beginning of next month? It's primarily up to you to decide.*

Professor Wang: *Wednesdays are fine with me.*

Dean Li: *OK, I will contact you in advance before the end of the month. Thank you.*
Professor Wang: *OK.* ***I will obey your order.***

In Example (21), by saying 'You just issue an order', Professor Wang fictionalizes himself as a subordinate and the addressee as his superior officer, instead of identifying them both as friends (the default identity). His identity work effectively elevates the addressee and establishes a jocular environment. However, Li does not react to this but continues to check the arrangements for the lecture with Professor Wang. The same type of identity work is performed by using 'I will obey your order' at the end of their conversation to construct the hearer as a superior. Here is another example:

(22) Context: Lu serves as a director in the faculty office. Master Ge is a temporary worker who has been hired to help in the office doing odd jobs.
鲁主任：葛总，去请李院长签一下字。
葛师傅：主任又拿我开心了。我这就去找李院长。
Director Lu: ***General Manager Ge***, *please go and ask Dean Li to sign this.*
Master Ge: *Director, you're kidding me again. I'll now go and find Dean Li.*

In Example (22), to enhance mutual rapport, Lu jocularly constructs a fictive superior identity for Master Ge, who is actually a temporary worker in the college and not a general manager, by addressing him as General Manager Ge. In response, Master Ge makes no explicit rejection of this form of address, understanding that Director Lu is just bantering ('Director, you're kidding me again'), but immediately proceeds to complete the task he has been asked to do (asking Dean Li to sign a document).

At times, Chinese communicators query, challenge or deny the truthfulness of the identity which has been constructed or fictionalized by the interlocutors (the speaker to the hearer, or vice versa) by making negative statements or interrogative utterances to fulfil particular transactional goals, or to challenge/impair rapport. Consider Example (23) (CCL, Ke Li, *Go Lala Go*):

(23) Context: Mao Ye's wife feels dizzy these days. Mao Ye is concerned about her and has asked her to see a doctor.
他老婆说："没关系，我自己知道。"
叶茂一挥手道："你知道什么！难道你是医生吗？过两天你和美兰说一下，我们俩要一起去检查一下身体，叫她给你两千块吧。"

他老婆吃了一惊道："厂子里今年不是组织我们做过体检了吗？再说，检查身体也要不了两千那么多呀。"

His wife said: 'It doesn't matter, I know.'

Mao Ye waved his hand and said: 'What do you know! **Are you a doctor?** *You had better ask Meilan for 2,000 yuan for a physical examination soon.'*

His wife said in surprise: 'Didn't the factory make us take an examination this year? Besides, it won't cost as much as two thousand for a physical examination.'

In Example (23), Mao Ye's wife declines his suggestion to see a doctor, as if she herself had medical knowledge ('It doesn't matter, I know'). In response, Mao Ye employs a strong rhetorical question ('Are you a doctor?') to challenge the perception of her physical state that she has fictionalized in her response, in an attempt to oppose her refusal and encourage her to accept his suggestion.

In addition, Chinese communicators can sometimes query, challenge or deny the truthfulness of a relational identity that has been assumed or constructed between the speaker and the hearer or a third party, by producing negative or interrogative identity-related utterances, often resulting in challenge or impairment to their mutual rapport. Consider Example (24) (CCL, Zijian Chi, *A Flock in the Wilderness*):

(24) Context: Sangsang is in the fourth grade and often argues with her parents.
桑桑不理睬我们，仍然端着饭回她的房间。
她吃完饭后叉着腰从房间出来，突然指着我说："你不是我亲妈妈，以后你不能再管我了。"
当时听完这句话我气得差点昏过去。我不是她亲妈，谁会是呢？我问她为什么会有这种怪念头。

Sangsang ignored us and carried her meal back to her room.

After the meal, she came out of her room with her arms akimbo and suddenly pointed at me and said: **'You are not my mother,** *and don't control me anymore.'*

I almost fainted when she said this. If I were not her mother, then who could it be? I asked her why she had such strange thoughts.

In Example (24), Sangsang is extremely determined and resents her mother's discipline because she was not controlled by her parents during her childhood. In the interaction, she denies the mother–daughter relationship to prevent her mother from disciplining her. The deconstruction of their mother–daughter relationship harms the harmonious relationship between them, causing her mother to almost faint.

6.5 Summary

The various strategies used to manipulate pragmatic identity that have been discussed above are generally based on the distinction between the default identity and some deviational identity. When a Chinese communicator performs identity work by adopting a specific strategy, more often than not he/she deliberately violates the Maxim of Identity (see Chapter 3) by adopting the default identity in the situated context concerned. In particular, the speaker's intentional switch from one identity to another in a dynamic interaction reflects the strategic nature of pragmatic identity manipulation.

It should be highlighted that even though the way in which speakers use various strategies to perform identity work has been the focus of this chapter, it is the joint efforts of all the participants in an interaction that contribute to identity work. Specifically, the goals of identity work cannot be achieved without the recipient's perception and endorsement, as testified by the recipients' responses in Examples (22) and (24). In some cases, the recipient's response is not particularly explicit or direct, because some of the original texts that have been presented in this chapter fail to record the recipient's physical or physiological responses, as illustrated in Example (23).

7

Identity work in interpersonal communication

This chapter focuses on the identity work that takes place in interpersonal communication between dyads or among multiparty participants. Drawing upon existing literature, this chapter begins with a discussion of the interconnection between identity work and relational work, and then explores in detail how various dimensions of identity can be used for rapport management. Authentic data on the way in which Chinese people propose a toast at the dinner table is presented as a case study, to further illustrate how identity work is performed in the social practice of urging others to drink as much as they can at three typical Chinese dinner parties.

7.1 Identity work as a means of relating

In verbal communication, participants do not always express their ideas directly. They may convey their meanings through an indirect speech act, by virtue of a conversational implicature or by the use of certain polite formulaic expressions. In terms of the connection between indirectness and politeness, scholars hold different views about the underlying motivation for being indirect, ranging from mitigating face threat, showing politeness (e.g. Brown and Levinson 1978, 1987), carrying out a socially approved conversational contract to fulfil one's conversational rights and obligations to be polite (e.g. Fraser 1990; Fraser and Nolan 1981), to promoting the chances of fulfilling one's communicational purposes via the use of expressions of politeness (e.g. Leech 1983, 2014). With the 'relational turn' (Enfield 2009; Spencer-Oatey 2011) featuring in politeness research during recent years, one common understanding that has gradually been shared by many scholars is to associate polite interactions with the ultimate goal of maintaining interpersonal relations, for relational work (Locher and Watts 2008) or rapport management (Spencer-Oatey 2000, 2008). This has given rise to the development of interpersonal pragmatics. For instance, Spencer-Oatey (2000, 2008) holds that people use linguistic politeness to manage rapport, rather than, as proposed by Brown and Levinson (1978, 1987), solely for maintaining face. In other words, according to her Rapport Management Model, other dimensions of interpersonal relations, such as benefit and cost, can also be managed (face is just one dimension of relations). She also points out that while Leech's politeness maxims appear to 'maintain the social equilibrium and the friendly relations' (Leech 1983: 82), in essence they act as pragmatic constraints on the management of the participants' potential face wants and sociality rights, and therefore, ultimately, they are not used for managing interpersonal relations but for fulfilling their communicative tasks. This means that linguistically polite behaviour in interactions can be beneficial for maintaining or promoting long-term interpersonal relations. (Admittedly, first-wave politeness research has also largely neglected the fact that impoliteness can threaten or harm mutual relations between participants.)

Take the performance of speech acts such as requesting and ordering as an example. Spencer-Oatey (2000, 2008) argues that the reason why these speech acts can influence interpersonal relations is that they threaten the participants' sociality rights and obligations, rather than their face. This differs from what is argued in Brown and Levinson's (1978, 1987) Face Theory, which holds that such speech acts threaten the hearer's negative face; that is, the speaker threatens the hearer's autonomy by imposing his/her own desires on the latter. According to Spencer-Oatey (2008), face is 'the positive social value a person effectively claims for himself by the line others assume he has taken during a particular contact' (Goffman 1967: 5), and therefore the performance of speech acts like requesting and ordering has nothing to do with face. Besides, unlike Leech's (1983) Politeness Principle, which regards the Tact and Generosity Maxims as dealing with cost-benefit issues, the Rapport Management Model advances the notion that cost-benefit issues differ in nature from sociality rights and obligations.

By focusing on the management of social relations, Spencer-Oatey (2000, 2005, 2008) proposes the Rapport Management Model (RMM hereafter). In its initial version, there are two motivations for rapport management: the management of face and that of sociality rights. Differing from its conception in Face Theory, face in the RMM is closely related to the participants' personal or social values and can be further divided into personal face (or quality face), relational face and collective face (these latter two can also be called identity face). The former, relating to other people's positive evaluations of one's personal qualities (competence, knowledge, appearance, etc.), is concerned with people's sense of personal worth, dignity, honour, reputation and so on. The latter two, relating to one's social identities or roles (close friend, valued customer, group leader, elder member, etc.), are concerned with people's sense of public worth. Communication can influence the participants' personal face, mutual face and collective face.[1]

Sociality rights and obligations in the RMM, which involve social expectancies, are concerned with the 'fundamental social entitlements that people effectively claim for themselves in their interactions with others' (Spencer-Oatey 2008: 336). They can be further divided into equity (including cost-benefit and autonomy-imposition) and association (including interactional involvement/interactional detachment and affective involvement/affective detachment).[2] The former relates to the belief that people have the right to be treated equally and therefore undue imposition on others should be avoided; the latter relates to the belief that people are entitled to associate with others and to maintain social relations.[3] Both equity rights and association rights can be influenced in communication, reflecting people's concerns about fairness, consideration and behavioural appropriateness.

Spencer-Oatey (2005) proposes three key elements that she believes can influence people's dynamic perceptions of rapport: behavioural expectations, face sensitivities and interactional wants, which are further adjusted in her 2008 book, *Culturally Speaking*. Notably, interactional wants not only involve momentary communicative goals (i.e. specific transactional tasks in specific interactions) but also include the interpersonal goals that participants attempt to achieve.

While reasonable elements in first-wave and second-wave politeness research are integrated in the RMM, it still needs to be viewed as a politeness theory (here 'politeness' is a neutral umbrella term, covering all types of situations, including polite, impolite, non-polite, not impolite, etc.), which goes beyond Leech's (1983: 82) definition of 'politeness' (i.e. 'to maintain the social equilibrium and the friendly relations'). The notion of politeness, therefore, becomes more inclusive, encompassing the management of face (personal/collective/group face), sociality rights and obligations, and interactional goals. Similarly, rapport management is not limited to positive and harmonious rapport orientation but also includes negative rapport orientation such as threatening or challenging social relations.

On the basis of a detailed examination of Spencer-Oatey's (2000, 2005, 2008) RMM, X. R. Chen (2018b) proposes a modified version of the model (see Figure 7.1).

As shown in Figure 7.1, participants often decide their rapport orientation at the very beginning of their communication. Also, they can adjust their rapport orientation as communication progresses.

After deciding upon the specific rapport orientation, the speaker will try to manage the hearer's face, benefits, rights and obligations, emotions or interactional goals (such management can involve more than one dimension at the same time). Depending on the rapport orientation, rapport management can be positively oriented (i.e. to satisfy others as much as possible) or negatively oriented (i.e. to hinder others as much as possible). It should be noted here that benefits have been separated from the association rights, under the assumption that benefits per se constitute an independent dimension of rapport management, which is also in accordance with Leech's (1983) Tact and Generosity Maxims. Moreover, emotions are added to the original list of rapport management dimensions, which differs from the approach taken by Spencer-Oatey (2005: 116), who considers emotional reactions to be the result of management evaluation rather than a dimension of management. Adding emotions to rapport management dimensions is supported by existing literature. The Sympathy Maxim (Leech 1983) and the Feeling-Reticence Maxim (Leech 2014), for instance, actually reflect the management of emotions.

After deciding upon a specific dimension of rapport management, the speaker resorts to various pragmatic strategies or observes maxims such as the Tact Maxim, the Generosity Maxim, the Approbation Maxim, the Modesty Maxim, the Agreement Maxim, the Sympathy Maxim (Leech 1983), the Obligation of S to O Maxim, the Obligation of O to S Maxim, the Opinion-Reticence Maxim and the Feeling-Reticence Maxim (Leech 2014). Whether following or violating those maxims, the adoption of certain strategies is realized by means of various discursive choices. Specifically, the speaker's choice-making takes place in one or more domains: the Illocutionary Domain, the Discourse Domain, the Participation Domain, the Stylistic Domain and the Non-verbal Domain. In other words, rapport management strategies are realized by (non-)linguistic choices made in different domains. Conversely, (non-)linguistic choices can reflect the speaker's specific orientations and dimensions of rapport management.

Finally, the hearer (including non-addressees, e.g. bystanders, eavesdroppers) evaluates the rapport orientation underlying the speaker's discursive choices, based on the social order or moral order that is appropriate for the current

Table 7.1 Identity Work and (Im)politeness Assessment

Relational work	Dimension of identity	Initiated by the speaker	(Im)politeness orientation	The hearer's (im)politeness assessment
Identity work	Attributes	This is what a true man does!	Positive	Polite
		Your son cannot go to school! … Can you still be counted as a man?	Negative	Impolite
		He is the only man in his family.	Neutral	Non-polite
	Membership	We're family!	Positive	Polite
		You are not one of us.	Negative	Impolite
		We six will march forward as one group.	Neutral	Non-polite
	Identification	We are fellow townsmen indeed!	Positive	Polite
		I dislike people from your place.	Negative	Impolite
		I'm Chinese. I love my country.	Neutral	Non-polite
	Role	You are the best teacher I've ever met!	Positive	Polite
		As a dad, how can you let such a thing happen to your child?	Negative	Impolite
		I was Xiao Mao's music teacher.	Neutral	Non-polite
	Doer	You did a great job as a host today!	Positive	Polite
		The activity you organized this time sucks!	Negative	Impolite
		This is my first time to host a program and I'm feeling a little nervous.	Neutral	Non-polite
	Status	We hope you will continue your work here. The company needs you.	Positive	Polite
		You're not qualified to speak here.	Negative	Impolite
		He's the most senior employee in the company.	Neutral	Non-polite
	Stance	Whatever your attitude is, I will support you.	Positive	Polite
		How can you understand the matter this way?	Negative	Impolite
		I know your opinions.	Neutral	Non-polite
	Image	You look terrific today!	Positive	Polite
		You look messy today.	Negative	Impolite
		You're dressed differently today.	Neutral	Non-polite
	Individuality	You are an extraordinary and special girl.	Positive	Polite
		Don't act too differently. You'd better follow the established practice.	Negative	Impolite
		I know you're a person of individuality.	Neutral	Non-polite

situated context. (Im)politeness judgements about the speaker's utterances are the result of this evaluation. Contextual variables, on the basis of which these judgments are made, encompass participant-related factors (e.g. power, distance, interactional roles, number of participants), task-related factors (e.g. cost-benefit considerations, degree of imposition), environmental factors (e.g. time, place) and other factors (e.g. interactional principles, pragmalinguistic conventions, activity types). This means that (im)politeness evaluation is not necessarily directly related to specific polite language or face strategies, as claimed in classic politeness theories, or directly related to interpersonal relations. Instead, the hearer needs to evaluate the rapport orientation underlying the speaker's specific linguistic or strategic choices in the first place, the result of which (i.e. whether polite or impolite) then influences interpersonal relations. In this way, some expressions that appear to impair the addressee's quality face or identity face at a superficial level will not actually harm interpersonal relations (e.g. jocular abuse, see X. R. Chen 2019b), as long as the hearer does not consider the speaker's rapport orientation to be negative.

(Im)politeness is, in essence, a form of evaluation, the result of which decides that of rapport management. Politeness and impoliteness form the polarities of a continuum. The idea of politeness as a continuum is in accordance with Leech's (1983) understanding of politeness in first-wave politeness, while its evaluative nature conforms to second-wave politeness. (Im)politeness evaluation depends on rapport management made possible by a specific discourse, reflecting the influence of a specific communicative behaviour on interpersonal relations. Such an influence is also a matter of degree and can be either positive or negative. If a certain communicative behaviour is believed to enhance mutual relations, it tends to be evaluated as polite. On the other hand, if a certain communicative behaviour is believed to damage mutual relations, it tends to be evaluated as impolite. Other behaviours lie somewhere in between. In this way, rapport management is then connected with (im)politeness evaluations. It is the rapport orientation (e.g. maintaining/enhancing/damaging mutual relations) behind a specific discourse that determines the hearer's (im)politeness evaluation of the speaker.

It is worth emphasizing here that the choice of (im)politeness evaluation, rapport orientation and rapport management strategy, and also (non-)linguistic choices, in the various domains all take place in, and depend on, the communicative context, which is governed by the presumed mutually shared social order or moral order.

Rapport Orientation	The Speaker's Rapport Management					Choices of Discourse Strategy	The Hearer's (Im)politeness Evaluations
	Dimensions of Management						
	Face	Benefits	Rights and Obligations	Emotions	Interactional Goals		
rapport enhancement ↕ rapport protection ↕ rapport neglect ↕ rapport challenge ↕ rapport impairment	enhance face as much as possible ↕ downgrade face as much as possible	give as many benefits as possible ↕ deprive as many benefits as possible	give as many rights as possible ↕ impose as many obligations as possible	attend to emotions as much as possible ↕ neglect emotions as much as possible	advance interactional goals as much as possible ↕ deter interactional goals as much as possible	illocutionary domain ↕ discourse domain ↕ participation domain ↕ stylistic domain ↕ non-verbal domain	polite ↕ impolite

Figure 7.1 Modified model of rapport management (X. R. Chen 2018b: 9)

However, notably, in the above RMM framework, identity is not taken as one dimension of management. While Spencer-Oatey's term 'identity face' has arguably related identity to face, her notion of identity only touches upon participant relations and the position of people within groups (involving identification and social roles), without mentioning the other dimensions of identity (attributes, membership, doers, images, stances, individuality, etc.). On the other hand, by failing to pay sufficient attention to how identity is dynamically constructed in interactions, it is hard to evaluate the influence of active identity work on rapport management. Therefore, it is argued here that identity needs to be incorporated into the RMM as yet another dimension of management in its own right, in parallel to the other dimensions (face, benefits, rights and obligations, emotions and interactional goals), so as to underscore the relationship between identity and politeness.

Fortunately, the past two decades have witnessed the intersection of politeness research and identity research, both of which have an inherent connection. However, until recently, research in the above two fields was conducted separately and independently. The reason for such a lack of communication is suggested by Garcés-Conejos Blitvich and Sifianou (2017: 227) as follows:

Despite its conceptual proximity to face, one of the core constructs of (im)politeness research, identity has not constituted a main focus of (im)politeness scholars until recently. Probably, that was due to the traditional approach of the two fields. Politeness scholarship mostly relied on Brown and Levinson's (1978, 1987) framework and was therefore top-down in orientation. Discursive identity models have been greatly influenced by constructionism and are thus bottom-up in orientation. This presented serious problems of incompatibility until the advent of discursive approaches in the 2000s (Eelen 2001; Mills 2003; Watts 2003) which adopted a bottom-up methodology to the study of (im)politeness. Not surprisingly, it was around this time when scholars started including identity in their accounts of (im)politeness.

Tracy (1990) also strongly suggests that face theorists should pay close attention to the self-presentation claims found in identity scholarship, as do Hall and Bucholtz (2013: 130), who state,

> We have titled this epilogue 'Facing identity' as a bidirectional call for a deeper consideration of the relationship between face and identity: to scholars of politeness to consider the place of identity in facework; and to scholars of identity to consider the place of face in identity work. Although we did not explicitly build politeness into our model of identity and interaction, we are now freshly reminded ... that facework, at once rational and emotional, is fundamental to the workings of identity, as human positioning is always sensitive to the reflection of one's image in the eyes of another.

It is exciting to see that a growing number of scholars have started to combine politeness research with identity research. For instance, Ting-Toomey and Kurogi (1998: 190) define face as a cluster of identity- and relational-based issues. Drawing upon Simon's (2004) self-respect model of identity, Spencer-Oatey (2007) investigates the insights that identity theories can offer for the study of face. Higgins (2007) explores, by drawing on Sacks's (1972) membership categorization analysis (MCA) and Antaki and Widdicombe's (1998) conceptualization of identity as identity-in-practice (i.e. the speaker's dynamic production of themselves and others), the relationship between the face of self and others and their social identities. Other scholars (e.g. Culpeper, Haugh and Kádár 2017: 238; Garcés-Conejos Blitvich 2013) have explicitly related (im)politeness assessments to identity. For example, Garcés-Conejos Blitvich argues that relational work is part of identity work. She demonstrates how the identities of the participants, which are co-constructed in discourse, are closely linked to (im)politeness assessments: specifically, whereas politeness evaluations can ensue as a result of identity verification and/or an implicit/explicit recognition of the authenticity/self-worth/self-efficacy attributes associated with one's identity, impoliteness evaluations can ensue as a result of identity either being partially verified or non-verified and/or a threat to the authenticity/self-worth/self-efficacy attributes associated with one's identity. Locher (2008), by combining relational work with identity construction, explores the relationship between (im)politeness and identity. Some common understandings shared by the above studies are listed as follows (see Culpeper, Haugh and Kádár 2017: 237–8):

a. (Im)politeness manifestations/assessments can be tied to identity (co-)construction, not just to face.
b. Identity and face are inseparable as they co-constitute each other.
c. (Im)politeness can be analysed as an index in identity construction.
d. Models developed for the analysis of identity construction can be fruitfully applied to the study of (im)politeness.

As highlighted by Culpeper, Haugh and Kádár (2017), identity and politeness are closely related to each other. X. R. Chen (2020a) argues that identity work – which refers to all aspects of the discursive work invested by individuals in the construction, maintenance, reproduction and transformation of interpersonal relationships among those engaged in social practice – can lead to politeness assessments, and therefore is one type of relational work. Relational work encompasses three types of orientation: positive orientation (e.g. being polite, refined, elegant), negative orientation (e.g. being impolite, rude, arrogant) and neutral orientation (e.g. being appropriate, normal). Accordingly, different identity work will also bring about three types of politeness assessment (see Table 7.1).

In daily communication, participants tend to choose a particular identity according to their communicative needs. The appropriacy and politeness assessment of the pragmatic identity chosen and the identity work performed will depend on the ongoing context, including the participants' power relations, activity types, environmental factors, the communicators' mental states and so on. In terms of power relations, addressing one's superior as '领导' (lingdao, leader) is only a neutral, unmarked practice; however, addressing a friend or colleague as '领导' will probably involve a politeness assessment. Likewise, the same identity work can lead to different politeness evaluations in different contexts. For instance, addressing one's superior directly by his/her name after an earthquake would be evaluated differently from doing the same thing in daily situations. Also, in certain institutional discourses, like an interrogation, the interrogator's direct utterances to someone of high rank would not cause a negative politeness evaluation. In addition, the speaker's pragmatic competence also influences the hearer's politeness evaluation of his/her identity work. For example, we normally would not evaluate a baby crying in public as being impolite.

7.2 Identity work for rapport management

Identity work can have an impact (e.g. enhance or impair) on different dimensions of rapport management, including face, benefits, rights, obligations, emotions and interactional goals. In the following section, the ways in which identity work can be performed in interactions as face work, a cost-benefit grounder, a rights-obligations rationalizer, emotional work, stance work and an interactional goal facilitator will be illustrated.

Identity work as face work

Before exploring how identity work can be employed to perform face work, we first need to define 'face'. In pragmatics literature, two important approaches for understanding face have been detailed, both influenced by Goffman.

The first approach is described by Brown and Levinson (1987: 61), who define face as 'the public self-image that every member wants to claim for himself', a type of 'emotional and social sense of self that everyone has and expects everyone else to recognize' (Yule 2000: 134). Face conceptualized in this way involves two related aspects: (i) negative face, namely 'the basic claim to territories, personal preserves, rights to non-distraction – i.e. to the freedom of action and freedom from imposition' (Brown and Levinson 1987: 61); and (ii) positive face, namely 'the positive consistent self-image or "personality" (crucially including the desire that this self-image be appreciated and approved of) claimed by interactants' (ibid.).

However, Brown and Levinson's (1978, 1987) conceptualization of face has been challenged by many scholars. Gu (1990, 1992), for instance, points out that in Chinese society, speech acts like inviting and offering are not considered to threaten the hearer's negative face and are even recognized as being polite. Mao (1994) suggests that there are two competing forces that influence interactions: the ideal social identity and the ideal individual autonomy. According to Spencer-Oatey (2008), Brown and Levinson's (1978, 1987) definition of face has placed too much emphasis on individual autonomy and freedom, which is not universally applicable to all cultures; moreover, such conceptualization has ignored the social or interpersonal aspects of face, since face can be personally oriented, group oriented or reciprocally oriented. As highlighted by some scholars (e.g. Gao 1996: 96), face not only involves personal concerns but also, more importantly, group concerns. Both Matsumoto (1988) and Ide (1989) stress the importance of social identity: in Japanese society, a person's position (I, others) in a group and his/her acceptance by others are more important than individual autonomy.

Following Spencer-Oatey, this book adopts Goffman's (1967: 329) definition of face, which is defined as 'the **positive** social value a person effectively claims for himself by the line others assume he has taken during a particular contact' (emphasis added). Such positive social value is reflected in the form of not only self-image but also self-worth (Ting-Toomey and Kurogi 1998). I agree that face is something that is emotionally invested, and can be lost, maintained or enhanced. It must be constantly attended to in interactions, underlying notions of being embarrassed, humiliated or 'losing face'. Defined in this way, face is no longer related to individual freedom of action or autonomy.

This book supports Goffman's (1981) view that face is related to a role or an identity. However, the relationship between face and identity can be either static or dynamic. Goffman appears to focus more on the static aspect of this relationship. For instance, people who are highly educated, have a particular occupation, have a high rank, have a good image or even come from a particular region and country often enjoy more respect and have more face. Face is the emotional advantage or disadvantage inherent in a particular identity. Locher (2008) argues that we can gain much from equating face with identity. Garcés-Conejos Blitvich (2013) also sees face and identity as mutual co-constituents. She even sees face as embedded in identity. From the constructionist point of view, Chaemsaithong (2011: 247) proposes that both face and identity are reflexive, indexed and constructed through the discursive accomplishment of the interactants' communication.

Unlike Goffman, this book focuses more on the dynamic relationship between face and identity. Specifically, it seeks to explore how identity work can enhance, threaten or even impair face by managing certain dimensions of identity. From a pragmatic perspective, performing identity work helps to maintain, promote, threaten, challenge or even impair the face of interlocutors (including that of the speaker, the addressee, a third party, etc.) through discursive practices. Since identity work often involves the interlocutors' face, performing identity work, to a large extent, also performs face work. As Joseph (2013: 51) rightly points out, 'separating identity work and face work' is very difficult.

By considering the analysis of identity dimensions and the definition of face presented in this book, it follows that the types of identity work detailed below can be viewed as face work, and will have a positive or negative impact (a neutral impact is also possible, i.e. maintaining face) on the face of the speaker, the hearer or a third party.

A. Beautifying people's image or praising their ability (as a doer) will enhance their personal/group face; vilifying people's image or depreciating their ability (as a doer) can threaten or even impair their personal/group face. For example:

(1) Context: Li and Wang are former classmates. They meet each other at a provincial conference.
王：李兄今天穿的是新西装吧？帅哥一枚！
李：是吗？这样说也真是太给面子了！

Wang: Brother Li, are you wearing a new suit? **A handsome guy!**
Li: Really? Indeed, your words give me a lot of face!

In Example (1), seeing Li wearing a new suit, Wang, his former classmate, makes an explicit comment about his appearance/image by saying that Li is 'a handsome guy'. His comment clearly pleases Li, as the latter directly responds by saying that Li's words give him 'a lot of face'.

(2) Context: Zhang organizes a conference, which Hu, a teacher from another university, also attends. As acquaintances, they have not met each other often.
胡：这次会议总体不错，但说实话，你闭幕式上的总结不够好啊。
张：哦，你这样看啊，这让我有点感到很没面子哦。

Hu: On the whole, the conference was not bad. But frankly, **your performance as the summary-maker at the closing ceremony was not very satisfactory**.
Zhang: Oh, that's how you evaluate the conference. I kind of feel like I've got no face.

In Example (2), Hu is very straightforward in expressing his somewhat negative evaluation of Zhang's performance, and his comments constitute a depreciation of Zhang's ability as the 'summary-maker'. This explains why Zhang feels rather offended, and considers Hu's words to have deprived him of face.

B. Promoting people's status can enhance their personal/group face; questioning, challenging or denying people's status can threaten or even impair their personal/group face. Consider the following two examples:

(3) Context: A group of card-playing friends gather together at a restaurant. Wang arranges the seats.

汪：老陈，你是咱们的会长，必须上座。

陈：哇，我好有面子！

Wang: Chen, **you're our president**, so you must take the big seat.

Chen: Wow, how much face I have!

In Example (3), Wang's seating arrangement is in accordance with Chinese etiquette: the most honourable guest is invited to sit next to the host on his/her right-hand side, or is even invited to take the host's seat (i.e. 'the big seat'). Since the participants at the dinner are just a group of friends who sometimes gather together to play cards, they are all equal. Even in such an equal setting, someone often needs to take 'the big seat'. To meet this need, the person organizing the gathering will try to find 'an excuse' to single out an appropriate person to take the seat. In this case, Wang deliberately elevates Chen by highlighting the 'leading role' that the latter often plays in uniting the friends for card-playing. Hearing Wang call him 'our president', Chen feels flattered and honoured, as shown by his response 'how much face I have!' Now consider Example (4):

(4) Context: Zhu and Ning are colleagues. Zhu is the deputy chair of the department. As required by the university, he needs to 'listen to' some of the classes of his young colleagues. He discusses with Ning his plan to go to her class. There have been some complaints about her class, largely because she is not a very sociable person and her classes are very dull. She is very annoyed about this plan and becomes very sensitive.

朱：宁老师，我明天下午想去听一下你的课，不知方便不方便？

宁：干嘛要听我的课啊？你以为你是谁啊，又不是学校督导，要听我的课也轮不上你来听啊！

朱：哎呀，宁老师，我也是按照系里的要求啊。你这样说让我好难堪啊。

Zhu: Ms Ning, I'd like to sit in your class tomorrow afternoon. I wonder if this is convenient for you?

Ning: Why sit in my class? **Who do you think you are? You're not a university teaching supervisor.** If someone has to come and sit in my class, it won't be you!

> Zhu: Oh, my! Ms Ning, I'm just doing what the department has asked me to do. Your words really embarrass me.

In Example (4), Zhu's proposal to sit in Ning's class is blatantly rejected, although it has been expressed with an adequate level of politeness, as indicated by the communication of tentativeness ('I wonder if this is convenient for you?'). In Chinese universities, this tentativeness is not often observed, as it is general practice for department leaders to sit in their faculty members' classes at least a couple of times, so that they can provide well-grounded feedback with the purpose of improving the quality of classroom teaching. Under normal circumstances, Zhu, as the deputy chair of the department, has both responsibility and eligibility to visit Ning's class, particularly as her class has been the target of complaint. This is why her refusal surprises Zhu. Furthermore, by challenging his qualification to supervise her class, she presents a significant threat to his face, as indicated by his reply 'Your words really embarrass me'.

Identity work as a cost-benefit grounder

According to Leech (1983), people engaged in communication often follow the Generosity Maxim to minimize benefit to self and maximize cost to self, as well as the Tact Maxim to minimize cost to others and maximize benefit to others. In Spencer-Oatey's RMM framework, cost-benefit, which is parallel to autonomy-imposition, is a part of equity rights. To Leech, the attention that participants pay to costs and benefits reflects their politeness considerations, the aim of which is to achieve a particular communicative goal (similar to Spencer-Oatey's specific interactional goals). However, to Spencer-Oatey, the ultimate goal of attending to cost-benefit is to maintain, enhance or threaten interpersonal relations, which are more enduring than the specific interactional goals. Of course, we might believe that immediate goals are related to long-term goals, and that the difference between the two is only relative. In other words, a temporary pragmatic strategy can also contribute to long-term interpersonal relations. On the other hand, we would argue that cost-benefit also needs to be separated from autonomy-imposition and equity rights so that it stands alone as an independent dimension of management in its own right (X. R. Chen 2018a). For example:

> (5) Context: NJ is visiting a university in another city to give a series of lectures, where the student SHS has collected her from the airport.

SHS: 您是客人，哪能让你买单呢？
NJ: 你不要客气，你是学生，不能让你破费的。
SHS: 您不用客气。我是会议工作人员，打的接客人是可以报销的。
NJ: 那好吧。
SHS: *You are the guest. How can I let you pay for this?*
NJ: *No need to act so politely. You're still a student, so **I can't let you pay**.*
SHS: *Please, I'm a conference staff member, and the taxi bill can be reimbursed later.*
NJ: *OK then.*

The interaction in Example (5) takes place when NJ goes to pay the taxi bill, and the student immediately declines her attempt to do so. By saying 'You are the guest', the student activates the Chinese cultural assumption that guests should be accorded a courteous reception, and therefore it would be inappropriate to let her pay the bill. In return, NJ also performs some identity work. By highlighting the other interactant's identity as a student, she is appealing to the latter's poor financial situation. While this interaction occurs between two individuals who are unfamiliar with each other, it might, nevertheless, influence the impression that each of them form of the other party and further facilitate their future relationship. In comparison to Example (5), Example (6) takes place between a supervisor and a visiting scholar who know each other quite well:

(6) Context: A visiting scholar asks a professor to check her research grant application.
访学老师：老师您好！我给你您发了邮件，我想申报一个课题，麻烦您帮我看下申报书。您是大忙人，您就帮我看看选题怎么样，好吗？
教授：没有问题，不用客气的。

Visiting scholar: *Morning, Professor. I have just sent you an email. I'm planning to apply for a research grant. Could you please have a look at my application form and give me some valuable suggestions when it's convenient for you to do so? I know **you're always a busy person**. Could you just help me by checking the topic I've chosen?*
Professor: *No problem. You are welcome.*

In Example (6), the visiting scholar tries her best to minimize the cost to the professor's workload that her request might incur by asking the professor to only check the topic that she has chosen for her grant application, instead of her whole application. By performing this identity work, she constructs the professor as someone who is 'always a busy person'. By doing so, she not only expresses her understanding of the professor's daily workload but also conveys her consideration for him and her reluctance to bother him. Such identity work helps to create a good impression, which might prove beneficial for their future relationship.

Identity work as a rights-obligations rationalizer

The management of rights-obligations, which are related to sociality rights, is similar to, but not the same as, the management of costs-benefits. A particular social identity often involves certain rights and obligations. Interlocutors sometimes perform identity work to manage the rapport of varied orientations by highlighting, questioning or challenging one's own, the other person's or even a third party's identity. Consider Example (7):

(7) Context: The son, a senior school student, returns home rather late. His father has been anxiously awaiting his return.
父亲：你怎么又这么晚才回家？
儿子：你怎么老管我啊。我是成人了。
父亲：可是我是你的监护人，当然得管啊。
Father: *You've come back home so late again!*
Son: *Why are you always trying to control my business?* **I'm already an adult.**
Father: **I'm your guardian**, *you see. Surely I have to discipline you.*

In Example (7), in reply to his father's question concerning his late return home, the son complains that his father has imposed too much control over him. By claiming that he is 'already an adult', the son tries to activate the assumptions about adult rights (i.e. making one's own decisions and taking responsibility for oneself), to infer that his father should give him more freedom. However, by announcing his identity as being his son's guardian, the father tries to activate the related assumptions about parental rights to discipline the child under his guardianship. In this case, their identity work is in opposite directions, and therefore could inevitably harm their relationship, even if just temporarily. Consider Example (8):

(8) Context: Neighbours Chen and Zhang are on close terms. They often help each other out. Chen is a university teacher, whereas Zhang is the owner of a store in their residential quarters.

陈：老张，麻烦你帮我接一下快递。我还在学校。

张：没问题。咱们是邻居，这点小事应该的。

Chen: *Lao Zhang, could you please take my delivery for me? I'm still at school.*

Zhang: *No problem.* **We're neighbours**. *It's just what neighbours are supposed to do.*

In comparison to the identity work in Example (7), Zhang's identity work in Example (8) highlights their identities as 'neighbours' in the interaction. This helps to improve mutual relations between the two interlocutors. To Zhang, neighbours have an obligation to help each other, and therefore he is supposed to help with matters such as taking Chen's delivery. Such identity work reflects Zhang's understanding of the obligations that are related to being neighbours and is beneficial for enhancing their mutual identification, thus shortening the psychological distance between them.

Identity work as emotional work

In previous literature, emotion is often viewed either as an important influence on the way communication is conducted or as the result of communication. In my proposed new version of the RMM (X. R. Chen 2018b), emotion is regarded as a dimension which is subject to the rapport management of interlocutors. Notably, identity work can also be realized in the form of emotional work and can have an impact on both the development and the outcome of communication. Specifically speaking, emotional work is primarily reflected in the following ways:

a. Enhancing mutual identification can strengthen mutual rapport;
b. Questioning, challenging or denying mutual deification can threaten or even impair mutual rapport.

Consider Example (9) (Feng 2020):

(9) Context: A couple have had an argument. The woman is about five months pregnant. They have called the police to handle the matter. The woman wants to end her relationship with the man.

民警：你们两个再拉拉？

女方：我的意思就是要分开，分手，把孩子打掉。

男方：我不同意，我们都是同学，这么多年了，感情还是很深的。

Police: *Will you two keep on?*

Woman: *I want to break up with him and to have an abortion.*

Man: *I don't agree.* **We were classmates**. *We've been together for so many years, and we have a deep emotional connection.*

In Example (9), the man does not accept the woman's decision to end their relationship. By stating that 'we were classmates', he is trying to promote his emotional identification with her to stress that he loves her, as indicated by the second part of his utterance ('we have a deep emotional connection').

Identity work as stance work

In some cases, Chinese communicators manage the rapport between themselves by expressing a convergence or divergence of attitude towards someone or something, which can be considered to be a form of identity work that is oriented towards stance. This can be termed 'stance work'. Specifically, highlighting a shared stance can strengthen mutual rapport; highlighting a different or even an opposing stance can threaten or even impair mutual rapport. Consider Example (10):

(10) Context: Members of a WeChat group, who are card-playing friends, are chatting after a game.

LH: @BYZ @QYZ @LF 三位高手厉害 👍👍

CXR: 是LF他们进步太快

BYZ: 书记过奖了。

BYZ: **LF进步飞快**。

LH: 会长，我们的确好久没磨合了，也难怪的！

LH: @BYZ 有同感！**LF进步飞快**

LH: @BYZ @QYZ @LF *You three are awesome!* 👍👍

CXR: *LF has made rapid progress.*

BYZ: *Secretary, you flatter me.*

BYZ: ***LF has made rapid progress***.

LH: *President, we haven't played cards together for a while. No wonder [we lost the game this time]!*

LH: @BYZ ***I agree! LF has made rapid progress***.

In Example (10), a group of friends are chatting in their WeChat group after playing a game of cards. LF and BYZ made up one team, and beat the team of LH and CXR. When CXR pays LF a compliment, both BYZ and LH echo his words and construct the same stance as him. While BYZ just repeats what CXR has said, LH uses an explicit marker to express the same stance, followed and intensified by repeating CXR's words. Such identity work serves to enhance their rapport.

Identity work as an interactional goal facilitator

People often have specific goals for interacting with others. 'Any failure to achieve them can cause frustration and annoyance' and 'can significantly affect their perceptions of rapport' (Spencer-Oatey 2008: 17). Therefore, facilitating the achievement of interactional goals is also a way of managing rapport. In Example (5), the student continued to perform identity work in her reply to the professor. By saying 'I'm a conference staff member', she emphasized that 'the taxi bill can be reimbursed later', thereby successfully persuading the other party to let her pay for the bill. Now consider Example (11):

(11) Context: ZT has randomly distributed red packets in a WeChat group of good friends.

WX：早起的鸟儿有虫吃！谢谢王老师的大红包！

LJL: @WX运气好啊。 👍👍👍

WX：@LJL 运气必须好！ 😄😁

ZT: 长江更应发红包 😄！大宴三天 😄

LJL: 支持王老师提议。 😄

(WX发红包)

WX: *The early bird catches the worm! Mr. Wang, thank you for your big red packet of money!*

LJL: *@WX You've got good luck!* 👍👍👍

WX: *@LJL That's for sure!* 😄😁

ZT: ***Changjiang Scholar*** *must give us a red packet* 😄 *! And treat us to dinner for three consecutive days as well!* 😄

LJL: *I fully support Mr. Wang's suggestion.* 😄

(WX gives out a bundle of red packets)

Example (11) begins with ZT giving out red packets of money in the chat group, and WX was very quick to seize one. LJL compliments WX on his good luck, which is echoed by WX himself. ZT then immediately suggests that 'Changjiang Scholar must give us a red packet' (WX has just been awarded the title of 'Changjiang Scholar' by the Ministry of Education, a very rare and prestigious honour for Chinese scholars). In China, when one has achieved something worth celebrating, one is supposed to treat other people. Therefore, by giving prominence to WX's new social identity, ZT proposes that WX should give each group member a red packet. This proposal, which sounds appropriate, is immediately supported by LJL, and successfully leads to WX giving out a bundle of red packets.

7.3 Identity work at the Chinese dinner table: A case study

One important behaviour that reflects Chinese food and drink culture is to urge others to drink at a banquet. Normally, urging others to drink needs to follow a routine sequence, based on age (i.e. starting with the eldest), rank (i.e. starting with the highest rank) and the host/guest identity at the dinner table (i.e. starting with the guests). This section presents a short discussion on the way in which identity work is performed to urge others to drink at the Chinese dinner table, based on my field notes. While utterances that propose a toast, urge others to drink and perform small talk all occur at the dinner table, I will only present examples involving identity work that has been performed to propose a toast and urge others to drink, in order to illustrate the points being made and to explore how particular identities are selected on these occasions (X. R. Chen 2018a).

(12)   Situation 1: A New Year's party for university associations in Nanjing is taking place. The leaders and employees of foreign language schools from a dozen Nanjing universities are participating. Partygoers not only drink with those sitting at their own table, but they also propose toasts to partygoers at other tables.
张老师：各位，我代表南邮的老师敬诸位一杯！
……
倪老师：你们都是搞语言学的，就我一人是文学方向。来，我敬你们各位语言学家们！
……
陆老师：章会长，我代表咱们学会的各位同仁敬你一杯！

Identity Work in Interpersonal Communication 161

……

王老师：吴老师、张老师，我们几个安徽的敬咱们的江苏同仁！

……

顾老师：老蔡，咱们哥们喝一个，感情深一口闷，感情浅舔一舔！

……

常老师：各位都是英语界的，就我一个是法语的，来，敬你们各位英语大师！

……

曹老师：来，我们几位美女敬一下各位帅哥！

……

汪老师：老田、老陈，我们上外的校友来一个！

Zhang: *Ladies and gentlemen, on behalf of the teachers of Nanjing University of Posts and Telecommunications, I'd like to toast you all!*

…

Ni: *You are all scholars of linguistics, only I myself am a researcher of literature. Please, allow me to propose a toast to every linguist here!*

…

Lu: *President Zhang, I'd like to toast you on behalf of our association members!*

…

Wang: *Mr. Wu, Mr. Zhang, we guys from Anhui would like to toast our colleagues from Jiangsu!*

…

Gu: *Lao Cai, let us brothers have a drink. Bottoms up if you feel our great friendship; otherwise just take a sip!*

…

Chang: *You all study English, and I'm the only one who studies French. So to every English master here, cheers!*

…

Cao: *OK, we beauties would like to toast you handsome guys here!*

…

Wang: *Lao Tian, Lao Chen, let us alumni of Shanghai International Studies University have a drink!*

In Example (12), each person proposing a toast highlights a specific identity, including a representative of the teachers of Nanjing University of Posts and Telecommunications (Zhang), a literature researcher (Ni), an association representative (Lu), colleagues from Anhui Province (Wang and others), a close friend (Gu), a French teacher (Chang), a beauty (Cao) and alumni of Shanghai International Studies University (Wang and others). As an old Chinese saying goes, '师出有名' (literally, 'to have a sufficient reason to dispatch troops to a war'), the same appears to be true of dinner table toasts. The Chinese seem to be fond of, and are very good at, finding 'excuses' when proposing dinner table toasts so that the other party will find it difficult to decline. Emphasizing some common identity is often an important way of constructing and strengthening the sense of being an 'insider'. The dinner table is an important space in which to promote relations in China, and, therefore, the identity adopted in toasts is often accepted and echoed by the other party. This is arguably one reason for the successful communicative effect that is achieved by employing identity strategies when proposing a toast or urging others to drink.

(13)   Situation 2: A group of university classmates are celebrating the twentieth anniversary of their graduation at a dinner party. Four former classmates (Zhao, Qian, Sun and Li), together with their spouses and children, are sitting around a table.

赵同学：我提议，我们几位同学一起敬一下各位家属、孩子！

……

钱同学：儿子，我们一起敬孙叔叔一家！

……

孙同学：来，我们几位男士敬各位女士一杯！

……

李同学：老赵，我们二班的敬一下一班的！

……

孙同学爱人：怎么样，我们几位家属也敬一下你们几位同学！

……

钱同学：我代表南京的同学，敬你们几位在扬州的同学！

……

孙同学：老李，我们老乡喝一个！

……

李同学：我们几个喝红酒的敬他们喝白酒的！

Zhao: *I suggest that we former classmates toast our spouses here!*

…

Qian: *Son, let's toast Uncle Sun's family!*

…

Sun: *Come, we four gentlemen shall toast the ladies at this table!*

…

Li: *Lao Zhao, we guys from Class 2 shall toast guys from Class 1!*

...

Sun's wife: *Alright, we spouses would also like to propose a toast to you!*

...

Qian: *On behalf of our classmates from Nanjing, I'd like to toast classmates from Yangzhou!*

...

Sun: *Lao Li, let us fellows from the same hometown have a drink!*

...

Li: *Let us guys with red wine toast those guys with liquor!*

In Example (13), the identities for self that are highlighted by the speakers include former classmates (Zhao), gentlemen (Sun), classmates in Class 2 (Li), spouses (Sun's wife), a representative of classmates in Nanjing (Qian), fellows from the same hometown (Sun) and people drinking red wine (Li). On the other hand, the identities of the addressees that have been highlighted by the speakers include spouses and children, a son, Uncle Sun, ladies, classmates in Class 1, classmates from Yangzhou, fellows from the same hometown and people drinking liquor. Of the identities that have been chosen and highlighted, some are relatively stable, like classmates and fellows from the same hometown, while others are more provisional, such as the representative of classmates in Nanjing, people drinking liquor or red wine, family member groups, gentlemen groups and even identities involving pragmatic empathy, as in the case when Qian adopts the identity of his son and addresses Sun as Uncle Sun. In effect, the employment of 'Lao' (literally means *old*), as in *Lao Zhao* and *Lao Li*, often conveys familiarity and respect in China, and can help promote mutual relations between old classmates. Now consider Example (14):

(14) Situation 3: Liu XX is toasting the guests at his son's wedding party. Unlike the proposal of a courtesy toast at the main dinner table, he is doing his best to urge those sitting at other tables to drink more as a demonstration of his hospitality.

刘1：舅舅，如果看得起外甥，你老人家今天无论如何要略微多喝一点。

刘2：老张，今天是老邻居家的大喜日子，今天要开心，多喝一点。

刘3：老同学，来，咱们再干一杯。明年喝你家儿子的喜酒！

Liu 1: *Uncle, if you think highly of **your nephew**, **you senior** please drink more than usual today.*

> Liu 2: *Lao Zhang, today is the wedding day of **your old neighbour**. You must drink more as a great rejoicing.*
>
> Liu 3: *Come on, **old classmate**, let's have one more glass of alcohol. Looking forward to attending your son's wedding next year!*

In Example (14), Liu is very happy and excited during his son's wedding. During such a celebration, Liu, as the host and joyous father, hopes that the guests will enjoy themselves to the full at the dinner table. As we can see from the example above, when urging his uncle to drink more alcohol, he uses 'your nephew' instead of 'me' as a self-reference, thus giving prominence to their relationship. By addressing him as '你老人家' ('you senior') instead of 'you uncle', Liu raises his uncle's identity, which demonstrates the great respect he has for him. In the case of Lao Zhang, Liu chooses to construct the relational identity of '老邻居' ('old neighbours'), which creates a favourable interpersonal effect in the Chinese context. There is a Chinese saying that 'Good neighbours are more valuable than gold and jewellery', so despite the occasional argument about a trivial matter, people generally cherish harmonious relations with their neighbours. In rural areas of north Jiangsu, where Liu lives, on big occasions like house warmings, weddings, funerals and birthday parties for the elderly, the host would treat neighbours to a free dinner. By following these customs, neighbours do not need to worry about giving gifts of money and are happy to drink to their heart's content. Therefore, Liu's employment of an 'old neighbour' identity could activate related cultural scripts, conveying his intention to urge his neighbour to have more alcohol. Finally, Liu chooses the address term '老同学' ('old classmate') to highlight the relationship between himself and his close friend when he approaches him to propose a toast. In addition, he uses the inclusive 'we' (*zan-men*, literally, 'us') to strengthen identification between insiders.

7.4 Summary

In this chapter, we have explored the various roles played by identity work in rapport management, and thus have specified the interconnections between identity, politeness and face. To be more specific, previous studies on politeness and identity tend to have been limited to one dimension of identity (e.g. image) or politeness (e.g. face), leading to an insufficient examination of both aspects.

However, in actual fact, identity involves various dimensions, and politeness is also concerned with more than one form of evaluation. Some scholars (e.g. Tracy 1990) point out that politeness theory needs to cover identity and other identity-related concepts (e.g. being capable, trustworthy, considerate), but that might involve impression management and self-presentation, which goes beyond the traditional theoretical scope of politeness (i.e. maintaining or promoting harmonious interpersonal relations). Nevertheless, the current discussion has broadened the notion of identity and has conducted a relatively comprehensive and detailed study of how identity is related to politeness, face and rapport management. In this way, this chapter has largely overcome the limitation mentioned in X. R. Chen (2018a) that existing literature has failed to clearly address the relationship between politeness, face and identity.

8

Identity work in institutional communication

In the previous chapter, we examined the identity work that takes place in interpersonal communication between social individuals. This chapter focuses on the identity work that communicators perform in institutional contexts, where one party or both/multiple parties to the communication are institutional (e.g. teachers, lawyers, judges, bank clerks). This form of communication takes place in an institutional context (e.g. a classroom, an office, a court, a bank). Since communicative purposes and interactional contexts vary, the ways in which the functions, types, representations and effects of identity work in institutional communication also vary are therefore worth investigating. Despite the complexities of identity work in institutional contexts, this chapter, due to space limitations, will only focus on identity work in relation to the default factor of institutional power, demonstrating how institutional communicators exercise or suspend institutional power via identity work. By including a case study, this chapter also demonstrates in some detail how related institutional communicators construct, or even highlight, their professional identities to achieve their goals of exerting influence in the institutional contexts concerned.

8.1 Identity work as a means of exercising institutional power

Identity is not only connected with a certain (identity) category-bound activity or obligation (Sacks 1972) but is also power-implicative as well. Some identities, such as experts, scholars, teachers and lawyers, have privileged levels of power and knowledge relative to the general public, laymen, students, clients and so on. Superiors and officials enjoy administrative power that is not available to their inferiors and the grassroots. Policemen and judges have legal power over ordinary citizens, and bosses have economic power over their employees.

Now that identity is power-implicative, identity work is naturally power-sensitive. In critical discourse analysis (CDA), language is assumed to be a means of power (Fairclough 1989). In this regard, I would contend that language in itself is not power, but its use can be, and the use of language for performing identity work can have power implications. At the risk of oversimplification, I only intend to focus on such institutional contexts as a police station and a law court to demonstrate how identity work is enacted for the purpose of exercising institutional power (in this case legal power).

Research has shown that various types of identity work are implemented as a form of legal power that is integral to the working of the police and judiciary. Some instances of identity work are concerned with highlighting the institutional identities of the police and judiciary, whereas others involve the ascription of a suspect's or client's situated identity. For example (CCL):

(1)　　Context: Jun Yu, who is a policeman, is walking down the street.
突然从一条小巷里跑出两个人来，一个说："东西搞到了，快走！"
喻军一愣，职业习惯使他警觉到：这两个人非扒即盗。他一个箭步追上去，双手同时抓住那两人的衣领，喝道："不许动！我是公安局的！"
不料，其中一个身高马大的家伙猛地转身朝他重击两拳，猝不及防的他急退两步，迅即欲拔出枪来。

Suddenly, two men came out of an alley. One said: 'I've got hold of it. Let's leave quickly!'

Jun Yu was taken aback. As a professional, he immediately became alert: The two guys must be thieves, if not robbers. He chased and caught the two men by their collars: 'Freeze! **Police!***'*

Unexpectedly, one of the men, a tall, large guy, suddenly turned around and smashed his fist into him. Unprepared, Yu Jun backed up quickly and produced his pistol.

In Example (1), upon realizing that the two men had probably committed a theft, Jun Yu, as a policeman, chases after them on professional impulse, eventually catching them. He identifies himself as police ('我是公安局的！') when he shouts '不许动' (Freeze!) at them. Such an identity claim entitles him to exercise his power as a policeman and, under normal circumstances, this would enable him to effectively scare the two men into either obeying him or fleeing from the scene. However, there are exceptions to this, as shown in Example (1), when one of the men refuses to surrender but fights back instead. Jun Yu is forced to produce his pistol to threaten the man. The following is another example:

(2) Context: The following dialogue occurs during the course of a courtroom interrogation.

审判员：现在进行法庭调查。被告人刘XX，刚才公诉人宣读的起诉书你是否听清楚了？与你收到的起诉书内容是否一致？

被告：一致。

审判员：（示意被告人坐下回答问题）被告人刘XX，你对起诉书指控的事实有什么意见吗？

被告：没有。

Judge: *Now let us begin the court investigation.* **Defendant** *Liu XX, have you clearly heard the indictment read by the* **public prosecutor**? *Is it in accordance with the one you received?*

Defendant: *Yes.*

Judge: *(motions for the defendant to sit down to answer the questions)* **Defendant** *Liu XX, do you have anything to say about the indictment?*

Defendant: *No.*

In Example (2), the judge does not address the defendant Liu XX solely by his name when interacting with him during the court investigation, as would normally be the case in everyday life. Rather, he adds the legal identity label 'Defendant' before his name. Similarly, he refers to the person who reads out the indictment as the 'public prosecutor', without mentioning his/her name. Thus, we can see that the judge is following normal practices in the courtroom context by using legal identity labels such as 'defendant' and 'public prosecutor'. The use of these labels helps to highlight the behavioural norms that are expected to be followed by the different parties in the courtroom interaction, thereby establishing power relations between them.

Interestingly, a non-institutional person sometimes deliberately highlights the institutional identity of the institutional person he/she is interacting with. In so doing, he/she demands them to enact their institutional rights or obligations, rather than allowing them to act in the name of non-institutional people. For example:

(3) Context: Zhang lives in an apartment on the ground floor of the same building as Chen. Annoyed by the constant noise caused by water from Chen's air-conditioning unit dripping onto her sunshade, Zhang calls the police.

警察：请问是你报警的？什么事呢？

张：403家的空调天天夜里滴水到我们家阳光棚上，吵得我们睡不着。我们跟他们家沟通了，但没有用。**你是警察**，这事你得管一管！

警察：可是你们的这个阳光棚属于违建啊，必须拆除的。不能怪403。

陈：是的啊。再说啦，这些天热得不得了，不开空调怎么过啊？

Policeman: *You called the police? What's up?*

Zhang: *Water from the air-conditioning unit of Room 403 keeps dripping on our sunshade every night. The noise makes it impossible to sleep. We've talked it over with the family, but have got no solution.* **You are a policeman,** *and must handle it!*

Policeman: *But your sunshade is an illegal construction and must be dismantled. You can't blame the noise on Room 403.*

Chen: *Exactly. What's more, it's so hot these days. How can we live without using an air conditioner?*

In Example (3), Zhang accuses Chen of refusing to prevent water from his air-conditioning unit from dripping onto her sunshade each night. Her highlighting of the policeman's institutional identity ('你是警察') is probably intended to solicit his institutional power as well as force Chen to stop his air-conditioning unit from making noise. However, her demand is rejected. Instead, the policeman tells Zhang that her sunshade is an illegal construction and must be dismantled.

8.2 Identity work as a means of suspending institutional power

Identity work is not only used to exercise institutional power, but it can also be used to suspend, weaken or even eliminate this power to achieve interpersonal effects such as constructing affinity, alignment, equality, amity and friendliness. In other words, institutional power can be used in reverse to satisfy particular communicative purposes. For example, some professors on thesis proposal or defence committees do not always enact the expert identity that is appropriate to the situation but instead choose to construct non-institutional identities by using self-referential terms such as 'personally' and 'as a researcher' when giving advice to doctoral students (Ren 2014). It has also been found that health consultants, from time to time, relinquish their institutional identity as an expert or consultant when answering calls to hotline radio programmes. Instead, they often adopt non-expert identities such as 'patient' and 'friend' when giving advice (Yuan 2011). Such identity work phenomena are too wide-ranging to cover in this chapter. Therefore, for demonstration purposes, we will cite only a few examples from J. Chen's (2019, 2020) research on institutional talk between student advisors and their students conducted in the former's office.

J. Chen (2018, 2019, 2020) finds that student advisors tend to construct a number of identities during individual consultations with their students. For example (J. Chen 2020):

(4) Context: A student goes to his advisor's office to ask her for some advice about how to improve his learning efficiency.

辅导员：然后就是你看看，老师又讲这么多啊，都让你没有说话的机会。你看看说了这么多之后，有没有这么一些想问的问题？

学生：问题，我想一想。就是我觉得吧，其实应该是一个，本来就是闲谈吧，我就随便问吧。就是有的人是适合自己学嘛，有的人是那种一看，然后有的人是适合听。我觉得我是适合听的那一种，就是别人跟我讲，我会吸收得特别快。就是如果让我自己去看的话，我会觉得效率很低。然后现在是，很多时候，大学是需要自己学嘛，然后我觉得，我要怎样改善呢？

*Student advisor: **Teacher** has talked so much and it seems that you haven't had a chance to speak. Do you have any questions that you want to ask?*

Student: Questions, wait a minute. Since this is an informal talk, I want to ask some casual questions. People are different. Some people excel at learning by themselves and others find it more suitable to study under the teacher's guidance. I prefer the latter. For me, I study more efficiently under the teacher's guidance, but if I study by myself, I feel that my learning efficiency is very low. And now, you know, as college students, we need to be able to study by ourselves in most cases. I can't think of how I can improve?

In Example (4), the student advisor addresses herself as 'teacher' instead of using the conventional 'I'. Her choice of self-referential term highlights the teacher–student relationship that exists between them. Although she provides advice on how to plan one's college life and how to live happily at college, thus fulfilling the role of an advisor, she tries to sound like she is talking on equal terms with the student. She even blames herself for talking too much ('Teacher has talked so much and it seems that you haven't had a chance to speak') and quickly gives the floor (i.e. the right to speak) to the student ('Do you have any questions that you want to ask?').

Unlike the case of identity work illustrated in Example (4), where the student advisor highlights her identity as a teacher, we sometimes find that student advisors do not highlight their institutional identities but instead construct personal identities, such as that of an individual, a friend or a parent. In other words, they do not appeal to institutional power but turn to personal sentiment to achieve their communicative goals. For example (J. Chen 2019):

(5) Context: A student advisor is talking to a student who has asked her advice on how to live a rich college life.

学生：我觉得自己上大学后就没有怎么好好读书，我觉得应该静下心来去拓展一些不同的领域，这也是非常有趣并且非常有意思的一件事情。

辅导员：是啊，大学应该是通识教育，不是一开始就让你钻在一个小课上，我个人是很推崇那种金字塔式的那种知识积累的过程，尤其是大一大二的时候，你就应该广泛涉猎，什么都看，然后你的底座基础打牢了之后，术业有专攻，是研究生，更多的是研究生时候的事情，所以其实本科就业的时候，专业不对口啊比例是非常高的，国内外都是。

Student: I don't think I have studied well after coming to college. I think I should explore some different fields. Such exploration can also be very interesting.

Student advisor: Yeah, liberal education is an essential part of higher education, instead of limiting you to a specific field from the beginning. **Personally speaking***, I appreciate the pyramid-like process of knowledge accumulation, and especially when you are a freshman or sophomore, you must read books extensively to lay a solid foundation. When you are a graduate student, you're better specializing in one area. In fact, for most undergraduates at home and abroad, when they are employed, their jobs have nothing to do with their specialism.*

In Example (5), the student advisor adopts an explicit personal identity marker ('personally') to emphasize to the student that she is not talking as a student advisor or teacher, even though institutional identities are appropriate in this situation. Such identity work helps to convey the message that her appreciation of 'the pyramid-like process of knowledge accumulation' is only her personal view, and is therefore not something that she wishes to impose on the student, who is free to agree or disagree, accept or decline. Clearly, her identity positioning as a result of suspending her institutional power may well give the student the freedom to choose and decide on her options, thus enhancing the harmonious relationship between them. Consider Example (6) (J. Chen 2018):

(6) Context: Tutor Wang and student Hua are having a one-to-one talk in the office.

辅导员：你现在大一哎。

学生：没有，但是我现在已经很大了。

辅导员：哦，但是问题是你现在还没有切实的做什么勤工助学什么的，你还没有设想别的，对吧？

学生：对对对。

辅导员：制定的还没有做，嗯，行啊，没问题。好像后面，但是做兼职要注意安全啊。我们做家长的，最担心的就是你们的安全了。

学生：嗯。

辅导员：第一个要注意安全，第二个，当然男生可能要稍微好一点，但是仍旧有人身安全的问题，第二就是那个，做兼职的话你可能要有一些取舍。就是不要什么都去做，第一价钱你肯定要考虑，千万不要充当廉价劳动力，第二要对自己今后发展有帮助的。

学生：对对。

Tutor: *You're a freshman.*

Student: *No, I'm older now.*

Tutor: *Oh, but the problem is that you haven't actually done any work placements or anything else. You haven't got any other plan, right?*

Student: *Yeah.*

Tutor: *What you had planned has not been carried out yet. En, ok, it doesn't matter. But pay attention to your safety when doing part-time jobs. This is what we, **as parents**, worry most about.*

Student: *OK.*

Tutor: *The first point you need to care about is safety, and the second also relates to personal safety issues, even though it may be slightly better for boys. Then you need to conduct some trade-offs when doing part-time jobs. Don't just do anything. You must first consider the salary, so as not to be treated as cheap labour, and secondly whether the experience will benefit your future development or not.*

Student: *Yes, yes.*

In Example (6), the student advisor constructs herself as a parent when inquiring about the student's participation in work placement activities. Her adoption of her parent perspective rather than her student advisor perspective when cautioning the student to be aware of safety issues makes her cautionary advice appear affect-motivated and not power-motivated. This ensures that her reminder is more favourably received by the student than it might otherwise have been, because, in China, it is a matter of course that parents are concerned with their children's safety, even when they are adults.

On other occasions, student advisors can construct both an institutional identity as a teacher and personal identities as individuals or friends. For example (J. Chen 2019):

(7) Context: A student advisor is having a one-to-one talk in her office with a student about his life and studies.
辅导员：那除了学习之外呢？
学生：生活方面吗？

辅导员：生活方面，你有没有什么困难啊？我们既是师生，更是朋友你有困难不妨直接说出来。

学生：有啊，我觉得，嗯……

辅导员：或者还有那个社会工作啊，等等。

Student advisor: What else do you want to talk about apart from your studies?

Student: My daily life?

Student advisor: Do you have any problems in your daily life? **We're not only teacher and student, but also friends**. Just let me know if you do.

Student: Yes, I think, mm …

Student advisor: Or, how about your social work? And so on.

In Example (7), when enquiring about whether the student has any problems in his daily life, the student advisor constructs a double identity of both a teacher and a friend by saying, 'We're not only teacher and student, but also friends.' The former is an institutional identity that is appropriate in the current context, while the latter is a non-institutional identity that is appropriate in daily interpersonal interactions. Her identity work of identifying the student as her friend, in addition to adopting her institutional identity as a teacher, serves to narrow the distance between them. This form of identity work performed by the student advisor is commonly found in interactional practices between student advisors and their students.

8.3 Identity work during Chinese reality TV mediation: A case study

This section reports on an empirical study into how Chinese experts perform identity work in reality TV (RTV) programmes for the purpose of successful mediation.

Mediation discourse has attracted a great deal of attention in recent decades due to its contextual and functional characteristics. Existing research focuses on its linguistic features, such as address terms (Jiang and Liu 2014; Ke 2013), discourse markers (Xu 2006), conversational sequences and structures (Greatbatch and Dingwall 1989, 1997; Heisterkamp 2006; Lü 2005; Stokoe and Sikveland 2016), discursive strategies (Jacobs 2002; Ke and Liao 2011; Rifkin, Millen and Cobb 1991; Tracy and Spradlin 1994; Wang 2012), pragmatic functions (Jiang 2016) and interactional features in terms of the power relations between disputants (Cheng 2009; Lü 2005). Most relevantly, some scholars have approached mediation discourse from the perspective of identity construction and have analysed the types of identities that are constructed and their discursive representations (e.g. Jiang and Liu 2014; Ke and Li 2014; Maley 1995; Wang 2012), and how the constructed identities influence the mediation process and consequences (Jiang and Liu 2014; Ke and Li 2014). However, to date, no study has investigated whether, how or why mediators construct identities that are appropriate to their professional backgrounds.

On a different front, few studies have explored the issue of identity construction during the course of mediation in an RTV mediation context that involves more than one mediator. RTV originated in 'actuality programming' in the United States during the 1940s (Garcés-Conejos Blitvich and Lorenzo-Dus 2013), with forerunners including *Candid Camera*, *Real People* and *The Gong Show* (Garcés-Conejos Blitvich and Lorenzo-Dus 2013). Although no consensus has been reached as to its definition (Garcés-Conejos Blitvich and Lorenzo-Dus 2013), RTV is generally viewed and analysed as 'factual media output' (p. 27) with a premise on 'viewer acceptance of there being strong connections between recording and reality' (ibid.). Academic critique of RTV is mixed (Garcés-Conejos Blitvich and Lorenzo-Dus 2013), with some applauding RTV for allowing citizens to have increasing access to the public domain of the media, and some criticizing its contribution to the 'demotic turn' (Turner 2010) and the exploitation of common people (e.g. Culpeper 2005). That said, RTV is still one of the most influential and popular TV genres (or sets of genres) in China, with popular programmes such as *Feichengwurao*, *Keep Running*, *Voice of China* and *Gold Medal of Mediation*. In connection with identity work, it is worthwhile exploring whether the RTV setting influences the construction of the mediators' identities.

Research questions

Based on a brief review of related literature on mediation and RTV, this case study seeks to address the following two research questions:

a. Do mediators from certain professions construct their current identities as mediators in relation to their professional backgrounds? In other words, do they construct their professional identities while mediating, and in what way?

b. What possible factors underlie the construction of a professional identity by mediators during an RTV programme, if any?

It is hoped that by answering these questions, this case study will provide both a new dimension for analysing identity construction in institutional interactions and a new perspective for understanding the nature and mechanism of Chinese RTV programmes.

Data source and collection

The data for this study was obtained from the RTV programme *Gold Medal of Mediation* (*GMM*), which first aired in 2011 and has continued to be one of the most popular RTV programmes in China. The programme generally includes two parties who are in dispute, the host, a Gold Medal mediator, and eight observational expert mediators from various professional backgrounds, such as lawyers, psychotherapists, college teachers, judicial cadres, radio programme hosts and social workers. In each episode (of approximately thirty-five minutes), two people (known as the 'two parties', instead of defendants or plaintiffs) are invited to present their dispute on stage, and the host and expert mediator group try to help them resolve the dispute. During this process, the programme aims to demonstrate the wisdom and art of resolving disputes and conflicts. All episodes of *GMM* are available online.

This study analyses the discursive practices used by mediators from two professional backgrounds, legal and psychotherapeutic, in order to reveal possible interconnections between the mediators' expertise, their identity construction and the effect that this identity construction has on the outcome of the mediation. Mediators from these two professions are selected because they are more likely to be identified as teachers and social workers from their possible explicit use of jargon and professional knowledge, than experts from some other professions.

To correctly understand the discursive identity construction of legal and psychotherapeutic mediators, it is important to have an adequate understanding of how the RTV programme *GMM* in particular, and mediation in general, progresses. In the following, a simplified account of the format of *GMM* is given, along with illustrations for each of the stages that are included. Table 8.1 presents the main stages in each episode of *GMM*.

Identity Work in Institutional Communication   177

Table 8.1 Mediation Steps in *Gold Medal of Mediation*

Step	Name	Participants	Main activities
1	Lead-in	Two parties in dispute	A short videotape introduces the two parties in dispute, which generally depicts the dispute as a mystery to be solved.
2	News-telling	(1) Host (2) Two parties in dispute	(1) The host introduces the two parties in dispute, the mediators, and herself. (2) The two parties in dispute present their accounts of the dispute and their mediation goals, one at a time, following the order indicated by the host. (3) Following the initial accounts of the dispute, the two parties elaborate on the dispute with relevant background information and details; this joint and mixed account is facilitated by the host's questions and ongoing repeats and summaries. (4) (optional) The host contacts certain informed people by phone for more information about the dispute.
3	On-stage mediation	(1) Host (2) Two parties in dispute (3) Gold Medal mediator (4) Observational mediators	(1) Gold Medal mediator conducts his mediation. (2) Some of the eight observational mediators volunteer to mediate. (3) During this process, the two parties in dispute reply to the mediators' questions, evaluations, advice, etc. or offer more information. (4) The host monitors the whole process and assigns turns.
4	Chamber mediation	(1) Two parties in dispute (2) Observational mediators	(1) The two parties in dispute are brought into a chamber one after the other, where certain observational mediators discuss with them their real thoughts on the dispute and their minimum mediation goals. (2) The two parties are brought into the chamber together by certain observational mediators to further discuss the issues at hand.
5	Conclusion	(1) Two parties in dispute (2) Host (3) Gold Medal mediator	(1) The host enquires about the result of the chamber mediation. (2) The two parties explain the result of the chamber mediation. (3) (optional) The two parties sign an agreement. (4) The Gold Medal mediator concludes.

On the basis of previous episodes of *GMM*, it can be seen that only a very small part of the chamber mediation process is shown on the RTV programme (which is understandable since chamber mediation is meant to be offstage). Thus, only data from the onstage part of the mediation process were collected for analysis in this study.

During data collection, one episode (episode 0221) was randomly chosen to be the starting point, and the following episodes were then watched in order until ten episodes involving the discursive practices of mediators with legal expertise and ten episodes involving the discursive practices of mediators with psychotherapeutic expertise were collected. Then, the sections containing the relevant discursive practices were transcribed using a crude version of Conversation Analysis (CA) conventions. A detailed description of the data (including episode theme, number of turns and words) for each of the two sets of episodes (legal and psychotherapeutic) is presented in Tables 8.2 and 8.3, respectively.

Data analysis

To provide answers to the two proposed research questions, the data were analysed in two ways.

Regarding the first research question, the data were scrutinized to ascertain the discursive practices that contributed to the construction of either a legal mediator identity or a psychotherapeutic mediator identity. The analytical framework used was modified according to Tracy and Robles's (2013) account of discursive practices for identity construction. However, as their account of discursive identity construction is based on the academic background of communication studies, it would not appear to be particularly applicable to the current study. Therefore, this study first focuses on only the linguistic (in the narrow sense) features, omitting discursive features such as the 'sight and sound of speech' in Tracy and Robles's (2013) framework. Furthermore, a data-driven approach is also adopted to identify additional linguistic features that might facilitate identity construction, wherever possible, adding new identity-indexing features like jargon and evidentials that indicate professional knowledge. Second, the 'content' aspect of discursive practices was considered, as it is closely related to expertise.

Table 8.4 presents the working analytical framework used.

Table 8.2 Information for Episodes Involving the Legal Mediator

Episode number	Episode theme	Numbers of turns	Numbers of words
0221	'A Childish Husband'	2	495
0222	'Domestic Abuse from Wife'	1	280
0227	'Why Ex-wife Extorted the Property'	1	641
0228	'Behind the Curtain of a Remarried Family'	1	418
0301	'A Wife's Gambling Addiction'	3	531
0302	'A Young College Girl's Mysterious "Campus Loan"'	1	568
0303	'Twilight Love'	1	625
0304	'Extreme Frugality'	1	598
0306	'An Unfair Property Notarization'	1	825
0308	'The Allocation of Family Property'	12	770

Table 8.3 Information for Episodes Involving the Psychotherapeutic Mediator

Episode number	Episode theme	Numbers of turns	Numbers of words
0221	'A Childish Husband'	1	420
0224	'A President's Gambling Addiction'	1	789
0225	'A Fearsome "Vampire"'	17	992
0226	'Our Daughter Is Growing Up'	1	359
0228	'Behind the Curtain of a Remarried Family'	3	580
0302	'A Young College Girl's Mysterious "Campus Loan"'	1	252
0306	'An Unfair Property Notarization'	5	310
0309	'Divorcing My Wife to Retaliate at My Mother'	1	608
0310	'A Husband's Lie'	1	478
0311	'Huge Debts from Nowhere'	1	484

Table 8.4 Discursive Practices Used for Identity Construction

Discursive practice	Description
Self-referencing practices	Words used to address self
Jargon or semi-jargon	Words indexing professional background
Evidentials	Words or expressions indicating expertise
Speech acts	Social acts performed through talk

Regarding the second research question, the discussion was centred on the goals of the RTV programme, particularly its entertaining and enlightening functions. Examples will be provided where necessary.

Results of the study

The following section reports on the identity work performed by the legal mediator and the psychotherapeutic mediator, respectively.

A. *The discursive practices used by the legal mediator to construct or highlight his professional identity*

By analysing the data collected, it was found that the legal mediator deployed four types of discursive practices to construct his professional identity: (i) self-referencing terms; (ii) jargon; (iii) evidentials; and (iv) speech acts, mainly including the speech acts of informing, counselling, evaluating and questioning (Table 8.5).

As can be seen from Table 8.5, in the ten episodes of *GMM* that involve the legal mediator, 145 discursive tokens are used to facilitate the construction of the speaker's identity as a legal mediator, including 1 professional self-reference, 69 instances of jargon or semi-jargon, 12 evidentials and 63 professionally bound speech acts (39 informing, 12 counselling, 4 evaluating and 8 questioning). The following are some examples taken from the data.

The only one professional self-referencing term that is used ('as a lawyer') occurs in episode 0306, 'An Unfair Property Notarization'. An excerpt is provided below.

> Excerpt 1 (episode 0306):
> 作为律师呢，我要表达的是，刚刚那份公证书是在你们婚后进行的，但同样是跟婚前的财产公证一样具备法律效力。
>
> **As a lawyer**, I want to state that although that notarial certificate was obtained postnuptially, it has the same legal force as a premarital property notarization.

As can be seen in the above excerpt, the legal mediator's use of a professional self-referencing term occurs at the beginning of his speech. Thus, by doing so, the legal mediator conveys a professional tone which serves to render his subsequent speech act (in this case, an informing speech act) authoritative and convincing to the disputants and, arguably, also to the RTV audience.

There are twelve evidentials in the data. During mediation, the legal mediator refers to the law or previous cases when providing relevant information, in order to examine the legal rights, obligations and consequences concerning certain acts and so on. Consider the two excerpts below:

Excerpt 2 (episode 0306):

但从法律上来讲的话，很遗憾，吴先生，您对这几栋房产，是没有分割权利的。

But **in terms of the law**, Mr Wu, I regret to say that you have no right to divide the property into several estates.

Excerpt 3 (episode 0221):

但是，根据我现有查到的案例，有一个和你非常相似的案例，而那个案件和你的事情的不同之处在于，警方在当事人　去取钱的过程中，抓获了。

However, **according to the cases I have seen**, there is one that is particularly similar to your situation, with the only difference being that the litigant was caught in the act by the police when the former went to fetch the money.

In the above two excerpts, the legal mediator's use of evidentials indicates his professional epistemological background, and renders the proposition authoritative and convincing.

In comparison to professional self-referencing terms (one instance) and evidentials (twelve instances), jargon (sixty-nine instances) occurs much more frequently in the legal mediator's utterances. Jargon is a useful indicator of a professional identity (Tracy and Robles 2013). In the data, jargon and semi-jargon occur as an integral part of the legal mediation utterances and are usually semantically self-explanatory, thus no explanation is provided in most cases. Excerpt 1, for example, contains jargon such as 'notarial certificate', 'postnuptially', 'legal force' and 'premarital property notarization'.

Sometimes, however, the legal mediator provides a further explanation for the legal terms he is using, as in Excerpt 4:

Table 8.5 Discursive Practices Used by the Legal Mediator to Construct or Highlight His Professional Identity

Discursive practice	Frequency	Examples
(1) Self-referencing terms	1	'as a lawyer (作为律师呢)'
(2) Jargon	69	'personal debt (个人债务)'; 'matrimonial debt (婚内共同债务)'; 'compensation of mental impairment (精神损害赔偿)'; 'lawsuit (诉讼案件)'; 'evidence (证据)'
(3) Evidentials	12	'According to the cases I have found (根据我现在查到的案例)'; 'In terms of the law (在法律上)'; 'It is not supported by the law (法律是不支持的)'
(4) Speech acts		
(4.1) Informing	39	'According to the law it is considered to be postnuptial personal debt (这个在法律上应当被认定为婚后的个人债务)'
(4.2) Counselling	12	'I think one practical solution is that … (我认为的话比较切实的方案就是 …)'; '(Based on the above discussion), my advice is that, this issue can be negotiated (那么最终我个人建议，就这个问题可以商量)'
(4.3) Evaluating	4	'As parents, we have an obligation to raise and educate our children, but from what I have heard just now, you have not established some (necessary) rules (作为父母来说，对于子女，我们有这种教育的义务，从你们刚刚谈的各种琐碎小事来说，包括教育孩子没有立好规矩)'
(4.4) Questioning	8	'That is a bank loan, right? (那是银行贷款，对吧？)'; 'Then did you two entertain friends together? That is, did your friends still consider you to be married? (那么你们对外，是不是共同接待各自的亲朋好友？就周围边的朋友是不是认为你们还是夫妻？)'
Total	145	

Excerpt 4 (episode 0308):

分关是个很古老的名词，新华字典明确的答复是，分家析产的文书，分家析产，分谁的？分父母的，既然是分父母的财产，自然不用征求子女的意见。

Fen Guan is an ancient term, which according to Xinhua Zidian means **document for dividing up family property** for the division of family property. Whose property? The parents. Since parents own the property, they need not ask for their children's opinions regarding its division.

In this excerpt, the legal mediator explains the meaning of the term 'Fen Guan', because it 'is an ancient term', and hence its legal implications may not be familiar to everyone.

In addition, four types of speech acts, used to facilitate the construction of the legal mediator's professional identity, are identified: questioning, informing, evaluating and counselling. Relevant questioning occurs eight times in the data. The legal mediator asks questions from a professional perspective to facilitate a legal assessment of the dispute. The reason for asking professional questions is that the two parties requiring mediation do not always provide adequate information, as observed by the legal mediator in Excerpt 5:

Excerpt 5 (episode 0301):

调解员：这个问题呢，作为一个诉讼案件来讲，是比较复杂，因为我们现在只是听你们口述，相关东西我们其实没有看到的。除了这份协议，离婚协议，你们平时就是在一起生活的时候，收支这块是混同的吗？

H女士：对。

调解员：那么你们对外，是不是共同接待各自的亲朋好友？就周边的朋友是不是认为你们还是夫妻？

X先生：是的。

Mediator: *This issue, as a lawsuit, is rather complicated, because we have only listened to your oral statements and have not seen the relevant documents. Except for this agreement, the divorce agreement, do you count your incomes and expenses together when living together?*

Ms H: *Yes.*

Mediator: *Then did you two entertain friends together? That is, did your friends still consider you to be married?*

Mr X: *Yes.*

In this episode, the legal mediator first observes that 'because we have only listened to your oral statements and have not seen the relevant documents', a legal assessment cannot be made. In Excerpt 5, the mediator asks two relevant professional questions over two turns, which the couple answer. Then, in a long turn (not included in the above excerpt), the mediator describes and assesses the dispute from a legal perspective before offering his professional advice.

When performing the speech act of informing,[1] the legal mediator describes, identifies and characterizes the disputes and relevant events from a legal perspective (Excerpt 6), provides background legal information (Excerpt 7) and highlights the legal consequences of the disputes and relevant events (Excerpt 8).

Excerpt 6 (episode 0221):
借款的问题，按照你们的陈述，场上男方至今那二十七万欠款，绝大部分用于个人的生活和挥霍。这个在法律上应当被认定为婚后的个人债务。

Regarding the debt, according to your statement, the man onstage still owes 270,000 yuan, which he has mostly squandered on personal enjoyment. **According to the law it is considered to be postnuptial personal debt.**

Excerpt 6 involves a dispute between a couple. The wife is seeking a divorce because her husband has generated a large amount of debt and is being irresponsible towards his family by lying and squandering. In the sentence set in boldface, the legal mediator identifies the husband's debt to be postnuptial personal debt (based on the couple's statement on how the money has been spent as well as relevant professional knowledge).

Excerpt 7 (episode 0227):
在民事方面的合同，它的评价有几点：第一个：是不是遭到了强迫胁迫而签订的；第二个，是不是显示公平；第三点，就在签订的时候，假如一方出现了违约责任，这种违约责任的条件是如何成就的，而成就之后，又是怎么处罚的。

A civil contract can be evaluated according to the following points: first, whether either party has been forced to draw up the contract; second, whether it reflects fairness; third, what behaviour is considered to be a violation of the contract and what the punishment is for that violation.

Excerpt 7 involves a divorced couple. The husband wants to take the estate, which he owns according to the couple's previous contract, back from his ex-wife, who still occupies the estate. In this excerpt, the legal mediator provides some relevant background information about how to evaluate a civil contract, because the contract previously drawn up between the couple is a civil contract.

> Excerpt 8 (episode 0228):
> 如果遭受家庭暴力的一方进行报警取证，将来离婚的时候，受害一方同样是可以请求精神损害赔偿。
> *If the party suffering domestic violence has reported it to the police and obtained evidence, the party will be able to request compensation for mental impairment when divorcing.*

Excerpt 8 involves a couple who are reconsidering their marriage. They have been married before to other people. The husband suffers domestic violence from his wife. In this case, the legal mediator points out the legal consequences of domestic violence.

Relevant evaluation occurs four times in the data. By an evaluative speech act, we mean that the speech act expresses the mediator's emotional and moral attitudes towards the dispute and the disputants. Excerpt 9 is a case in point:

> Excerpt 9 (episode 0228):
> 作为父母来说，对于子女，我们有这种教育的义务。从你们刚刚谈的各种琐碎小事来说，包括教育孩子，你们没有立好规矩。
> *As parents, we have an obligation to raise and educate our children, but from what I have heard just now, you have not established some (necessary) rules.*

In Excerpt 9, the mediator begins by emphasizing the parents' obligation to raise their children, as stipulated in law, and then passes the evaluation that the two parties have not fulfilled their duty in regard to educating their children properly.

In addition to questioning, informing and evaluating, the legal mediator also provides advice based on his understanding of the dispute at hand and the law. Expert advice is typically provided before the close of a matter, and is generally preceded by informing (Excerpt 10) and sometimes by evaluating (Excerpt 11).

> Excerpt 10 (episode 0227):
> 在民事方面的合同，它的评价有几点：第一个：是不是遭到了强迫胁迫而签订的；第二个，是不是显示公平；第三点，就在签订的时候，假如一方出现了违约责任，这种违约责任的条件是如何成就的，而成就之后，又是怎么处罚的。…… 我认为的话比较切实的方案就是首先，第一点，你们双方的话，站在一个角度，考虑一下房子给谁，另外一方补钱，当

双方争执不下的时候，谁也拿不出钱来的时候，那么很简单，那就是拍卖，各自拿走各自的钱。

A civil contract can be evaluated according to the following points: first, whether either party has been forced to draw up the contract; second, whether it reflects fairness; third, what behaviour is considered to be a violation of the contract and what the punishment is for that violation. ... In my opinion one practical solution would be, first, the two parties together think about and decide who will own the estate and the other will then receive financial compensation, and if you cannot reach an agreement or do not have adequate money, then another simple solution is to auction the estate and split the money.

In Excerpt 10, the legal mediator provides advice for the resolution of the dispute concerning estate ownership after providing relevant information about the legal force of the couple's previous contract. This advice appears at the end of the matter and before the legal mediator turns his attention to the implementation of compensation or newly agreed ownership. In this latter session, he first provides legal information and then provides advice (not included in the above excerpt).

Excerpt 11 (episode 0306):
那么对于吴先生来说，他的确是会觉得有一点吃亏。...... 大致上主要的财产，是女方所有，但是不是能把它朝双方共有的这个层面发展？

Thus for Mr Wu, it is justifiable that he might, to a certain degree, feel that he has been taken advantage of. ... Sure, the main part of the property is owned by the female party, but I wonder if it is at all possible that ownership of the property could be tilted just a bit further in the direction of co-ownership?

Excerpt 11 involves a couple who are in dispute over a seemingly unfair property notarization, that is, the wife owns the majority of the property. After identifying the nature of the dispute and relevant details from a legal perspective (not included in the above excerpt), the legal mediator evaluates that the husband is indeed justified in claiming that he is being taken advantage of (the first sentence in the above excerpt), and, at the end of his turn, the legal mediator provides advice for solving the dispute.

B. The discursive practices used by the psychotherapeutic mediator to construct or highlight her professional identity

Table 8.6 presents the type and frequency of the discursive practices deployed by the psychotherapeutic mediator to construct her professional identity in the ten relevant episodes. In total, 129 discursive tokens are used to facilitate the construction of a psychotherapeutic mediator identity, including 46 instances of jargon, 2 evidentials and 81 speech acts (26 informing, 19 counselling, 14 evaluating and 22 questioning).

In the ten episodes involving the psychotherapeutic mediator, no professional self-address terms are used to indicate the mediator's psychotherapeutic background because there is no such special address form available in Chinese.

Two evidentials occur in the data. In Excerpt 13, the psychotherapeutic mediator cites empirical data from a physiopsychological experiment when accounting for the male party's psychological issue (i.e. his addiction to gambling), while in Excerpt 14 the mediator resorts to a psychological hypothesis to support her argument.

> Excerpt 13 (episode 0224):
> 当一个人赌博，以及在催眠状态下狂欢的时候，多巴胺分泌量达到百分之一千两百。这是实验室数据。
>
> *When one is gambling or revelling under hypnosis, one's dopamine level is at 1,200 percent.* **This is laboratory data.**
>
> Excerpt 14 (episode 0226):
> 我们经常在心理学里面解读一个女孩子，她为什么会无数次的早恋，实际上就是因为这个家庭缺爱的一个结果，就是跟父亲的链接产生了裂痕。
>
> *In psychology, we often interpret this type of girl who falls in love a lot at an early age as suffering from a lack of parental love. Specifically,* **her relationship with her father is damaged**.

The psychotherapeutic mediator uses a great deal of jargon in her mediation attempts (forty-six times in the data). Like the professional lexical choices made by the legal mediator, the majority of these lexical items are not explained (e.g. Excerpt 15). It is only on some occasions that additional explanations are provided (e.g. Excerpt 16).

> Excerpt 15 (episode 0302):
> 这个心理阴影是什么呢？是我们在最初的时候，这种生存的需要被否定，她有一个很强烈的湮灭恐惧，导致孩子产生强烈的不安全感。

Table 8.6 Discursive Practices Used by the Psychotherapeutic Mediator to Construct or Highlight Her Professional Identity

Discursive practice	Frequency	Examples
(1) Self-referencing terms	0	
(2) Jargon	46	'psychological characteristics (心理特点)'; 'dopamine (多巴胺)'; 'annihilation fear (湮灭恐惧)'; 'insecurity (不安全感)'; postnatal depression (产后抑郁)'
(3) Evidentials	2	'This is laboratory data (这是实验室数据)'; 'in psychological (research) (在心理学里面)'
(4) Speech acts		
(4.1) Informing	26	'What are Mr Wang's (main) psychological characteristics? They include, first, an avoidance defence mechanism, second, a childlike affection evaluation system (王先生的特点是什么？第一，回避式的防御机制；第二，儿童式的情感评价体系)'
(4.2) Counselling	19	'Based on her current physiological basis, the best solution is to assuage her emotionally and with love …. (基于她这样的生理基础，所以最好的办法就是，多做情绪上的情感上的安抚…)'
(4.3) Evaluating	14	'There is no real difference between you, only that your husband is worse (跟你讲，没什么区别，只是你丈夫做得更恶劣一点)'; 'From what I have heard today, I know your parents love you too much and control you too much, I admit there is a "too much" (整场听得下来，你父母太爱你了，太控制你了，确实是要加这个太字)'
(4.4) Questioning	22	'What is the relationship between you really like? What is its fundamental cause? (究竟你们之间，要是一种怎样的关系？你们之间内心最真实的原因是什么？)'
Total	129	

What is this **psychological shadow**? When our survival need is denied at the very beginning of our lives, we form an intense **annihilation fear**, causing us to feel great **insecurity**.

Excerpt 16 (episode 0228):

王先生的特点是什么？第一，回避式的防御机制；第二，儿童式的情感评价体系；回避式的防御机制是什么？你不跟你的前妻过了，你就要走，逃到哪去？随心所欲啊。逃到这个女人的身边，和另外一个女人的身边，无所谓啊。……这叫回避式防御机制。儿童式评价体系是什么？儿童的对人的评价体系，不包括是非，不包括道德，只包括我在你身边的感觉，谁对我好，我就说谁好，我就跟谁在一起。

What are Mr Wang's (main) psychological characteristics? They include, first, an avoidance defence mechanism, second, a childlike affection evaluation system. What is an avoidance defence mechanism? When you do not want to live with your ex-wife, you run away. Where? You don't care. Run to this woman or to that woman? You don't care. … This is an avoidance defence mechanism. What is a childlike affection evaluation system? A child's evaluation of a person does not include right or wrong, it does not include morality. It only includes my feelings when I am around you. When a person is nice to me, I will say he is good, and I will be with him.

In terms of the speech acts used by the mediator to construct her psychotherapeutic identity, four types are found in the data: informing, counselling, evaluating and questioning.

During mediation, the psychotherapeutic mediator utilizes a number of psychotherapeutic techniques and tools (e.g. Excerpt 17).

Excerpt 17 (episode 0225):

李金萍（心理咨询师）：你们俩给这沙盘起个名字吧。你给这个沙盘起个名字叫什么？

母：家园吧。

李金萍（心理咨询师）：叫家园。你呢？

小郑：平安。

……

李金萍（心理咨询师）：妈妈觉得这个沙盘摆得怎么样？

母：还好吧。

李金萍（心理咨询师）：有没有不太满意的地方？

母：（短暂沉默）

李金萍（心理咨询师）：没有？

母：没有，我喜欢。

Mediator: **Would you name your own sandbox?** *(To the mother)* **What would you name your sandbox?**

Mother: *I'd call it home.*

Mediator: *Home. (To the daughter) What about you?*

Daughter: *Peace.*

…

Mediator: *What do you think about the sandbox (referring to the daughter's sandbox), mother?*

Mother: *All right.*

Mediator: **Is there anything you do not like?**

Mother: (Silence)

Mediator: *No?*

Mother: *No, I like it.*

This episode involves the dispute between a mother and her young rebellious adopted daughter. During the mediation, the psychotherapeutic mediator conducts a sandbox game, a psychoanalytical game, to analyse the relationship between the mother and daughter and its psychological causes. After the mediator introduces the rules of the sandbox game, the two parties arrange the objects in their separate sandboxes. When they are finished, the mediator asks them questions about the names they have given their sandboxes, the way in which they have arranged the objects in their sandboxes and so on, in a total of thirteen questions (Excerpt 17 contains the first five questions).

In Excerpt 17, the mediator asks five questions about the naming of the sandboxes and the mother's opinion of how her daughter has arranged her sandbox. On the basis of their performance in the sandbox game and their answers to the questions, the psychotherapeutic mediator then forms preliminary judgements about their relationship (not included in the excerpt): for example, the daughter wants her parents to resume their marriage (the four puppets in her sandbox); the mother wants some private space (only one puppet in her sandbox); the mother tends to compromise on her daughter's requests (evaluating the daughter's sandbox positively even though she does not really like it).

The psychotherapeutic mediator also performs the speech act of informing, for the purpose of identifying and describing certain psychological characteristics of the disputants (Excerpt 18), providing background psychological knowledge

(Excerpt 19) or pointing out the psychological causes behind certain events (Excerpt 20).

Excerpt 18 (episode 0228):
王先生的特点是什么？第一，回避式的防御机制；第二，儿童式的情感评价体系。

What are Mr Wang's (main) psychological characteristics? They include, first, an avoidance defence mechanism, second, a childlike affection evaluation system.

Excerpt 19 (episode 0228):
儿童式评价体系是什么？儿童的对人的评价体系，不包括是非，不包括道德，只包括我在你身边的感觉，谁对我好，我就说谁好，我就跟谁在一起。

What is a childlike affection evaluation system? A child's evaluation of a person does not include right or wrong, it does not include morality. It only includes my feelings when I am around you. When a person is nice to me, I will say he is good, and I will be with him.

Excerpt 20 (episode 0226):
我们经常在心理学里面解读一个女孩子，她为什么会无数次的早恋，实际上就是因为这个家庭缺爱的一个结果，就是跟父亲的链接产生了裂痕。

In psychology, we often interpret this type of girl who frequently falls in love at an early age as suffering from a lack of parental love. Specifically, her relationship with her father is damaged.

The psychotherapeutic mediator evaluates the disputes and the parties involved from her professional perspective. Excerpt 21 provides an example:

Excerpt 21 (episode 0225):
只要失去了这个前提，其他的就叫自己自作自受，自己不想好。

Without this premise (gratitude for a parent's love), I can only say that you're to blame for your own behaviour and the results.

The speech act of counselling occurs nineteen times in the data. The advice that the psychotherapeutic mediator provides is often related to psychological aspects (Excerpts 22 and 23).

Excerpt 22 (episode 0221):

所以你要搞清楚，你自己究竟是个什么样的人，你要过什么样的生活，你们的婚姻走到今天，到底是你心里的哪个特点在作祟，让你愿意这样生活。

So you have to figure out what kind of person you really are and what kind of life you really want, what psychological characteristics brings your marriage to this state.

Excerpt 23 (episode 0310):

基于她这样的生理基础，所以最好的办法就是，多做情绪上的情感上的安抚。

Based on her current physiological foundation, the best solution is to assuage her emotionally.

Discussion

Despite their different professional backgrounds, the legal and psychotherapeutic mediators both agree on how to construct a (professional) mediator identity based on their respective expertise. The question then arises: why do they construct their identities as legal or psychotherapeutic mediators? In other words, what factors form the basis of this professional identity construction? We provide tentative answers to these questions from two perspectives.

First, the discursive construction of a professional identity is conducive to dispute resolution. When mediating via their professional discourse, mediators provide information, an evaluation and advice for the parties involved in the dispute. Thus, in a sense, they are trying to persuade the parties to resolve the dispute. The discursive construction of a professional identity, whether a legal or psychotherapeutic one, gives the mediators a certain degree of authority. According to social psychological research (e.g. Myers et al. 2014), this can increase the persuasiveness of the utterance. From *GMM*, it can be seen that often the responses given by the disputants testify to the persuasiveness of the mediation discourse and the effects created by professional identity construction.

According to social psychological research, an increase in persuasiveness only occurs when the speaker is an authority on the topic he/she is discussing. Naturally, when expert mediators present arguments from their own professional perspectives, they discursively construct a professional identity, but, when they present arguments from perspectives that deviate from their own professional expertise, they do not actively construct themselves as professionals. To exemplify, when the legal mediator discusses legal issues, he identifies himself 'as a lawyer' (episode 0306), but when he discusses living a quality life (episode 0303), he identifies himself instead as 'a post-1980s youth', a generation that is widely known for its emphasis on quality of life. In comparison, when the psychotherapeutic mediator discusses a topic about financial management (not her area of expertise), she uses none of the discursive practices that index her professional identity, with the exception of one speech act that weakly implicates her psychotherapeutic background.

Second, the discursive construction of a professional identity can help achieve the goals of the RTV programme. According to its promotional advertising, one goal of *GMM* is to demonstrate to the general public 'the wisdom and art of resolving dispute and conflict'. Indeed, this echoes the evaluation of RTV in previous research as containing 'a mixture of surveillance and collective learning activity which seems both entertaining and enlightening' (Shei 2013: 45). By inviting experts from various professions to be observational mediators, and as a result of the construction of distinct professional identities, *GMM* provides its audience with both entertainment and enlightenment. It is entertaining because when mediators with different professional identities tackle the same problem, disagreements or even conflict can sometimes emerge (e.g. episode 0302), which creates a certain dramatizing effect that is welcomed by the RTV audience. At the same time, it is enlightening because *GMM* provides the audience with professional knowledge by engaging them in the collective learning activity of how to tackle a dispute from different professional perspectives. In this process, the construction of professional identities can facilitate the audience's learning process by emphasizing the authority of the information source and, hence, emphasizing the reliability of the knowledge. This care and commitment that the RTV programme offers its audience can be seen in the way in which the legal and psychotherapeutic mediators refer to the parties involved in the disputes as 'parties on stage' (episode 0221) and 'the female guest [of the show]' (episode 0222), and the way they refer to themselves as 'teachers attending [the show]'.

8.4 Summary

In this chapter, we have demonstrated how identity work can appropriately exercise or suspend institutional power in a variety of institutional contexts. For that purpose, 'institutional' people tend to claim or emphasize the institutional identity that is appropriate to the setting in question when interacting with those over whom they enjoy institutional power. While this is generally the practice, we have indicated that 'institutional' people can sometimes opt out of constructing an institutional identity, instead constructing a more personal identity. When this happens, they are deliberately performing identity work that suspends or weakens their institutional power. In effect, they are resorting to non-institutional forces such as friendship, kinship and empathy to achieve their communicative goals, despite the fact that they are interacting in institutional contexts. Thus, as communicators, 'institutional' people have an agency and a potency in their identity choice, except in some specialized contexts such as courtroom proceedings. To some extent, these findings are all supported by the reported case study in which a lawyer and a psychotherapist discursively construct their professional identities as a legal mediator and a psychotherapeutic mediator, respectively, in the RTV programme *Gold Medal of Mediation*. It has been argued that the construction of a professional identity by legal and psychological experts helps to facilitate dispute resolution and contributes to the entertaining and enlightening effects created by the RTV programme.

9

Identity work in public communication

In the previous two chapters, I have explored identity work in interpersonal communication and institutional communication, respectively. This chapter will focus on identity work in public communication, to reveal how it is used as a means of persuasion and an image management device in public spheres.

By 'public sphere', Verschueren (2016: 143) denotes 'communication in the context of shared media, networks, organizations, institutions, states and state-like structures'. In this book, I use the term to refer to 'public places, public media, public networks, etc., which are open and accessible to the public and which are subject to the general public's observation and supervision' (X. R. Chen 2020b: 1). Public places include airports, railway, coach or bus stations, parks, museums, cinemas, theatres, sports centres, banks, shops, supermarkets, hotels, post offices, telecommunication offices, hospitals, streets, roads and so on. Public media include newspapers, magazines, television, radio and so on. Public networks include internet-based blogs, bulletins and so on. Public discourse is then any 'discourse that occurs in these public spaces and that provides the general public with access to public information' (ibid.). Essentially, public discourse is the genre of language used in public spheres by various social bodies (administrative, commercial, financial, educational, etc.) for the primary purpose of transmitting public information or messages. It is the most frequent and encompassing form of language used in daily social life, compared with institutional discourse like courtroom and classroom discourses or interpersonal discourse in face-to-face or non-face-to-face encounters.

Public discourse falls into several important types. In terms of content, for example, it comprises advertising or promotional discourse, advocating discourse (including all forms of slogans), journalistic discourse, public signs, news reports and commentaries, commodity descriptions or instructions and so on (Wang and Yuan 1999). Even shop names, brands, plate names, labels and public notices belong to the genre of public discourse. Public discourse can be either written or spoken. Whereas posters, public signs, tourist brochures, written advertisements, news reports and the like are generally written, news broadcasting and advertising on TV or radio, oral announcements of messages in public places and so forth are primarily spoken.

9.1 Identity work as a means of persuasion

Being 'socially situated and publicly oriented' (X. R. Chen 2020b: 1), public discourse has many functions. For example, advertising discourse is meant to persuade potential purchasers to buy products; public signs are intended to persuade the public to follow all types of directions for the sake of orderliness, safety, efficiency and so on. Thus, a large portion of public discourse involves the need to persuade. While many persuasive strategies have been identified in previous literature, such as the use of rhetorical devices (e.g. McQuarrie and Glen 1996), interdiscursivity (e.g. Guo 2008), code-mixing (e.g. Yang 2008), personalization (e.g. X. R. Chen 2013b) and metadiscourse (e.g. Fuertes-Olivera et al. 2001), numerous studies have found that advertisements involve identity construction (e.g. Caldas-Coulthard 2008; Fellows and Rubin 2006; Harmon-Kizer 2016; Piller 2001; Pomering and White 2011; Rodney 1997; Wang 2013, 2015; Xiong 2008). It has been found that advertisers persuade the potential purchasers by adopting identity-related strategies such as identity distancing (Harmon-Kizer 2016) and constructing an indigenous identity (Pomering and White 2011). Fellows and Rubin (2006) are explicit in claiming 'identities for sale'.

Now, let us consider a few specific examples from the Chinese context. I have found that Chinese advertisers often construct the manufacturers of some products as '专家' ('experts'), as shown below:

(1) 九牧王，西裤专家
    Jiumuwang, an expert in suit pants
(2) 方太，中国高端厨电专家与领导者
    Fangtai, an expert and leader in top-end kitchen appliances in China

An identity, particularly in terms of status, is associated with social influence. The construction of a particular identity amounts to evoking the corresponding influence. This explains not only why advertisers often employ celebrities as their spokesmen but also why they construct expert or leader identities for the product manufacturers concerned, as indicated by Examples (1) and (2). Now consider Example (3):

(3) 我们不生产水 我们是大自然的搬运工 (农夫山泉)
   We don't manufacture water. We are just porters for nature (Nongfu Shanquan)

In Example (3), the advertiser adopts the perspective of a manufacturer, that is, that of Nongfu Shanquan, a well-known mineral water producer. By means of a self-narrative, the advertisement communicates the identity message that the mineral water producer is a 'porter' who brings clean, natural water to the consumer, thus implying that the manufacturer does not use additives and takes preventative measures against pollution.

In addition to advertising discourse, some public signs in China also involve the construction of identity, in most cases for the public. Consider the following examples:

(4) 做文明人，请勿随地乱扔垃圾。（上海某公园）
   Be a civilized man: No Littering. (seen in a Shanghai park)
(5) 做一名文明的乘客，今天你先下后上了么？（南京地铁）
   As a civilized passenger, did you let others off first before getting on today? (seen in metro stations in Nanjing)

It is worth noting that '文明人' (literally translated as 'a civilized person') in Example (4) and '文明的乘客' (literally translated as 'a civilized passenger') in Example (5) are projected identities for the public, conveying the expectation that they will behave in civilized ways (e.g. not littering, getting on the metro after other passengers have got off). Clearly, the act of projecting the target audience as 'civilized' serves to enhance the quality of their face in the Chinese context. When members of the public see these types of signs, they tend to follow the instructions on them to create or maintain their positive public image.

9.2 Identity work as a means of public image management

Image is 'an identity-related feature, presented by individuals in interaction, which conforms to or runs counter to others' expectations' (X. R. Chen 2020a: 5).

It can be constructed and transmitted via the use of discourse in interactions. For instance, by analysing the request emails sent by some leaders to their subordinates in a Hong Kong public educational institute, Ho (2010) reveals a variety of personal identities (equivalent to image here) that these leaders constructed for themselves, such as an accountable leader, a rational leader, an authoritative leader, an understanding, considerate and polite leader and a capable leader. Ren (2014) investigates how Chinese experts construct authoritative, modest or amiable images during dissertation proposal or defence meetings. X. R. Chen (2013c, 2020b) explores the identity construction of China's post-1990s generation in online news headlines and, from the perspective of critical pragmatics, criticizes media discourse for constructing negative images of this generation. As a matter of fact, numerous studies (e.g. Ekström and Lundell 2011; Garcés-Conejos Blitvich 2009; Jo 2018; Persson 2019; Wang and Ge 2020; Wiik 2009; You 2011) indicate that news discourse (including headlines, news texts, interviews, etc.) is concerned with identity construction, with the image subjects being the nation (e.g. Wang and Ge 2020; You 2011), reporters (e.g. Ekström and Lundell 2011; Wiik 2009) or some other individuals (e.g. Jo 2018; Persson 2019).

In addition to news reports, various discursive practices are used in public spheres to construct an image by means of identity work. We will focus on some common examples in the following section.

First, let us consider notification discourse, which includes announcements, notices, circulars and the like that are issued to public groups by departments or organizations. Compare the following two notices, issued by the same property management company of a residential community:

(6) a. 居民朋友们：

您好！为了营造安全、整洁、有序的车辆停放环境，也为了邻里和谐，凡在车棚长期存放的旧自行车、旧电瓶车等物品，请自行认领取走，7月30日前将对该车棚进行清理，逾期不拿走的，有关执法部门予以清理，由此造成的一切损失及责任将由您自行承担。谢谢您的配合！

二号新村小区
2020年7月21日
21 July 2020

Dear **resident friends**:
Hello! To create a safe, tidy and orderly space for parking bicycles, and to promote harmonious relationships between neighbours, please remove from the shed all bikes and electric bikes that have been parked there for a long time. We will clean the shed before 30 July and the law enforcement department will remove all overdue vehicles, with all losses being the responsibility of the owners. Thank you for your cooperation!

No. 2 New Village Community

b. 各位居民，你们好！为了大家的安全，请不要飞线充电，近期有关部门将清理飞线，感谢大家的配合。

二号新村小区

2020年7月

July 2020

Hello, **residents**! For the sake of safety, please do not charge your vehicles by connecting them to hung wires. In the near future, the relevant department will remove the wires. Thank you for your cooperation.

No. 2 New Village Community

Address terms are used in both these notices. However, in Example (6a), the property management company calls the residents of the community 'dear resident friends', constructing the relational identity of a friend in addition to conveying the default identity relationship between the manager and the managed residents. In Example (6b), the property management company calls the inhabitants 'residents', merely constructing the default identity relationship between the manager and the managed residents. In comparison, the address term in (6a) performs additional identity work and helps to construct a friendlier image for the manager, instead of only constructing a matter-of-fact image for the management company.

The identity work discussed above also tends to take place in hospital management discourse. For example (X. R. Chen 2018a: 157):

(7) Context: In the CT waiting room of a Nanjing hospital.
尊敬的病友：您好！！
欢迎您来到CT室，请您在我们护士的安排下，坐在座椅上耐心等候，我们会尽快为您安排检查。当喊到您的名字时，穿好鞋套，进入机房。
（敬请没有被喊到的病友不要进入操作间，以免X线辐射。）谢谢您的合作！！

Hello!! Distinguished **patient friends**:

Welcome to the CT room. Please wait patiently on your seats according to our nurses' instructions. We will arrange your examination as soon as possible. When your name is called, please put on your shoe covers and enter the machine room.

(Please do not enter the operation room if your name is not called to avoid exposure to X-ray radiation.) Thank you for your cooperation!!

In Example (7), the CT room not only employs such honorifics as '尊敬的' (distinguished) and '您' (the honorific form of 'you') but also addresses the patients in a deviational manner, that is, 'patient friends', instead of the default 'patients'. This type of identity work helps to construct a civilized and enthusiastic image for the staff in the CT room, thus maintaining and strengthening the harmonious relationship between doctors and patients. Undoubtedly, such identity work is a pragmatic practice which is particularly worth advocating in the current Chinese context, where the doctor–patient relationship can at times be tense.

In addition, similar identity work can be seen to be performed in managerial discourse at Chinese airports and train and bus stations. For instance (X. R. Chen 2018a: 158):

(8) Context: At Hongqiao station in Shanghai.
电子指示牌：请旅客朋友们按顺序排队进站上车

*Electronic signboard: **Passenger friends**, please get in line while entering the station and boarding your train.*

In this case, the station managers adopt the deviational 'passenger friends', instead of the default 'passengers', to address the passengers, thereby constructing their relational identity as a friend of the passengers, and conveying an amiable and friendly image of themselves. In contrast, the default address form does not possess an identity or image construction function.

Finally, let us consider the identity work performed in city promotional discourse on television or in other media in some Chinese cities, and its role in constructing an image of each city.

(9) a. 牡丹之都，好汉之乡 （菏泽）
Capital of peonies, the home of heroes (Heze)
b. 墨子故里，美丽滕州
Hometown of Mozi, the beautiful Tengzhou

c. 走进孔子，游学曲阜
   Walk to Confucius, travel and study in Qufu
d. 山东好客，沂水情长
   Hospitable Shandong, Friendly Yishui

The sentences in Example (9) are promotional slogans from four cities or counties in Shandong. In (9a), Heze is described as the 'home of heroes' as many historical 'heroes' lived in Heze (their origins are in *Heroes of the Marshes*, a classical masterpiece written by Nai'an Shi). The heroic image of this region is constructed by activating memories of relevant historical figures. The slogan in (9b) portrays Tengzhou as the 'hometown of Mozi', one of the most famous thinkers in Chinese history, thus indirectly conveying the cultural image of Tengzhou as an ideological cradle. In (9c), Qufu is portrayed as the hometown of Confucius, founder of Confucianism, and is therefore constructed as the origin of thought and education in China. The slogan in (9d) not only highlights the hospitable image of Shandong as a large province but also indicates that the county Yishui represents Shandong's hospitality. As shown above, the four counties or cities employ different discursive practices (e.g. literary allusion, reference to celebrities, direct description of unique identity features) to perform identity work, to achieve the same goal of self-promotion by presenting favourable images to attract domestic and foreign tourists.

9.3 Identity work in Chinese real estate advertisements: A case study

In this section, a case study of Chinese real estate advertisements[1] will be presented, and by exploring the identity work performed in these advertisements, it will be revealed how real estate advertisers perform identity work by means of various discursive practices in an attempt to persuade potential purchasers into buying commercial housing.

As we are all aware, over the past twenty years, the real estate industry has formed the backbone of China. Naturally, it is also an extremely competitive industry, with advertisements being a common sight. To promote sales and maximize profits, advertisers try their utmost to make their advertisements attractive, touching and thrilling. It is safe to say that real estate advertisements in contemporary China are the 'cream' of advertising, as they involve all sorts of captivating strategies and persuasive skills.

Falling squarely within the scope of public discourse, real estate advertising can be investigated by considering language theories. In actual fact, linguistic researchers have conducted numerous studies of real estate advertising from different perspectives, which have improved our understanding of this use of language, but few studies focus on identity construction in real estate advertisements. On the strength of existing research, this section adopts a critical pragmatic perspective, in conjunction with the Pragmatic Identity Theory (X. R. Chen 2013a, 2014, 2018a), as its theoretical tool. It focuses on the types, distribution and discursive strategies of identity construction in a sizable database of real estate advertisements. By uncovering the adaptation features behind these advertisements, this case study reveals the 'identity traps' that real estate advertisers sometimes use. It is hoped that this study will contribute to our understanding of the generic features and persuasive art of real estate advertising, and our appreciation of the pragmatic efficacy of identity construction in commercial contexts.

Research background

Numerous studies have explored real estate advertising from various linguistic perspectives. For instance, a number of scholars have examined real estate advertising from the perspective of critical discourse analysis. Drawing upon Fairclough's (1989) three-dimensional conception of discourse analysis, Wang (2007) critically analyses real estate advertisements from the perspective of transitivity, indicating that when promoting housing products, real estate advertisements cater to people's emotional needs and shape their lifestyles and attitudes towards life. F. Chen (2008) explores word choices, address terms, modality, theme-rheme and content in real estate advertisements, revealing how they influence and manipulate the ideology and thoughts of potential house buyers through the above means. Dong (2011) investigates how real estate advertising caters to the emotional needs of consumers through word choices, transitivity and social contexts. Y. Li's (2014) critical analysis of real estate advertising focuses on the transitivity system, mood-modality system, theme system and so on, revealing underlying ideologies, social relationships and values, the emotional needs of consumers, and emotional and psychological identification.

The above review of literature, although far from exhaustive, demonstrates that existing studies, in some aspects, could be further enhanced. First, even though previous critical discourse analyses have found that real estate advertisers intentionally cater to identity needs (e.g. Dong highlights that real estate advertisers cater to the emotional needs of consumers in their social identities), no studies have explored this issue from the perspective of identity construction. Second, while a number of pragmatic studies involving real estate advertising are critical, the identity perspective has not yet been adopted. For instance, although X. R. Chen (2013c) investigates various 'pragmatic traps' in real estate advertisements and Shu (2016) addresses the way in which Chinese real estate advertising employs numerous devices of pragmatic presupposition to deceive consumers, neither of these studies are empirical. Third, while some studies (e.g. Cheng 2016) examine pragmatic identity construction in real estate advertisements, and have found that this form of advertising constructs such identities as narrator, judge and interlocutor, thereby displaying a high degree of contextual adaptability, they are not critical. Fourth, existing critical studies on real estate advertising are not based on sufficiently ample first-hand data to systematically conduct a critical analysis. For example, Y. Li's (2014) dataset is composed of only twenty-three real estate advertisements, while Wang (2007) examines a mere four real estate advertisements. To fill the above research gaps, this section will explore the types and distribution of identities that are constructed for potential house buyers by real estate advertisers in a sizable dataset of real estate advertisements and, from a critical perspective, will analyse the motivations of real estate advertisers that underlie the construction of related identities for purchasers.

Methodology

Research questions

The aim of this study is to reveal the way in which real estate advertisers construct identities for potential house buyers in an attempt to promote sales. Therefore, I will endeavour to answer the following questions by analysing the collected data:

a. What identities do real estate advertisers construct for potential house buyers in their advertisements? What is the distribution of these identities?
b. What pragmalinguistic devices do real estate advertisers use in their advertisements to construct these identities for potential house buyers?

c. What particular values held by potential house buyers do real estate advertisers exploit when constructing identities by certain discursive means?

Data collection

A total of 407 advertisements were collected for this study. From 31 March to 2 April 2018, Baidu (an internet search engine) was searched using the keyword 'real estate advertisement', and real estate advertisements were collected using the 'real estate advertisement selection' on Sina Weibo. The data were then screened and processed. Screening the data involved removing advertisements that only contained basic information such as price and house type (e.g. Zhongxin Hongshushan – a community with all three-room cottage-quality apartments of 85–100m^2 on sale), and processing the data involved transcribing collected advertisements such as posters.

Analytical methods

After collecting the data, analytic induction and statistical analysis were used to analyse the data. For analytic induction, I employed discourse analysis, focused on the content and form of the real estate advertisements, and recognized and identified the types of identities constructed for the potential house buyers by real estate advertisers. Specifically, I considered whether the advertisement directly portrayed the identity of the potential house buyers, as shown in Example (10), or whether it constructed their identities by displaying their personalities, images, roles or expectations, as demonstrated in Examples (11) and (12):

(10) 您将成为东方高层人士
You will be a VIP of the Orient
(11) 这是您的写意空间，还是您洽谈商务之地？
Will this be a space where you can relax or negotiate business?
(12) 把家轻轻放在大自然中
Gently place your home in nature

If advertisements specifically emphasized the function or quality of the house, they were removed from the data, as shown in Examples (13)–(15):

(13) 居住改变生活
Residence changes lives

(14) 共筑品质，共享生活
 Improve quality together, enjoy life together
(15) 4个阳台的4种幸福时光
 Four kinds of happy times on four balconies

Without doubt, determining the types of identities constructed for potential house buyers in real estate advertisements is a challenging task. Different researchers might well propose different categorizations depending on the objectives of their research. While not denying the possibility that there are other methods of classification, in this study I have used the identity needs which previous studies have highlighted in relation to real estate advertisements (e.g. F. Chen 2008). In addition, I have also considered a number of mainstream values and concerns held by residents in modern China. To avoid unnecessary overlapping, I have classified identity types as broadly as possible. For instance, the category of 'successful people' includes social elites, emerging rich people, high-level people and so on.

After determining the types of identities that were constructed in the real estate advertisements, I counted the frequency of occurrence of each identity and evaluated these frequencies in terms of percentages.

In the following sections, I will discuss the types, distribution and discursive practices of the identities constructed in real estate advertisements for potential house buyers by advertisers, thus revealing how the latter exploit certain buyer values to promote sales. Furthermore, the influence of the social context of modern China and the underlying goals of real estate advertisements will be investigated.

Results

Types of identities constructed for potential house buyers by real estate advertisers

Table 9.1 details the types and distribution of the identities constructed for potential buyers by real estate advertisers as found in the data.

From Table 9.1, we can see that of the 407 real estate advertisements that were collected, 120 of them either directly or indirectly constructed identities for potential house buyers. Given that the main function of an advertisement is to provide objective information about a product or service, it is worth noting that identities are constructed for potential house buyers in a significant proportion of the real estate advertisements. The motivations behind this are worth exploring.

In addition, Table 9.1 also indicates that of the types of identities constructed, 'natural environment lovers' is by far the most common (45 per cent), followed by 'successful people' (23.3 per cent), 'family-oriented people' (15 per cent), 'individuality advocators' (14.2 per cent) and 'sports enthusiasts' (2.5 per cent). In the discussion, we shall explore the underlying reasons for this distribution.

In the following section, I will present specific examples of the above identity types in decreasing order of frequency.

A. Natural environment lovers

When constructing identities, advertisements of this type cater to the expectations that potential house buyers have of the natural environment. For example:

(16) 亲近自然，享受自然
Get close to nature, enjoy nature
(17) 让你每天也可细听海涛，抱拥大海
You can also listen to waves and embrace the sea every day
(18) 您禁得起绿色的诱惑么？
Could you resist the temptation of the green?

The above examples exploit the potential house buyer's love of the natural environment from several angles. Example (16) directly mentions the closeness and enjoyment of nature. Example (17) implies the potential house buyer's desire to listen to waves near the sea. Similarly, Example (18) implies the potential buyer's love of green houses. It can be seen that advertisements of this kind assume that potential house buyers are lovers of the natural environment.

B. Successful people

When constructing identities, this type of advertisement exploits the expectations that potential house buyers have of success. For instance:

(19) 为每个成功的广州人建造一间别墅！
*Build a villa for each **successful person in Guangzhou**!*
(20) 您将成为东方高层人士
*You will be **a VIP of the Orient***

Table 9.1 Types and Distribution of the Identities Constructed (N = 407)

Type of identity	Number of advertisements	Frequency
Natural environment lovers	54	45%
Successful people	28	23.3%
Family-oriented people	18	15%
Individuality advocators	17	14.2%
Sports enthusiasts	3	2.5%
Total	120	100%

(21) 这是您的写意空间，还是您洽谈商务之地？
Will this be a space where you can relax or **negotiate business**?

In different ways, the above examples identify potential house buyers as successful people, either currently or in the future. Example (19) considers potential buyers to be successful people, Example (21) implies that the buyer is a successful businessman, while Example (20) indicates that the house will lead buyers to business success.

C. Family-oriented people

This category of advertisements caters to the buyer's love of, and yearning for, a happy family life when constructing his identity. For instance:

(22) 爱家的男人住百合
The man who loves his family lives in Baihe
(23) 回家的感觉真好
It feels great to come home
(24) 守候家的温馨
Secure the warmth of your home

Example (22) describes the potential house buyer as a 'man who loves his family', Example (23) expresses the feeling the buyer will have of coming home and Example (24) implies that the buyer will be happy because of the warmth of his home. These advertisements all exploit the potential buyer's pursuit of a warm, comfortable residence.

D. Individuality advocators

This type of advertisement involves the expectations that potential house buyers have of themselves when constructing their identities. For example:

(25) 为自己而存在的地方
 A place which only exists for you
(26) 生活由我定义
 Life is defined by me
(27) 拥有一片自己的天空
 Own a sky which belongs to yourself

With a specific target in mind, these examples feature keywords such as 'me' and 'yourself', which cater to the individual thoughts and needs of the potential house buyer.

E. Sports enthusiasts

When constructing identities, this type of advertisement targets the enthusiasm that potential house buyers have for sports. For instance:

(28) 运动就在家门口
 Play sports right in front of the door
(29) 享受临海的高尔夫乐趣
 Enjoy the fun of golfing near the sea

The above examples identify potential buyers as sports enthusiasts, and thus 'sports' in general is mentioned, as in Example (28), or a specific (high-class) sport is mentioned, as in Example (29).

So far, examples have been provided of the different types of identities that have been constructed for potential buyers by the real estate advertisers. Our presentation is clearly not exhaustive and it is not the only feasible categorization or analysis. However, the above analysis demonstrates quite adequately that identity construction is an important persuasive strategy for real estate advertisers. In the next section, we will examine the discursive practices and motivations behind this strategy.

Discursive practices used by real estate advertisers when constructing identities for potential house buyers

The discursive practices employed by real estate advertisers when constructing particular identities for potential buyers can vary from time to time. At times they are direct, and other times indirect, with different degrees of specificity. For instance, while the discursive practices employed to construct the identity of successful people are overt, those adopted to construct the identity of natural environment lovers are comparatively covert; discursive practices between these two extremes are used to construct the identities of family-oriented people, individuality advocators and sports enthusiasts.

A. Overt devices in identity construction

In our data, the overt devices adopted by real estate advertisers when constructing identities for potential house buyers include

a. a modifier to indicate a certain identity, for example, a 'family-loving' man in Example (22); and
b. a predicate to indicate identity, for example, (You will be) 'a VIP of the Orient' in Example (10) and 'standing on the summit' in 'You cannot see the summit because you are standing on the summit'. Overall, few overt devices are used in the construction of a potential buyer's identity.

B. Covert devices in identity construction

Based on the data, the covert devices employed by real estate advertisers when constructing identities for potential house buyers include, primarily,

a. presupposition to imply identity-related information, for example, in Example (17), 'also' is used as a presupposition trigger, which can trigger the inference that potential buyers love to listen to waves near the sea (i.e. are natural environment lovers); the use of an interrogative sentence in Example (18) not only presupposes that the house being presented is a green product but also assumes that buyers will love the green residential environment; the alternative question in Example (21) presupposes that potential house buyers will either relax or negotiate business in their new homes; and

b. implicature to convey identity-related information, for example, Example (19) delivers the implicature that if you are successful, you can buy a villa in Guangdong, and covertly constructs potential buyers as successful people; Example (25) delivers the implicature that the houses being advertised will meet the buyers' needs to pursue individuality, thus covertly constructing their identities as individuality pursuers or advocators.

It is worth noting that, apart from the few times that overt devices are employed, for the majority of the time real estate advertisers use covert devices, particularly presupposition, to construct identities for the potential buyers. In the following section, we will discuss the possible motivations for the discursive practices used in identity construction.

Critical discussion

Mey indicates that, as a social science, pragmatics should help people understand the imbalance of power in language use and language discrimination, thus encouraging them to terminate these phenomena (Mey 1993: 320). He believes that to find the goal of language use, we have to know who the language users are in the context, what conditions of language use they are facing and what impact these conditions have on them, thus understanding how they 'word the world' (Mey 1985: 166). Therefore, Mey (1993: 320) proposes the term 'critical pragmatics' and notes that the goal of critical pragmatics is to improve language users' awareness of power structure and language conditions, so as to promote their freedom and independence, that is, realizing the so-called 'linguistic emancipation'.

It should be noted that the term 'critical pragmatics' which Mey uses covers all the critical studies that are concerned with the relationship between language and social issues (e.g. power relationship, domination, bias, domestication). It is a 'denominator' of various approaches to critical analysis (Mey 1993: 316), including Teun van Dijk's studies and Norman Fairclough's studies. To distinguish between critical analysis from the perspective of pragmatics and critical analysis from the perspective of systemic-functional linguistics, X. R. Chen (2009, 2013c, 2020b) suggests that the former could be termed critical pragmatic analysis, while the latter could be termed critical discourse analysis, and these two forms of critical analysis are part of critical linguistics (which also includes critical cognitive analysis, etc.). According to X. R. Chen's (2009, 2013c,

2020b) redefinition of critical pragmatics, critical pragmatic analysis points to the discussion on language, guided by pragmatic theories, which influences people's actions and thoughts. As Mey (1993) states, from the perspective of critical pragmatics, the key to examining speech acts in social contexts is not to categorize them or explore their felicity conditions but to investigate what people want to do by performing certain speech acts, how to do it and how to do it properly. Critical pragmatic analysis does not avoid subjectivity, but this subjectivity is not casual. It is a 'considered subjectivity' (Mey 1993: 315).

Critical pragmatics investigates primarily the ideologies, values and so forth. behind language use in social contexts, with the aim of promoting proper societal pragmatic practices and criticizing the power suppression, social bias and political or economic fraud behind language use, thus contributing to the building of a societal pragmatic civilization (X. R. Chen 2009, 2013c, 2020b). Thus, being similar to critical discourse analysis, critical pragmatic research can focus on discourse with positive societal meaning (e.g. all types of humane public signs and polite service discourse) and discourse with negative societal meaning, with the focus being on the latter.

Let us now return to the earlier discussion. It was shown in the previous data analysis that real estate advertisers sometimes construct identities for potential house buyers in their advertisements. This finding is not accidental. For instance, Lei (2003), F. Chen (2008) and Yang (2009) have obtained the same finding. Besides, real estate advertisers have preferences when constructing identities for potential buyers. For example, F. Chen (2008) notes that real estate advertisements use address terms such as 'social elites', 'emerging rich', 'IN humans', 'absolute minorities', 'intellectual rich', 'people in the air', 'Chopin' and 'beautiful women' to construct the corresponding identities; Yang (2009) indicates that real estate advertisements are inclined to presuppose the consumers' identities as rich people. Our study has shown that real estate advertisers frequently construct the identities of potential buyers as 'natural environment lovers', 'successful people', 'family-oriented people', 'individuality advocators' and so on. The question is, why?

From the perspective of critical pragmatics, the deep motivation underlying the tendency of real estate advertisers to construct these identities for potential house buyers is to adapt to the mental needs (e.g. pursuing health, getting ahead in life, face, individuality, leading a happy life) in the mental world of the buyers. Real estate advertisements appeal to those mental needs that guide and control the ideology of consumers (Lei 2003). In actual fact, these mental needs are closely related to a number of social mentalities resulting from the increasing economic tide of recent years and the issue of environmental pollution in modern China. As a matter of fact, the identities (e.g. 'high-level elites') that are constructed by real estate advertisers are not necessarily faithful reflections of the needs of potential house buyers. Sometimes, they can be total inventions to stimulate customers, thus promoting sales. Therefore, this form of adaptation is a 'negative adaptation' in nature with a negative social meaning!

Moreover, the previous data analysis illustrates that when constructing identities for potential house buyers, real estate advertisers use covert devices such as presupposition and implicature. F. Chen (2008) also demonstrates that real estate advertisers often employ address terms which are indistinct and blurry, identity symbols or abstract identity images, but this covert practice can encourage consumers to assume these tempting titles based on unrealistic evaluations of themselves. This practice is somewhat misleading. If house buyers are not careful, they can easily fall into the 'pragmatic traps' (X. R. Chen 2013c) that some real estate advertisers have constructed.

In conclusion, the identities that real estate advertisers construct for their consumers can be termed an 'identity trick'. This trick is reflected in three ways: first, advertisers construct the identities of potential house buyers to stimulate their identity needs in order to promote sales; second, the types of identities constructed cater to a few salient values that are championed by certain people in modern China; and third, covert devices are adopted to construct these identities so that potential house buyers unconsciously 'take the bait'.

9.4 Summary

This chapter has explored identity work in a variety of public discourses, in particular advertising discourse. On the strength of the Pragmatic Identity Theory, I have attempted to exemplify how we can approach the purposeful construction of identity by Chinese communicators in public spheres. In particular, via the use of a case study, I have demonstrated how a range of identity work in Chinese real estate advertisements can be interpreted and critically analysed. It is hoped that the case study will serve as a reference for conducting similar critical research.

It must be conceded, however, that one of the limitations of the case study lies in the lack of a reliable standard for analysing and categorizing the identities in some real estate advertisements. Recognition of the constructed identities was based primarily on the advertisers' identification of the potential house buyer's personality, image, role and expectations. Although a number of previous studies were referenced, there was still a degree of subjectivity involved. In future studies, it would be worth interpreting these advertisements from other perspectives.

10

Conclusion

So, identity work works! It works not because identity functions in itself, but because it can be contextually and discursively chosen, (de)constructed and used to perform communicative work.

To further clarify and underscore this point, this conclusion will summarize the main lines of work and arguments from the preceding chapters, along with necessary caveats. It will highlight some remaining issues, and a number of directions for future research will be suggested after acknowledging a few crucial limitations of the current study.

10.1 Recap of the study

In retrospect, I have accomplished the following in this book:

- Defined the core notion of identity work on the basis of the multidimensional and constructionist conceptualization of identity or, more precisely, pragmatic identity. It is argued that the identity work that occurs in communication is not always a predetermined act of simply or mechanically mapping a certain identity with corresponding discourse, or the other way around, but rather a purposeful, active, dynamic and bilateral process. It is purposeful because people (de)construct a certain identity or identities to accomplish certain goals – transactional, interpersonal or both. It is active because people not only exploit their pre-existing identities but also deviate from them by either appropriating a non-real identity or inventing a false identity. It is dynamic because people often shift from one identity to another at different points in time during the same communicative event. It is bilateral or even multilateral because the success or failure of identity work is not wholly in the hands of the initiator, but rather it is also subject to the responder's or responders' uptake.

- Formulated the generative mechanism of identity work by integrating insights from X. R. Chen's (2013a, 2018a) conception of pragmatic identity and Verschueren's (1999, 2012) representation of the structure of pragmatic theory. The proposed construct comprises the following: the locus of identity work (in which identity choices are motivated by certain communicative needs arising in certain contexts and then realized by discursive choices); the process of identity work (which pertains to the dynamic feature of identity choice-making, as indicated by the shift from one identity to another as a result of changes in communicative needs); and the salience or status of identity work (which means that context-bound identity choice-making or shifting during the service of certain communicative needs is a more or less conscious process). In addition, a Maxim of Identity is proposed with a view to assisting in the assessment of the speakers' awareness of the identity work that they are enacting. Also discussed is the metapragmatic awareness of identity work, as indicated by the use of various identity markers.
- Presented a variety of discursive choices for the identification and categorization of identity work by merging insights from Tracy (2002), X. R. Chen (2018a, 2018b) and Spencer-Oatey (2000, 2008). These discursive choices are made from either a single communicative domain or a combination of domains, notably the address and referential domain, the illocutionary domain, the stylistic domain, the participation domain and the non-verbal domain. While the exploration of the discursive practices in these domains may not be exhaustive or fully conclusive, it helps to operationalize and objectivize the recognition of identity work being enacted in the speech event concerned.
- Categorized identity work from different perspectives, such as its direction, targets, dimensions and rapport orientations. This categorization facilitates the visualization of venues and paths through which communicators can consider performing identity work for some communicative purposes. It also enables a deeper understanding of the complexities and subtleties of identity work that Chinese communicators might engage in. While not excluding the possibility of other equally or more meaningful and significant categorizations, the classificatory work presented in this book may serve as a necessary point of departure for analysing identity work in the (Chinese) communicative context.

- Categorized a variety of strategies for performing identity work with respect to different aspects such as manipulating identity salience (including foregrounding and backgrounding), manipulating identity similarity (including alignment and misalignment), manipulating identity closeness (including identity proximization and identity distancing) and manipulating identity truthfulness (including identity fabrication, identity challenge and identity denial). Again, the categorization of these strategies cannot be deemed exhaustive because it has been formulated on the basis of limited data and has been derived by depending heavily on introspection. Nevertheless, in conjunction with the above categorization of identity work, it provides an adequate range of strategic options that people can avail themselves of to increase their chances of communicative success.

Two additional caveats follow. First, identity work is a continuum in terms of explicitness. Explicit identity work plays on certain identities, while implicit identity work implicates the construction of identity for certain communicative purposes. Second, identity work can be very complex, encompassing various dimensions of identity. Although we might appear to have a precise analysis of just one dimension, such an analysis should not obscure the fact that identity work can involve many dimensions simultaneously.

It should be stressed that identity work is a bilateral process, although our analysis has, for the majority of the time, focused on the speaker rather than the hearer as well.

10.2 Remaining issues

A number of issues pertaining to the topic of identity work have not been adequately addressed or even touched upon in the main body of this book. While I have chosen to leave some critical issues (e.g. the delineation, appropriacy and efficacy of identity work) open, I will briefly discuss the following three issues.

The cultural issue

Is identity work a universalist phenomenon or a culturally unique phenomenon? Despite a lack of conclusive evidence, I would venture to claim the former, in the sense that communicators from all types of cultural backgrounds can enact identity work. While this book explores identity work in Chinese communication, it by no means implies that identity work does not take place in communication in other languages or cultures. Consider, for example, the following extract from *Ally McBeal* (season 1, episode 2), an American TV series:

> And I stood over him. Well, I've had my successes **as a lawyer**. I've given money to charities. I've performed public services that brought me enormous gratification **as a human being**. But **as a man**, medieval as this may sound, **as a man**, the most satisfying moment of my life was that punch.

The above extract is taken from a case in which a defence attorney is defending his client. The accused boy had punched the ex-boyfriend of his date because he had verbally insulted her. In order to win the support of the jurors, the attorney highlights two identities, one being his professional identity (a lawyer) and the other being their (the lawyer's and defendant's) personal identities (a human being and a man). The attorney's identity shift, and a conscious and purposeful shift at that, from the former professional identity to the latter personal identity is both relevant and significant to his defence of the boy. Such identity work is likely to win the jury's emotional support because it exploits their common sense.

It is not only American attorneys who perform identity work, but American presidents appeal to identity strategies as well. Consider the following extract from Barack Obama's victory speech in Chicago, given after his first presidential win:

> A little bit earlier this evening, I received an extraordinarily gracious call from Sen. McCain. Sen. McCain fought long and hard in this campaign. And he's fought even longer and harder for the country that he loves. He has endured sacrifices for America that most of us cannot begin to imagine. We are better off for the service rendered by **this brave and selfless leader**.

In this case, Barack Obama constructs a decidedly positive identity (image in particular) for Sen. John McCain, his presidential campaign rival: someone who has 'fought even longer and harder for the country that he loves' and who has 'endured sacrifices for America that most of us cannot begin to imagine'. Most notably, he describes Sen. McCain as a 'brave and selfless leader'. By virtue of such 'gracious' identity work, he is attempting to improve rapport with his rival.

Having claimed the universality of identity work, I must proceed to argue that such work is probably culturally specific as well. Specifically, the way in which and to what extent identity work is enacted can vary, perhaps more quantitatively than qualitatively, across different cultures. For example, in Chinese, a speaker tends to use a kinship term to construct a kinship-based relational identity for someone who is not related to the speaker. This 'kinship term generalization' (Chen and Ren 2020; Ren and Chen 2019) practice as a form of identity work, while also found in Laotian, Korean and many other societies (e.g. Enfield 2007; Sun-Young 2007), generally occurs more frequently in Chinese society than in most, if not all, other societies. Similarly, the use of an official title like 'Director' ('局长', '主任', etc.) for someone who is actually a vice director (He and Ren 2016) represents another form of identity work that is more widely and frequently observed in Chinese society than most, if not all, other societies.

Thus, like face work, identity work is culturally bound in many ways and in many cases. Whereas many of the identity work practices that I have discussed in this book have deep Chinese cultural underpinnings, others clearly have their counterparts in other cultures.

The variability issue

A closely related issue is whether identity work varies intralingually and intraculturally, and in what way. Falling within the scope of variational pragmatics (Barron 2005; Barron and Schneider 2009; Schneider and Barron 2008), this issue is grounded on my preliminary observations that different Chinese social groups (with respect to age, gender, occupation, education and suchlike) display all sorts of variations when performing identity work, in terms of their targets, dimensions, direction, rapport orientations and strategies. For example, a Chinese university student advisor might project him-/herself as a family member of his/her student during individual consultations to enhance solidarity between the two parties (J. Chen 2018), whereas Chinese professors more often depict themselves as research colleagues when chatting to their students for the same purpose of solidarity enhancement. Moreover, like politeness phenomena (X. R. Chen 2017), identity work can vary due to contextual or generic differences. For example, Chinese professors might portray themselves as laypeople to show modesty or to avoid misguidance when commenting on a thesis or dissertation in an oral defence setting.

Thus, as a complex form of discursive practice, identity work is inherently variable. Nevertheless, such variability does not contradict the existence of the various patterns and regularities behind identity work. This is why we find identity work to be so doable and comprehensible.

The conventionalization issue

Finally, identity work can become somewhat conventionalized in one way or another and to varying degrees. There are different lines of evidence. For example, the constant need to address a non-kin person as kin, which is generally performed as a form of identity work, underlies the phenomenon of kinship term generalization mentioned above. Similarly, in Chinese, English and perhaps most, if not all, languages, there exist common linguistic markers of identity work, such as '作为 …' (as …) and '代表 …' (on behalf of …). Moreover, the constant practice of identity work might give rise to the lexicalization of identity connotations in some lexicons. For example, we might jocularly use '视察' (inspect) to describe the casual visit from a non-official person (see X. R. Chen 2019a) in an attempt to strengthen solidarity. Even structurally, at least in both English and Chinese, an appositional construction can be used to perform identity work, as in '我们老师们应该关心学生' (**We teachers** should care for the students).

The existence and use of identity-indexing expressions or structures suggest an interaction between identity work and the language system. Such interaction provides new evidence for the need and rationale to conduct research on the pragmatics–grammar interface.

10.3 Limitations and future directions

This book leaves open the possibility of future research due to its descriptive and explanatory inadequacies. Amongst other things, there has been insufficient discussion about the interactional or social effects of identity work in different contexts. Much of the related analysis and interpretation has been largely speculative or introspective in nature. Although interlocutor responses were occasionally cited to illustrate or prove the consequences of identity work, proof was rather lacking in other cases. For this reason, I would like to call on future researchers to conduct further empirical research on this particular aspect. Another potential area of improvement might involve expanding the scope of the Chinese data to examine whether different Chinese social groups, at present or in the past, vary in their performance of identity work across different genres. While I exemplified the analysis of identity work in interpersonal, institutional and public domains, further systematic treatment is needed to discover nuanced differences within and beyond these domains. In the same vein, it might be interesting to observe how people from different cultural backgrounds differ in their enactment of identity work, particularly when they are engaged in intercultural communication. Pragmatic failures, such as the improper use of a generalized kinship term to perform identity work, might be expected to occur at times in these contexts. Hence, a degree of linguistic and cultural knowledge of identity work could prove essential to intercultural communication.

Notes

1 Introduction

1 According to Brubaker and Cooper (2000: 10–11), strong versions of identity place an emphasis on sameness over time or across people, whereas soft versions view identity as being multiple, unstable, fragmented, negotiated, and so on. By and large, the dichotomy between essentialism and (social) constructionism corresponds to the strong vs weak versions. Tracy (2002) appears to reconcile these two versions by highlighting the complexity and diversity of identity. Thus, her characterization of identity includes both the stable properties people possess prior to communication and those dynamic and situated ones that are discursively constructed and change with the situation (2002: 17).

2 Defining key terms

1 This is my translation. It was originally presented in Chinese as follows: '在特定环境、场合或事件中所处的地位'.
2 Sometimes, one can construct one's own identity by constructing or deconstructing the interlocutor's identity. For example, Li and Ran's (2016) study finds that participants in Chinese televised debating discourse can construct their professional self-identity by deconstructing their other-identity.
3 Due to limited space, only the target turns are presented in each of the examples, with less relevant turns in the context being omitted.
4 'Qin' is a form of address that has its origins in Taobao, an extremely popular online shopping website. 'Qin' is the abbreviation of 'qin'ai de' (亲爱的, which literally means 'dear') and is generally used by customer service staff.

3 Generative mechanism of identity work

1 When the hearer adopts an identity after understanding the speaker's utterance, the discursive aspect is implicit, as it is only mentally represented or processed.

2 Brown and Yule (1983) distinguish between the transactional and interpersonal functions of language, with the former involving the transfer of factual or propositional information. While the successful delivery of information is the main concern of communicators, the latter function deals with coordinating the role relationship and the friendly peer relationship, as well as the saving and maintaining of face, etc. However, this differentiation does not cover effort-saving and aesthetic needs.
3 But, as some studies (e.g. Butler and Fitzgerald 2010; Li and Chen forthcoming) have suggested, communicators can consciously activate some form of membership to serve particular communicative purposes in some contexts, such as family meals and gatherings of friends.
4 In the case of deviational identity, two different situations need to be differentiated: (i) where deviational identity is a strategy which is deliberately adopted by the speaker, which can also be called strategic identity; and (ii) where deviational identity is caused by pragmatic failure due to inadequate pragmatic competence on the part of the speaker, which can also be called problematic identity.
5 Henceforth, sources of examples taken from the CCL's Modern Chinese Corpus will be cited as 'CCL'.

4 Discursive practices of identity work

1 Li (2010) explores the role of a deictic perspective in the construction of identity.
2 When a person gives out a red packet, he/she is giving out cash for the WeChat group members to grab. Usually, the amount of cash grabbed by 'lucky' members is not the same as everyone else's.
3 It would appear that style switching (Cheng 2007) is sometimes used interchangeably with style shifting (Li 2003; Yin 2007). The current study adopts the former and equates the latter to style mixing.
4 On the surface, the source of the information provided by John is Ann. In fact, Ann may not be the exact source. She may have given John this information after listening to a particular university department whose information might have been provided by a higher-level department. Therefore, it is sometimes difficult, or even impossible, to trace the primary source of the information. This study is not concerned with this dilemma.
5 The utterer of an utterance can be either real or virtual (the latter is considered to be an imaginary utterer). Sometimes in our daily routines, we borrow someone's 'mouth' by which to talk, particularly when we want to refuse somebody or something. In fact, it does not necessarily mean that a person has actually said something. This strategy is exploited to construct a virtual speaker.

7 Identity work in interpersonal communication

1 In Spencer-Oatey's later version, in addition to personal value and social value, face also involves relational value. Therefore, face can be divided into personal face, group face and relational face (Yuan 2016).
2 As to equity rights and association rights, what counts as an appropriate level varies according to the nature of the relationship, as well as sociocultural norms and personal preferences. Interlocutors' assessments also vary according to the specific contexts and communicative goals.
3 According to Spencer-Oatey (2000, 2008), managing sociality rights can be differentiated from managing face, since an infringement of the sociality rights of other people would not lead to face threats or loss of face. Within the framework, equity involves cost-benefit but is broader in scope and is not limited to autonomy-imposition issues.

8 Identity work in institutional communication

1 According to our data analysis, it is worth noting that the speech act of informing appears to enjoy a distinguished status in the construction of a legal mediator identity, as this speech act occurs in all but one of the episodes of *GMM* mediation that involve a legal mediator. In each case, the legal mediator explicitly identifies himself, not as a legal mediator, but as a 'post-1980s youth' (this will be elaborated upon in the discussion). All other discursive practices previously discussed are frequently absent in more than one episode.

9 Identity work in public communication

1 This case study is based on my Chinese article written entitled ' "Identity traps" in Commercial Ads: A Critical Pragmatic Study', published in *Shandong Foreign Language Teaching* (Chen 2018c, 5: 24–33).

References

Antaki, C., and S. Widdicombe, eds (1998), *Identities in Talk*, London: Sage.
Bamberg, M., A. De Fina and D. Schiffrin (2011), 'Discourse and Identity Construction', in S. Schwartz, K. Luyckx and V. Vignoles (eds), *Handbook of Identity Theory and Research*, 177–99, Berlin: Springer.
Barron, A. (2005), 'Variational Pragmatics in the Foreign Language Classroom', *System*, 33(3): 519–36.
Barron, A., and K. P. Schneider (2009), 'Variational Pragmatics: Studying the Impact of Social Factors on Language Use in Interaction', *Intercultural Pragmatics*, 6(4): 425–42.
Benwell, B., and E. Stokoe (2006), *Discourse and Identity*, Edinburgh: Edinburgh University Press (reprinted in 2007).
Blommaert, J. (2005), *Discourse: A Critical Approach*, Cambridge: Cambridge University Press.
Blum-Kulka, S., J. House and G. Kasper, eds (1989), *Cross-cultural Pragmatics: Requests and Apologies*, Norwood, NJ: Ablex.
Bou-Franch, P., and P. Garcés-Conejos Blitvich (2014), 'Conflict Management in Massive Polylogues: A Case Study from YouTube', *Journal of Pragmatics*, 73: 19–36.
Boxer, D., and F. Cortés-Conde (1997), 'From Bonding to Biting: Conversational Joking and Identity Display', *Journal of Pragmatics*, 27: 275–94.
Brewer, M., and W. Gardner (1996), 'Who Is This "We"? Levels of Collective Identity and Self Representations', *Journal of Personality and Social Psychology*, 71(1): 83–93.
Brown, G., and G. Yule (1983), *Discourse Analysis*, Cambridge: Cambridge University Press.
Brown, P., and S. Levinson (1978), 'Universals in Language Usage: Politeness Phenomenon', in E. Goody (ed.), *Questions and Politeness: Strategies in Social Interaction*, 56–310, New York: Cambridge University Press.
Brown, P., and S. Levinson (1987), *Politeness: Some Universals in Language Usage*, Cambridge: Cambridge University Press.
Brubaker, R., and F. Cooper (2000), 'Beyond "Identity"', *Theory and Society*, 29: 1–47.
Bublitz, W., and A. Hübler, eds (2007), *Metapragmatics in Use*, Amsterdam: John Benjamins.
Bucholtz, M., and K. Hall (2004), 'Language and Identity', in A. Duranti (ed.), *A Companion to Linguistic Anthropology*, 369–94, Oxford: Blackwell.
Bucholtz, M., and K. Hall (2005), 'Identity and Interaction: A Sociocultural Linguistic Approach', *Discourse Studies*, 7(4–5): 585–614.

Bucholtz, M., and K. Hall (2008), 'Finding Identity: Theory and Data', *Multilingua*, 27(1–2): 151–163.

Bucholtz, M., and K. Hall (2010), 'Locating Identity in Language', in C. Llamas and W. Dominic (eds), *Language and Identities*, 18–28, Edinburgh: Edinburgh University Press.

Butler, C. W., and R. Fitzgerald (2010), 'Membership-in-Action: Operative Identities in a Family Meal', *Journal of Pragmatics*, 42: 2462–74.

Butler, J. (1990), *Gender Trouble: Feminism and the Subversion of Identity*, New York: Routledge.

Caffi, C. (1984), 'Metapragmatics', Special Issue of *Journal of Pragmatics*, 8(4): 433–592.

Caffi, C. (1994), 'Metapragmatics', in R. E. Asher (ed.), *The Encyclopedia of Language and Linguistics*, 2461–66, Oxford: Pergamon Press.

Caffi, C. (2006), 'Metapragmatics', in K. Brown (ed.), *Encyclopedia of Language and Linguistics*, 2nd edn, 83–8, Amsterdam: Elsevier.

Caldas-Coulthard, C. R. (2008), 'Body Branded: Multimodal Identities in Tourism Advertising', *Journal of Language and Politics*, 7(3): 451–70.

Chaemsaithong, K. (2011), 'Accessing Identity through Face Work: A Case Study of Historical Courtroom Discourse', *International Review of Pragmatics*, 3(2): 240–67.

Chamani, F. (2014), 'Gender Differences in the Use of Apology Speech Act in Persian', *International Journal of Linguistics*, 6(6): 46–63.

Chen, F. (2008), '*Zhongwen fangdichan guanggao de pipingxing yupian fenxi* 中文房地产广告的批评性语篇分析' [A Critical Discourse Analysis of Chinese Real Estate Ads], *Journal of Mudanjiang Education College*, 5: 35–6.

Chen, J. (2018), '*Fudaoyuan qinshulei shenfen dingwei xianxiang yu fenxi* 辅导员亲属类身份定位现象与分析' [Student Advisors' Identity Positioning as Family Members], *Journal of Henan Science and Technology College*, 38: 105–9.

Chen, J. (2019), '*Fudaoyuan gebie tanhua zhong de feizhiye shenfen xuanze ji dongji tanjiu* 辅导员个别谈话中的非职业身份选择及动机探究' [Investigating Student Advisors' Choices of Non-professional Identities and Their Underlying Motivations in Individual Consultations], *Journal of Zhejiang International Studies University*, 5: 39–44.

Chen, J. (2020), *Gaoxiao fudaoyuan gongzuo tanhua zhong de shenfen xuanze yanjiu* 高校辅导员工作谈话中的身份选择研究 [Investigating Student Advisors' Choices of Identities in Consultations], Nanjing: Nanjing University Press.

Chen, R., and X. R. Chen (2020), 'Introduction', *East Asian Pragmatics*, 5(1): 1–5.

Chen, X. R. (1998), '*Huihua jiaozheng celue de shiyan yanjiu* 会话矫正策略的实验研究' [An Experimental Study of Conversation Corrective Strategies], in Z. A. Chen, J. R. Liu and X. Wen (eds), *Pragmatics: Language Understanding, Social Culture and Foreign Language Teaching*, 327–33, Chongqing: Southwest Normal University Press.

Chen, X. R. (2004a), '*Lun yuyong pingheng* 论语用平衡' [On Pragmatic Balance], *Foreign Language Research*, 6: 42–7.

Chen, X. R. (2004b), *Huihua xinxi guoliang xianxiang de yuyong yanjiu* 会话信息过量现象的语用研究 [The Pragmatics of Interactional Overinformativeness], Xi'an: Shanxi Normal University Press.

Chen, X. R. (2009), 'Piping yuyongxue: Mubiao, duixiang yu fangfa 批评语用学: 目标、对象与方法' [Critical Pragmatics: Aims, Objects and Methods], *Foreign Languages and Their Teaching*, 12: 10–12.

Chen, X. R. (2013a), 'Yuyong shenfen: Dongtai xuanze yu huayu jiangou 语用身份：动态选择与话语建构' [Pragmatic Identity: Dynamic Choice and Discursive Construction], *Foreign Language Research*, 4: 27–32, 112.

Chen, X. R. (2013b), 'Guanggao yuyong de gerenhua quxiang: Yixiang lishi yanjiu 广告用语的个人化趋向：一项历时研究' [The Trend of Personalization in Advertising Discourse: A Diachronic Study], *Foreign Language Learning Theory and Practice*, 3: 26–32, 81.

Chen, X. R. (2013c), *Piping yuyongxue shijiao xia de shehui yuyong yanjiu* 批评语用学视角下的社会用语研究 [Critical Pragmatic Studies on Public Discourse], Shanghai: Shanghai Foreign Language Education Press.

Chen, X. R. (2014), 'Yuyongxue shijiao xia de shenfen yanjiu: Guanjian wenti yu zhuyao lujing 语用学视角下的身份研究——关键问题与主要路径' [Current Research on Identity from the Pragmatic Perspective: Key Issues and Main Approaches], *Modern Foreign Languages*, 5: 702–10.

Chen, X. R. (2015), 'Emailing Requests to International Scholars: The Construction of Identity by Chinese EFL Graduate Students', in Y. Chen, D. V. Rau and G. Rau (eds), *Email Discourse among Chinese Using English as a Lingua Franca*, 115–34, New York: Springer.

Chen, X. R., ed. (2017), *Politeness Phenomena across Chinese Genres*. Sheffield: Equinox.

Chen, X. R. (2018a), *Yuyong shenfen lun: Ruhe yong shenfen huayu zuo shi* 语用身份论——如何用身份话语做事 [Pragmatic Identity: How to Do Things with Words of Identity], Beijing: Beijing Normal University.

Chen, X. R. (2018b), 'Yanyu jiaojizhe guanxi guanli moshi xinni 言语交际者关系管理模式新拟' [A Revised Model of Interactants' Rapport Management], *Foreign Language Learning Theory and Practice*, 163(3): 7–14.

Chen, X. R. (2018c), 'Shangye guanggao zhong "shenfen taolu" de piping yuyong fenxi 商业广告中"身份套路"的批评语用分析' ['Identity Traps' in Commercial Ads: A Critical Pragmatic Study], *Shandong Foreign Language Teaching*, 5: 24–33.

Chen, X. R. (2019a), 'Shenfen lilun shijiao xia de cihui yuyong wenti yanjiu 身份理论视角下的词汇语用问题研究' [Exploring Lexical Pragmatics from the Perspective of Pragmatic Identity Theory], *Studies in English*, 9: 23–33.

Chen, X. R. (2019b), 'You're a Nuisance! Patch-Up Jocular Abuse in Chinese Fiction', *Journal of Pragmatics*, 139: 52–63.

Chen, X. R. (2020a), 'Shenfen gongzuo yu limao pingjia 身份工作与礼貌评价' [Identity Work and Politeness Evaluation], *Journal of PLA University of Foreign Studies*, 2: 1–10.

Chen, X. R. (2020b), *Critical Pragmatic Studies of Chinese Public Discourse*, London: Routledge.

Chen, X. R. (2020c), '*Jiyu yuanyuyong de yuanhuayu fenlei xinni* 基于元语用的元话语分类新拟' [A New Taxonomy of Metadiscourse based on Metapragmatics], *Foreign Languages and Their Teaching*, 4: 1–10, 24.

Chen, X. R., and Y. H. Qian (2011), '*Duomotai fenxifa zai yuyongxue yanjiu zhong de yingyong* 多模态分析法在语用学研究中的应用' [The Application of Multimodal Discourse Analysis in Pragmatic Research], *Foreign Languages in China*, 5: 89–93.

Chen, X. R., et al. (2013), *Yuyongxue shijiao xia de shenfen yu jiaoji yanjiu* 语用学视角下的身份与交际研究 [Identity and Interaction: A Pragmatic Perspective], Beijing: Higher Education Press.

Chen, X. R., and J. J. Ren (2020), 'A Memetic Cultural Practice: The Use of Generalized Kinship Terms in a Research Seminar Attended by Chinese Graduate Students', *Lingua*, 245: 1–11.

Cheng, Y. (2007), '*Yuti zhuanhuan jiqi yuyong gongneng fenxi* 语体转换及其语用功能分析' [Style-Switching and Its Pragmatic Functions], *Journal of Shenyang University*, 3: 47–50.

Cheng, Y. (2016), '*Fangdichan guanggao huayu yuyong shenfen jiangou de yujing shunyi ngxing* 房地产广告话语用身份建构的语境顺应性' [The Contextual Adaption of the Construction of Pragmatic Identity in the Case of Real Estate Advertisements], *Journal of Bengbu University*, 5(5): 58–63.

Cheng, Z. Y. (2009), '*Fating tiaojie huayu yu quanli yanjiu* 法庭调解话语与权力研究' [Analysis of Judicial Mediation Discourse and Power Relation], *Journal of Law Application*, 7: 39–43.

Chiles, T. (2007), 'The Construction of an Identity as "Mentor" in White Collar and Academic Workplaces: A Preliminary Analysis', *Journal of Pragmatics*, 39: 730–41.

Clifton, J., and D. Van De Mieroop (2010), '"Doing" Ethos: A Discursive Approach to the Strategic Deployment and Negotiation of Identities in Meetings', *Journal of Pragmatics*, 42(9): 2449–61.

Côté, J. (2006), 'Identity Studies: How Close Are We to Developing a Social Science of Identity: An Appraisal of the Field', *Identity: An International Journal of Theory and Research*, 6(1): 3–25.

Culpeper, J. (2005), 'Impoliteness and Entertainment in the Television Quiz Show: The Weakest Link', *Journal of Politeness Research*, 1: 35–72.

Culpeper, J., and M. Haugh (2014), *Pragmatics and the English Language*, Basingstoke: Palgrave Macmillan.

Culpeper, J., M. Haugh and D. Z. Kádár (2017), *The Palgrave Handbook of Linguistic (Im)politeness*, London: Palgrave Macmillan.

De Fina, A. (2003), *Identity in Narrative: A Study of Immigrant Discourse*, Amsterdam: John Benjamins.

De Fina, A. (2010), 'The Negotiation of Identities', in M. A. Locher and S. Graham (eds), *Interpersonal Pragmatics*, 205–24, Berlin: Mouton de Gruyter.

De Fina, A., D. Schiffrin and M. Bamberg, eds (2006), *Discourse and Identity*, Cambridge: Cambridge University Press.

Dolón, R., and J. Todolí, eds (2008), *Analyzing Identities in Discourse*, Amsterdam: John Benjamins.

Donaghue, H. (2018), 'Relational Work and Identity Negotiation in Critical Post Observation Teacher Feedback', *Journal of Pragmatics*, 135: 101–16.

Dong, L. Y. (2011), '*Cong pipingxing yupian fenxi shijiao jiexi fangdichan guanggao* 从批评性语篇分析视角解析房地产广告' [An Interpretation of the Real Estate Advertisements from the Perspective of Critical Discourse Analysis], *Overseas English*, 13: 289–90.

Eelen, G. (2001), *A Critique of Politeness Theories*, Manchester: St Jerome.

Eisenstein, M., and J. W. Bodman (1986), ' "I Very Appreciate": Expressions of Gratitude by Native and Non-native Speakers of American English', *Applied Linguistics*, 7(2): 167–85.

Ekström, M., and Å. K. Lundell (2011), 'The Joint Construction of a Journalistic Expert Identity in Studio Interactions between Journalists on TV News', *Text and Talk – An Interdisciplinary Journal of Language, Discourse and Communication Studies*, 31(6): 661–81.

Enfield, N. J. (2007), 'Meanings of the Unmarked: How "Default" Person Reference Does More than Just Refer', in N. J. Enfield and T. Stivers (eds), *Person Reference in Interaction: Linguistic, Cultural, and Social Perspectives*, 97–120, Cambridge: Cambridge University Press.

Enfield, N. J. (2009), 'Relationship Thinking and Human Pragmatics', *Journal of Pragmatics*, 41(1): 60–78.

Erikson, E. H. (1968), *Identity: Youth and Crisis*, New York: Norton.

Fairclough, N. (1989), *Language and Power*, London: Longman.

Fearon, J. (1999), 'What Is Identity (as We Now Use the Word)?', unpublished paper, Stanford University.

Fellows, K. L., and D. L. Rubin (2006), 'Identities for Sale: How the Tobacco Industry Construed Asians, Asian Americans, and Pacific Islanders', *Journal of Intercultural Communication Research*, 35(3): 265–92.

Feng, W. J. (2020), '*Yuyong shenfen jiangou de youxiaoxing pingjia: Yi jingcha tiaojie huayu weili* 语用身份建构的有效性评价——以警察调解话语为例' [The Evaluation of the Validity of Pragmatic Identity: Evidence from Police Mediation Discourse], *Journal of PLA University of Foreign Studies*, 2: 26–33.

Fraser, B. (1990), 'Perspectives on Politeness', *Journal of Pragmatics*, 14: 219–36.

Fraser, B., and W. Nolan (1981), 'The Association of Deference with Linguistic Form', in J. Walters (ed.), *The Sociolinguistics of Deference and Politeness*, 93–111, The Hague: Mouton.

Fuertes-Olivera, P. A., M. Velasco-Sacristan, A. Arribas-Bano and E. Samaniego-Fernandez (2001), 'Persuasion and Advertising English: Metadiscourse in Slogans and Headlines', *Journal of Pragmatics*, 33(8): 1291–307.

Gao, G. (1996), 'Self and Other: A Chinese Perspective on Interpersonal Relationships', in W. B. Gudykunst, S. Ting-Toomey and T. Nishida (eds), *Communication in Personal Relationships across Cultures*, 81–101, Thousand Oaks, CA: Sage.

Garcés-Conejos Blitvich, P. (2009), 'Impoliteness and Identity in the American News Media: The "Culture Wars"', *Journal of Politeness Research. Language, Behaviour, Culture*, 5(2): 273–304.

Garcés-Conejos Blitvich, P. (2013), 'Introduction: Face, Identity and Im/politeness. Looking Backward, Moving Forward: From Goffman to Practice Theory', *Journal of Politeness Research*, 9(1): 1–33.

Garcés-Conejos Blitvich, P., and N. Lorenzo-Dus (2013), 'Reality Television: A Discourse-Analytical Perspective', in N. Lorenzo-Dus and P. Garcés-Conejos Blitvich (eds), *Real Talk: Reality Television and Discourse Analysis in Action*, 9–23, London: Palgrave Macmillan.

Garcés-Conejos Blitvich, P., and M. Sifianou (2017), '(Im)politeness and Identity', in J. Culpeper, M. Haugh and D. Z. Kádár (eds), *The Palgrave Handbook of Linguistic (Im)politeness*, 227–56, London: Palgrave Macmillan.

Garcés-Conejos Blitvich, P., N. Lorenzo-Dus and P. Bou-Franch (2010), 'A Genre Approach to Impoliteness in a Spanish Television Talk Show: Evidence from Corpus-Based Analysis, Questionnaires and Focus Groups', *Intercultural Pragmatics*, 7 (4): 689–723.

Garcés-Conejos Blitvich, P., P. Bou-Franch and N. Lorenzo-Dus (2013), 'Identity and Impoliteness: The Expert in the Talent Show *Idol*', *Journal of Politeness Research*, 9(1): 97–121.

Garfinkel, H. (1967), *Studies in Ethnomethodology*, Englewood Cliffs, NJ: Prentice Hall.

Goffman, E. (1955), 'On Facework: An Analysis of Ritual Elements in Social Interaction', *Psychiatry: Journal for the Study of Interpersonal Processes*, 18 (3): 213–31.

Goffman, E. (1967), *Interaction Ritual: Essays on Face to Face Behavior*, New York: Anchor Books.

Goffman, E. (1981), *Forms of Talk*, Philadelphia: University of Pennsylvania Press.

Grad, H., and L. M. Rojo (2008), 'Identities in Discourse', in R. Dolón and J. Todolí (eds), *Analyzing Identities in Discourse*, 3–28, Amsterdam: John Benjamins.

Graham, S. L. (2007), 'Disagreeing to Agree: Conflict, (Im)politeness and Identity in a Computer-Mediated Community', *Journal of Pragmatics*, 39: 742–59.

Greatbatch, D., and R. Dingwall (1989), 'Selective Facilitation: Some Preliminary Observations on a Strategy used by Divorce Mediators', *Law and Society Review*, 23(4): 613–41.

Greatbatch, D., and R. Dingwall (1997), 'Argumentative Talk in Divorce Mediation Sessions', *American Sociological Review*, 62(1): 151–70.

Grice, P. (1975). 'Logic and Conversation', in P. Cole and J. Morgan (eds), *Syntax and Semantics*, Vol. 3, 41–58, New York: Academic Press.

Gu, Y. G. (1990), 'Politeness Phenomena in Modern Chinese', *Journal of Pragmatics*, 14(2): 237–57.

Gu, Y. G. (1992), '*Liqi de xiucixue lilun* 利奇的修辞学理论' [Leech's Theory of Rhetoric], *Journal of Foreign Language Research*, 4: 17–21.

Guo, X. H. (2008), '*Guanlian-shunying shijiao xia de guanggao ticai huwenxing jiedu* 关联-顺应视角下的广告体裁互文性解读' [The Interdiscursivity of Advertisements from the Relevance-Adaptation Perspective], *Guizhou Gongye Daxue Xuebao (Journal of Guizhou University of Technology)*, 2: 124–6.

Guo, Y. D. (2020), '*Chongtu huayu zhong shenfen gongzuo de shehui renzhi jiexi* 冲突话语中身份工作的社会认知解析' [A Socio-cognitive Interpretation of Identity Work in Conflict Talks], *Journal of PLA University of Foreign Studies*, 2: 11–19.

Hall, S. (1989), 'Ethnicity: Identity and Difference', *Radical America*, 23: 9–20.

Hall, S. (1996a), 'Introduction: Who Needs Identity?', in S. Hall and P. D. Gay (eds), *Questions of Cultural Identity*, 1–17, London: Sage.

Hall, S. (1996b), 'Cultural Identity and Cinematic Representation', in H. A. Baker, M. Diawara and R. Lindeborg (eds), *Black British Cultural Studies: A Reader (Black Literature and Culture)*, 210–20, Chicago: Chicago University Press.

Hall, S., and M. Bucholtz (2013), 'Epilogue: Facing Identity', *Journal of Politeness Research*, 9(1): 123–32.

Harmon-Kizer, T. R. (2016), 'Identity Distancing and Targeted Advertisements: The Black Sheep Effect', *Journal of Promotion Management*, 22(3): 321–48.

Haugh, M. (2010), 'When Is an Email Really Offensive? Argumentativity and Variability in Evaluations of Impoliteness', *Journal of Politeness Research*, 6 (1): 7–31.

Haugh, M. (2015), *(Im)politeness Implicatures*, Berlin: Mouton de Gruyter.

He, Z. R. (2015), '*Shenme shanshang chang shenm ge: Shehui yuyong shenfen jiangou yu rentong* 什么山上唱什么歌——社会语用身份建构与认同' [Where and What to Say? On Identity Construction and Recognition in Societal Pragmatics], *Foreign Language and Literature Research*, 1: 12–19.

He, Z. R., and W. Ren (2016), 'Current Address Behaviour in China', *East Asian Pragmatics*, 1(2): 163–80.

Hecht, M. L., M. J. Collier and S. Ribeau (1993), *African American Communication: Ethnic Identity and Cultural Interpretation*, Newbury Park, CA: Sage.

Heisterkamp, B. L. (2006), 'Conversational Displays of Mediator Neutrality in a Court-based Program', *Journal of Pragmatics*, 38(12): 2051–64.

Heritage, J., and S. Clayman (2010), *Talk in Action: Interactions, Identities and Institutions*, Malden, MA: Wiley-Blackwell.

Higgins, C. (2007), 'Constructing Membership in the In-group: Affiliation and Resistance among Urban Tanzanians', *Pragmatics*, 17 (1): 49–70.

Ho, V. (2010), 'Constructing Identities through Request E-mail Discourse', *Journal of Pragmatics*, 42: 2253–61.

Holmes, J. (1995), *Women, Men and Politeness*, London: Routledge.

Holmes, J. (2007), 'Whose Perspective Counts? Sociopragmatics and Identity Construction at Work', paper presented at the 11th International Conference, 12–17 July 2007, University of Melbourne.

Hübler, A., and W. Bublitz (2007), 'Introducing Metapragmatics in Use', in W. Bublitz and A. Hübler (eds), *Metapragmatics in Use*, 1–26, Amsterdam: John Benjamins.

Ide, S. (1989), 'Formal Forms and Discernment: Two Neglected Aspects of Universals of Linguistic Politeness', *Multilingua*, 8: 223–48.

Jacobs, S. (2002), 'Maintaining Neutrality in Dispute Mediation: Managing Disagreement while Managing not to Disagree', *Journal of Pragmatics*, 34(10): 1403–26.

Jiang, T. (2016), '*Taidu xitong shiyu xia zhongcaiyuan tiaojie huayu de renji yiyi fenxi* 态度系统视阈下仲裁员调解话语的人际意义分析' [On Interpersonal Meanings in Arbitrators' Mediation Discourse: An Attitude System Perspective], *Modern Foreign Languages*, 2: 188–97+291–2.

Jiang, T., and J. J. Liu (2014), '*Tiaojie huayu zhong zhongcaiyuan de shenfen jiangou: Yi chenghuyu de yuma zhuanhuan wei shijiao* 调解话语中仲裁员的身份建构——以称呼语的语码转换为视角' [Mediators' Identity Construction in Mediation Discourse: From the Perspective of Code Switching in Address Terms], *Social Science Research*, 3: 91–6.

Jin, Y. Z., and X. R. Chen (2020), '"*Mouren*" ("Somebody") Can be You-Know-Who: A Case Study of Mock Referential Vagueness in Chinese Weibo Posts', *Journal of Pragmatics*, 163: 1–15.

Jo, J. (2018), 'Korean "Formality" Endings "-supnita/-supnikka" and "-eyo" in the Negotiation of Interactional Identity in the News Interview', *Journal of Pragmatics*, 136: 20–38.

Joseph, J. E. (2013), 'Identity Work and Facework across Linguistic and Cultural Boundaries', *Journal of Politeness Research*, 9 (1): 35–54.

Karafoti, E. (2007), 'Politeness, Gender and the Face of the Speaker', *Camling*, 1: 120–6.

Ke, X. B. (2013), '*Fating tiaojie chengweiyu limao boyi yanjiu* 法庭调解称谓语礼貌博弈研究' [A Game-Theoretical Study of Polite Address Terms in Court-Related Mediation], *Hubei Social Sciences*, 11: 118–21.

Ke, X. B., and Z. L. Li (2014), '*Fating tiaojie faguan huayu juese zhuanhuan yanjiu* 法庭调解法官话语角色转换研究' [Analysis of Judge's Switching of Discoursal Roles in Judicial Mediation], *Hubei Social Sciences*, 5: 153–8.

Ke, X. B., and M. Z. Liao (2011), '*Fating tiaojie huayu boyi jiaoji yanjiu* 法庭调解话语博弈交际研究' [A Game-Theoretical Study of Court-Related Mediation Discourse], *Foreign Language Research*, 5: 70–5.

Kroskrity, P. (2000), 'Identity', *Journal of Linguistic Anthropology*, 9: 111–14.

Labov, W. (1966), *The Social Stratification of English in New York City*, Washington, DC: Center for Applied Linguistics.

Lakoff, R. (1989), 'The Limits of Politeness: Therapeutic and Courtroom Discourse', *Multilingua – Journal of Cross-Cultural and Interlanguage Communication*, 8(2-3): 101–30.

Leech, G. (1983), *Principles of Pragmatics*, London: Longman.

Leech, G. (2014), *The Pragmatics of Politeness*, Oxford: Oxford University Press.

Lei, Q. L. (2003), '*Shen fen, shichang ji qita: Cong shanghai fangdichan guanggao kan xiaofei yishi xingtai de jiangou* 身份、市场及其他——从上海房地产广告看消费意识形态的建构' [Identity, Market and Other: The Construction of Consumption Ideology in Shanghai Real Estate Ads], *Contemporary Writers Review*, 6: 64–73.

Li, C. T. (2008), '*Huayu biaojiyu "ma" de yuyong gongneng* 话语标记语"嘛"的语用功能' [A Study of the Pragmatic Functions of the Discourse Marker 'Ma'], *Modern Foreign Languages*, 2: 150–6.

Li, C. T. (2010), '*Zhishiyu xuanze de shidian dingwei yu shenfen goujian* 指示语选择的视点定位与身份构建' [Stancetaking and Identity Construction of Indexicality in Verbal Interaction], *Foreign Language Education*, 5: 15–19.

Li, C. T., and Y. P. Ran (2012), '*Taren shenfen de yinhan fouding jiqi renji hexie de yuyong quxiang* 他人身份的隐含否定及其人际和谐的语用取向' [A Pragmatic Study of Implicit Negation of Other-Identity in Interaction], *Foreign Languages in China*, 5: 34–40.

Li, C. T., and Y. P. Ran (2016), 'Self-professional Identity Construction through Other-Identity Deconstruction in Chinese Televised Debating Discourse', *Journal of Pragmatics*, 94: 47–63.

Li, J. W. (2003), '*Yuti zhuanhuan yu juese dingwei* 语体转换与角色定位' [Style-Shifting and Identity-Projection], *Journal of PLA University of Foreign Studies*, 1: 6–10.

Li, J., and X. R. Chen (forthcoming), 'The Performance and Relational Role of Toast Intervention in Chinese Dining Contexts', *Pragmatics and Society*.

Li, W. (1999), *Nuerhachi*, Beijing: China Drama Press.

Li, Y. (2014), '*Cong piping huayu fenxi shijiao kan fangdichan guanggao de wenhua suqiu* 从批评话语分析视角看房地产广告的文化诉求' [The Cultural Appeal of Estate Advertisement from the Perspective of Critical Discourse Analysis], *Journal of Shenyang Agricultural University (Social Sciences Edition)*, 16(4): 500–2.

Locher, M. (2008), 'Relational Work, Politeness, and Identity Construction', in G. Antos and E. Ventola (eds), *Handbook of Interpersonal Communication*, 509–40, Berlin: Mouton de Gruyter.

Locher, M. A., and S. Hoffmann (2006), 'The Emergence of the Identity of a Fictional Expert Advice-Giver in an American Internet Advice Column', *Text and Talk*, 26(1): 67–104.

Locher, M. A., and R. J. Watts (2008), 'Politeness Theory and Relational Work', *Journal of Politeness Research*, 1(1): 9–13.

Lorenzo-Dus, N. (2009), '"You're Barking Mad, I'm Out": Impoliteness and Broadcast Talk', *Journal of Politeness Research*, 5(2): 159–87.

Lorenzo-Dus, N., and P. Garcés-Conejos Blitvich (2013), 'Discourse Approaches to the Study of Reality Television', in N. Lorenzo-Dus and P. Garcés-Conejos Blitvich (eds), *Real Talk: Reality television and Discourse Analysis in Action*, 24–42, London: Palgrave Macmillan.

Lü, W. Y. (2005), '*Sifa tiaojie huayu zhong de chongtuxing daduan* 司法调解话语中的冲突性打断' [Conflicting Interruption in Judicial Mediation], *Journal of PLA University of Foreign Languages*: 26–30+86.

Lucy, J. (2000), 'Reflexivity', *Journal of Linguistic Anthropology*, 9: 212–15.

Macaulay, M. (2001), 'Tough Talk: Indirectness and Gender in Requests for Information', *Journal of Pragmatics*, 33(2): 293–316.

Maley, Y. (1995), 'From Adjudication to Mediation: Third Party Discourse in Conflict Resolution', *Journal of Pragmatics*, 23(1): 93–110.

Mao, L. R. (1994), 'Beyond Politeness Theory: "Face" Revisited and Renewed', *Journal of Pragmatics*, 21: 451–86.

Marcia, J. E. (1980), 'Identity in Adolescence', in J. Adelson (ed.), *Handbook of Adolescent Psychology*, 159–87, New York: Wiley.

Matsumoto, Y. (1988), 'Reexamination of the Universality of Face: Politeness Phenomena in Japanese', *Journal of Pragmatics*, 12: 403–26.

McCall, G. J., and J. L. Simmons (1978), *Identities and Interactions*, New York: Free Press.

McQuarrie, E. F., and M. D. Glen (1996), 'Figures of Rhetoric in Advertising Language', *Journal of Consumer Research*, 4: 424–38.

Mey, J. (1985), *Whose Language? A Study in Linguistic Pragmatics*, Amsterdam: John Benjamins.

Mey, J. (1993), *Pragmatics: An Introduction*, Oxford: Blackwell.

Mills, S. (2003), *Gender and Politeness*, Cambridge: Cambridge University Press.

Moody, S. J. (2014), '"Well, I'm a Gaijin": Constructing Identity through English and Humor in the International Workplace', *Journal of Pragmatics*, 60: 75–88.

Myers, D., N. Haslam, W. Louis, F. Allen, T. Denson, G. Karantzas and L. Zinkiewicz (2014), *Social Psychology*, North Ryde, NSW: McGraw-Hill Education.

Ochs, E. (1990), 'Indexicality and Socialization', in J. Stigler, R. Shweder and G. Herdt (eds), *Cultural Psychology: Essays on Comparative Human Development*, 287–308, Cambridge: Cambridge University Press.

Ochs, E. (1993), 'Constructing Social Identity', *Research on Language and Interaction*, 26(3): 287–306.

Ochs, E. (2012), 'Experiencing Language', *Anthropological Theory*, 12(2): 142–60.

Ogi, N. (2014), 'Language and an Expression of Identities: Japanese Sentence-final Particles *ne* and *na*', *Journal of Pragmatics*, 64: 72–84.

Parisi, C., and P. Wogan (2006), 'Compliment Topics and Gender', *Women and Language*, 29(2): 21–8.

Perry, J., ed. (1975), *Personal Identity*, Berkeley: University of California Press.

Persson, G. (2019), 'Speaking on Behalf of Oneself and Others: Negotiating Speaker Identities in Journalistic Discourse on Refugee Activism in Sweden', *Discourse and Society*, 30(2): 1-17.

Piller, I. (2001), 'Identity Constructions in Multilingual Advertising', *Language in Society*, 30(2): 153-86.

Pomering, A., and L. White (2011), 'The Portrayal of Indigenous Identity in Australian Tourism Brand Advertising: Engendering an Image of Extraordinary Reality or Staged Authenticity?' *Place Branding and Public Diplomacy*, 7(3): 165-74.

Rees-Miller, J. (2011), 'Compliments Revisited: Contemporary Compliments and Gender', *Journal of Pragmatics*, 43(11): 2673-88.

Ren, J. J., and X. R. Chen (2019), 'Kinship Term Generalization as a Cultural Pragmatic Strategy among Chinese Graduate Students', *Pragmatics and Society*, 10(4): 615-40.

Ren, Y. X. (2012), 'Constructing Identities in Academic Advising Interaction: An Adaptationist Account', unpublished PhD dissertation, School of Foreign Studies, Nanjing University, Nanjing.

Ren, Y. X. (2014), *Xueshu jianyi zhong de shenfen jiangou* 学术建议中的身份建构 [Constructing Identities in Academic Advising Interaction], Tianjin: Nankai University Press.

Richards, K. (2006), '"Being the Teacher": Identity and Classroom Conversation', *Applied Linguistics*, 27: 51-77.

Rifkin, J., J. Millen and S. Cobb (1991), 'Toward a New Discourse for Mediation: A Critique of Neutrality', *Mediation Quarterly*, 9(2): 151-64.

Rodney, H. J. (1997), 'Marketing the Damaged Self: The Construction of Identity in Advertisements Directed Towards People with HIV/AIDS', *Journal of Sociolinguistics*, 1(3): 393-418.

Rorty, A., ed. (1976), *The Identities of Persons*, Berkeley: University of California Press.

Sacks, H. (1972), 'An Initial Investigation of the Usability of Conversational Data for Doing Sociology', in D. Sudnow (ed.), *Studies in Social Interaction*, 31-74, New York: Free Press.

Sarangi, S., and C. Roberts (1999), *Talk, Work and Institutional Order*, Berlin: Mouton de Gruyter.

Schneider, K. P., and A. Barron, eds (2008), *Variational Pragmatics: A Focus on Regional Varieties in Pluricentric Languages*, Amsterdam: John Benjamins.

Schnurr, S. (2009), 'Constructing Leader Identities through Teasing at Work', *Journal of Pragmatics*, 41: 1125-38.

Searle, J. (1969), *Speech Acts*, New York: Cambridge University Press.

Shei, C. (2013), 'How "Real" Is Reality Television in China? On the Success of a Chinese Dating Programme', in N. Lorenzo-Dus and P. Garcés-Conejos Blitvich (eds), *Real Talk: Reality Television and Discourse Analysis in Action*, 43-65, London: Palgrave Macmillan.

Shu, S. C. (2016), '*Duomotai shijiao xia zhongwen fangdichan guanggao zhong yuyong yushe de qipianxing* 多模态视角下中文房地产广告中语用预设的欺骗性' [The

Deceptivity of Pragmatic Presupposition in Chinese Real Estate Ads from the Multimodal Perspective], *Overseas English*, 329(13): 204–6.

Simon, B. (2004), *Identity in Modern Society: A Social Psychological Perspective*, Oxford: Blackwell.

Spencer-Oatey, H. (2000), 'Rapport Management: A Framework for Analysis', in H. Spencer-Oatey (ed.), *Culturally Speaking: Managing Rapport through Talk across Cultures*, 11–46, London: Continuum.

Spencer-Oatey, H. (2005), '(Im)politeness, Face and Perceptions of Rapport: Unpackaging Their Bases and Interrelationships', *Journal of Politeness Research*, 1: 113–37.

Spencer-Oatey, H. (2007), 'Theories of Identity and the Analysis of Face', *Journal of Pragmatics*, 39: 639–56.

Spencer-Oatey, H., ed. (2008), *Culturally Speaking: Culture, Communication and Politeness*, London: Continuum.

Spencer-Oatey, H. (2009), 'Face, Identity and Interactional Goals', in F. Bargiela-Chiappini and M. Haugh (eds), *Face, Communication and Social Interaction*, 137–54, London: Equinox.

Spencer-Oatey, H. (2011), 'Conceptualising "the Relational" in Pragmatics: Insights from Metapragmatic Emotion and (Im)politeness Comments', *Journal of Pragmatics*, 43(14): 3565–78.

Spencer-Oatey, H., and D. K. Kádár (2016), 'The Bases of (Im)politeness Evaluations: Culture, the Moral Order and the East-West Debate', *East Asian Pragmatics*, 1(1): 73–106.

Sperber, D., and D. Wilson (1986/1995), *Relevance: Communication and Cognition*, London: Blackwell.

Stokoe, E., and R. O. Sikveland (2016), 'Formulating Solutions in Mediation', *Journal of Pragmatics*, 105: 101–13.

Stryker, S. (1980/2002), *Symbolic Interactionism: A Social Structural Version*, Caldwell, NJ: Blackburn Press.

Stryker, S. (1987), 'Identity Theory: Developments and Extensions', in K. Yardley and T. Honess (eds), *Self and Identity: Psychosocial Perspectives*, 89–104, Chichester: Wiley.

Sun-Young, O. (2007), 'The Interactional Meanings of Quasi-pronouns in Korean Conversation', in N. J. Enfield and T. Stivers (eds), *Person Reference in Interaction: Linguistic, Cultural, and Social Perspectives*. 203–25, Cambridge: Cambridge University Press.

Tajfel, H. (1974), 'Social Identity and Intergroup Behavior', *Social Science Information*, 13: 65–93.

Tajfel, H. (1981), *Human Groups and Social Categories*. Cambridge: Cambridge University Press.

Tajfel, H., ed. (1982), *Social Identity and Intergroup Relations*, Cambridge: Cambridge University Press.

Tajfel, H., and J. C. Turner (1986), 'The Social Identity Theory of Inter-group Behavior', in S. Worchel and W. G. Austin (eds), *Psychology of Intergroup Relations*, 7–24, Chicago: Nelson-Hall.

Tannen, D. (1990), *You Just Don't Understand: Women and Men in Conversation*, New York: Morrow.

Ting-Toomey, S., and A. Kurogi (1998), 'Facework Competence in Intercultural Conflict: An Updated Face-negotiation Theory', *International Journal of Intercultural Relations*, 22(2): 187–225.

Tracy, K. (1990), 'The Many Faces of Facework', in H. Giles and W. P. Robinson (eds), *Handbook of Language and Social Psychology*, 209–26, Oxford: John Wiley and Sons.

Tracy, K. (2002), *Everyday Talk: Building and Reflecting Identities*, London: Guilford Press.

Tracy, K., and J. S. Robles (2013), *Everyday Talk: Building and Reflecting Identities*, New York: Guilford Press.

Tracy, K., and A. Spradlin (1994), 'Talking like a Mediator: Conversational Moves of Experienced Divorce Mediators', in J. P. Folger and T. S. Jones (eds), *New Directions in Mediation: Communication Research and Perspectives*, 110–32, Thousand Oaks, CA: Sage.

Turner, G. (2010), *Ordinary People and the Media: The Demotic Turn*, London: Sage.

Turner, J. C., M. A. Hogg, P. J. Oakes, S. D. Reicher and M. S. Wetherell (1987), *Rediscovering the Social Group: A Self-categorization Theory*, Oxford: Blackwell.

Verschueren, J. (1995), 'Metapragmatics', in J. Verschueren, J. Ostmanand and J. Blommaert (eds), *Handbook of Pragmatics. Manual*, 367–71, Amsterdam: John Benjamins. Republished 2010 in Handbook of Pragmatics Online.

Verschueren, J. (1999), *Understanding Pragmatics*, London: Arnold.

Verschueren, J. (2000), 'Notes on the Role of Metapragmatic Awareness in Language Use', *Pragmatics*, 10: 439–56.

Verschueren, J. (2012), *Ideology in Language Use: Pragmatic Guidelines for Empirical Research*, Cambridge: Cambridge University Press.

Verschueren, J. (2016), 'Humanities and the Public Sphere: A Pragmatic Perspective', *Pragmatics and Society*, 7(1): 141–61.

Wang, H., and Y. F. Ge (2020), 'Negotiating National Identities in Conflict Situations: The Discursive Reproduction of the Sino-US Trade War in China's News Reports', *Discourse and Communication*, 14(1): 65–83.

Wang, J. H., and G. F. Yuan (1999), '*Jianxi shehui yongyu de tezheng* 简析社会用语的特征' [A Brief Analysis of the Features of Public Discourse], *Yuyan Wenzi Yingyong (Applied Linguistics)*, 3: 55–9.

Wang, W. Q. (2007), '*Qianxi zhongwen fangdichan guanggao zhong de yishi xingtai: Yi pipingxing yupian fenxi lilun wei shijiao* 浅析中文房地产广告中的意识形态——以批评性语篇分析理论为视角' [An Analysis of Ideology in Chinese Real Estate Ads from the Perspective of Critical Discourse Analysis], *Journal of Guangdong University of Foreign Studies*, 18(1): 98–101.

Wang, X. Y. (2012), 'Guanggao quanshuo zhong de yuanhuayu ziyuan he shenfen jiangou 广告劝说中的元话语资源和身份建构' [Metadiscourse and Identity Construction in Advertisements], *Journal of Tianjin Foreign Studies University*, 19(3): 1–7.

Wang, X. Y. (2013), 'Guanggao yupian zhong guanggaozhu shenfen jiangou de lishi yanjiu 广告语篇中广告主身份建构的历时研究' [Advertisers' Identity Construction in Advertising Texts: A Diachronic Study], unpublished PhD dissertation, School of Foreign Studies, Nanjing University, Nanjing.

Wang, X. Y. (2015), 'Shangye guanggao yupian zhong de shenfen jiangou bianqian: Lishi shejiao yuyongxue shijiao 商业广告语篇中的身份建构变迁:历史社交语用学视角' [Changes of Identity Construction in Commercial Ads: A Historical Pragmatic Perspective], *Contemporary Foreign Language Studies*, 9: 39–43.

Watts, R. (2003), *Politeness*, Cambridge: Cambridge University Press.

Wetherell, M. (2007), 'Community Cohesion and Identity Dynamics: Dilemmas and Challenges', in M. Wetherell, M. Lafleche and R. Berkeley (eds), *Identity, Ethnic Diversity and Community Cohesion*, 1–14, London: Sage.

Widdicombe, S. (1998), 'Identity as an Analyst's and a Participant's Resource', in C. Antaki and S. Widdicombe (eds), *Identities in Talk*, 191–206, London: Sage.

Wiik, J. (2009), 'Identities under Construction: Professional Journalism in a Phase of Destabilization', *International Review of Sociology*, 19(2): 351–65.

Xiao, S. (n.d.), *Sinicism Family*, available online: https://zhidao.baidu.com/question/513393791.html.

Xiong, T. (2008), 'Nvxing shenfen de guanggao huayu jiangou 女性身份的广告话语建构' [The Construction of Female Identity in Advertisements], *Journal of Changsha University*, 6: 79–80.

Xu, Y. P. (2006), 'Huayu biaojiyu zai fayuan tiaojie guocheng zhong de zuoyong: Guanlian lilun jiaodu de fenxi 话语标记语在法院调解过程中的作用——关联理论角度的分析' [Functions of Discourse Markers in Judicial Mediation: A Relevance Theoretic Perspective], *Rhetoric Learning*, 4: 52–5.

Yang, L. (2009), 'Fangdichan guanggao dui xiaofeizhe fugui shenfen de yushe qingxiang 房地产广告对消费者富贵身份的预设倾向' [The Presupposition Trend of Consumers' Honourable Identity in Real Estate Ads], *News World*, 6: 88–9.

Yang, Y. H. (2008), 'Guanggao yuyan zhong de yuma hunyong yanjiu 广告语言中的语码混用研究' [Code-Mixing in Advertising Language], *Zhongguo Waiyu (Foreign Languages in China)*, 3: 34–7.

Yin, B. H. (2007), 'Huihua zhong yuti zhuanhuan xianxiang fenxi 会话中语体转换现象分析' [Analysis of Style-Shifting in Conversations], *Friend of Science Amateurs*, 1: 110–11.

You, Z. S. (2011), 'Huayu, Shenfen jiangou yu zhongguo dongmeng guanxi: Renmin ribao xinwen biaoti fenxi 话语、身份建构与中国东盟关系:《人民日报》新闻标题分析' [Discourse, Identity Construction and China-ASEAN Relations: An Analysis of News Headlines in *People's Daily*], *Southeast Academic Research*, 5: 240–8.

Yuan, Z. M. (2011), '*Shunyinglun shijiao xia yiyao zixun guwen yuyong shenfen jiangou de shizheng yanjiu* 顺应论视角下医药咨询顾问语用身份建构的实证研究' [An Empirical Study of Medical Consultants' Pragmatic Identity Construction from the Adaptationist Perspective], unpublished PhD dissertation, School of Foreign Studies, Nanjing University, Nanjing.

Yuan, Z. M. (2012), '*Zichengyu de yuyong shenfen jiangou: Zuowei yuyong xingwei de shenying* 自称语的语用身份建构: 作为语用行为的顺应' [Pragmatic Identity Construction of Self Address Forms: Adaptation as a Pragmatic Act], *Foreign Language Education*, 5: 33–40.

Yuan, Z. M. (2016), '*Guanxi guanli lilun jiqi yunzuo* 关系管理理论及其运作' [Rapport Management Theory and Its Operation], *Foreign Languages in China*, 1: 41–7.

Yuan, Z. M. (2020), 'Identity Rhetoric in Chinese Radio-Mediated Medical Consultation', *East Asian Pragmatics*, 5(1): 41–65.

Yuan, Z. M., and X. R. Chen (2013), '*Yuyan shunyinglun shijiao xia de yuyong shenfen jiangouyanjiu* 语言顺应论视角下的语用身份建构研究' [A Study of Pragmatic Identity Construction from the Perspective of Linguistic Adaptation Theory: A Case Study of Medical Consultations], *Foreign Language Teaching and Research*, 4: 518–30.

Yuan, Z. M., and Z. X. Fang (2008), '*Yanyu jiaoji zhong de shenfen jiangou jiqi liju yanjiu* 言语交际中的身份建构及其理据研究' [On Identity Construction and Its Motivation in Verbal Communication], *Journal of Nanjing University of Posts and Telecommunications (Social Science)*, 3: 56–9.

Yule, G. (2000), *The Study of Language*, 2nd edn, Beijing: Foreign Language Teaching and Research Press.

Zhong, X. Y. (2013), '*Zhapianzhe xujia shenfen de huayu jiangou* 诈骗者虚假身份的话语建构' [Discursive Construction of Deceivers' Fake Identity], in X. R. Chen (ed.), *Identity and Interaction: A Pragmatic Perspective*, 64–78, Beijing: Higher Education Press.

Zhong, X. Y., and Y. T. Zeng (2020), '"Guess Who I Am": Constructing False Identities for Fraudulent Purposes in the Chinese Context', *East Asian Pragmatics*, 5(1): 99–122.

Zimmerman, D. H. (1992), 'The Interactional Organization of Calls for Emergency Assistance', in P. Drew and J. Heritage (eds), *Talk at Work: Interaction in Institutional Settings*, 418–69, Cambridge: Cambridge University Press.

Zimmerman, D. H. (1998), 'Identity, Context and Interaction', in C. Antaki and S. Widdicombe (eds), *Identities in Talk*, 87–106, London: Sage.

Index

activity type 47, 58, 146, 149
address form 29, 38, 40–6, 59–60, 62–3, 68, 72, 113, 131, 134, 188, 202
address term 61–2, 81, 88–89, 128–9, 136, 164, 174, 201, 204, 213, 214
addressing 25, 43–4, 113, 137, 149, 164
affective detachment 143
affective involvement 143
approaches to identity
    cognitive 9
    discursive 5
    pragma-rhetorical 4
    psychological 9
    social 52
    socio-cognitive 9
    sociological 9
argot 60, 69

bilateral negotiability 20

civic dialect 10
code 51, 58, 60, 68–9, 198
code switching 68–70, 72
communication dependency 19
communication strategy 22
communicative effect 19, 38–39, 162
communicative equilibrium 7
communicative event 6, 51, 53, 217
communicative goals 28, 73, 119, 120, 143, 171, 195, 225
    illocutionary 7
    interactional 3, 15, 17, 19–22, 31, 143–144, 147, 150, 154
    interpersonal 143
    practical 15
    transactional 7, 137
communicative need viii, 3, 6, 7, 21, 33, 34, 35–40, 42–3, 46–9, 52, 55, 85, 111, 112, 117, 135, 149, 218
communicative value ix, 39
comprehension process 54
context viii, ix, 3, 5–7, 15–22, 24–7, 30–55, 62–3, 65–72, 74, 76–83, 85–139, 149, 152–9, 164, 167–9, 171–5, 194–5, 197–9, 201–2, 204–5, 207, 212–13, 217–18, 221–5, 230, 235, 241
    background assumption 54
    behavioural expectations 143
    channel of communication 58
    cognitive environment 54
    communicative viii, ix, 34, 39–40, 46–8, 53, 83, 85, 146, 218
    co-text 35, 53–5
    environmental factor 146, 149
    interactional 20, 167
    linguistic channel 53–5
    mental world 35, 53, 213
    physical world 52–4
    sequential 53
    situational 54
    social world 35, 52–3
    sociocultural factor 6
context-adaptive 54
context formation 54
contextual assessment 52
contextual constraint 19
contextual correlate 52, 53
contextual factor 6
contextual norm 19
contextual resource 35, 55
conversation analysis (CA) 2, 5, 178
conversational implicature 48, 141
critical linguistics 212
    critical cognitive analysis 212
    critical discourse analysis (CDA) 168, 204, 212–13
    critical pragmatics 200, 212–13
    negative critical pragmatic analysis 28–9
    positive critical pragmatic analysis 28

data for pragmatic analysis
    Contemporary Chinese Language Corpus 5
    field notes 5, 160
    Modern Chinese Corpus 50, 224

ready-made corpora 5
real estate advertisement 8, 65, 203–8, 213–14
reality TV (RTV) 5, 174
real-life data 4, 6
self-built database 5, 7
deixis 29, 52, 61, 63, 68
descriptive adequacy 58
dialect 10, 54, 58, 60–1, 69–70
discourse
  advertising 198–9, 214
  advocating 197
  appropriacy of 24
  felicity of 23
  identity 22, 48
  interactional 13
  jocular 137, 146, 222
  journalistic 197
  legitimacy of 27
  mediation 174–5, 193
  professional 193
  promotional 197, 202
  public 8, 197–8, 204
  truthfulness 27
discourse analysis
  contextual analysis 49
  critical analysis 168, 204–5, 212–13
  critical pragmatic analysis 28–9, 212–13
  membership categorization analysis (MCA) 148
  multimodal pragmatic analysis 5
  qualitative analysis 5
  quantitative analysis 5
discourse authenticity 27
discourse legitimacy 27
discourse organization 59
discourse role 17
discursive accomplishment 25, 151
discursive choice 3–4, 33–4, 40, 42, 52, 59, 144, 218
discursive construction ix, 19, 193–4
discursive device 48–9
discursive effort ix
discursive formulae 79
discursive practice 4–5, 7, 10, 18, 57–60, 68, 81, 83–5, 114, 151, 176, 178, 181, 183, 188–9, 194, 200, 203, 207, 210–12, 218, 221, 224–5

domains of identity work 61
  address and referential 59, 61, 68, 84, 218
  illocutionary 61, 64, 84, 218
  non-verbal 57, 61, 80, 84, 218
  participation 61, 78, 84, 218
  stylistic 61, 68, 84, 218

East Asian Pragmatics 4
emotional positioning 11
evidential 178, 181–3, 188–9

face
  collective 143
  group 143, 152–3, 225
  identity 143, 146–7
  negative 142, 150
  personal 142–3, 225
  positive 150
  quality 142, 146
  relational 143, 225
familiarizer 63
felicity conditions/ rules 23
  essential condition 23
  preparatory condition 23
  propositional content condition 23
  sincerity condition 23
footing 13, 15, 61

group membership 10

honorifics 61

identity
  as attribute 10
  collective 10, 13, 17, 85, 88–9, 91–3
  communicative 17
  constructed viii, 3, 37, 82, 88
  contextualized 18
  default 17, 46–8, 69, 112, 133, 137, 139, 201
  deviational 17, 47, 139, 224
  discourse 17
  as doer 11
  emergent 1–2, 18
  fabricated 17
  fragmental viii
  group 13, 17
  as identification 10

as image 12
image- 12
individual 6, 13, 17, 85–7, 89, 92–93
as individuality 13
institutional 80, 83, 169–70, 173–4, 194–5
interactional 11, 17
interpersonal 13
intersubjective viii, 3, 18
master 10, 54
as membership 10
non-default 20, 47
personal 12–13, 172, 195, 220
pragmatic viii–ix, 3, 15, 17–19, 21–2, 25, 27–31, 38, 40, 42, 46–7, 50, 55, 57, 59, 68, 70, 75, 80–2, 139, 149, 204–5, 214, 217–18
pre-existing nature of viii–ix, 1–2, 217
professional 20, 117, 126, 130, 176, 181–184, 188–9, 193–5, 220, 235
relational 13, 17, 28, 45, 70, 77, 85, 87–90, 92–4, 96–8, 100, 117, 123–4, 129, 134, 138, 164, 201–2, 220
as role 11
role 11, 104
situated 11, 168
social 11, 18, 38, 150–151, 156, 160
as stance 12
as status 12
words of 2
identity address term 129
identity attribute 12
identity awareness 46
identity category 167
identity choice 3, 33–5, 39, 46, 52, 54–5, 58, 134, 195, 218
identity choice-making 46, 218
identity construction 2, 4–5, 11, 25, 30, 41, 43, 50, 58–60, 64–5, 67–9, 71, 74–8, 80, 85, 89, 92–3, 149, 175–6, 178, 181, 193, 198, 200, 204–5, 210–12
identity feature 12, 203
identity indexing 2, 64, 178, 222
identity-in-practice 148
identity-marked 21
identity marker 34, 50, 61, 67–8, 75, 86, 119–20, 124, 128, 130, 133, 172, 218
identity positioning 120, 172
identity resource 6, 22

identity rhetoric 3, 52, 119
identity schema 48
identity selection 34, 39, 43–4, 46, 49–50
identity statement 85, 87, 96, 129
identity theories 148
   constructionist view 19, 30
   discursive turn 1
   essentialist view 1
   Identity Maxim 6, 40, 46–9, 139, 218
   membership categorization device 46
   pragmatic approach ix–x, 6
   Pragmatic Identity Theory 15, 22, 30
   rhetorical approach 3–4
   Self-Aspect Model 9, 13
   self-categorization theory 11
   social constructionism 18, 223
   Social Identity Theory 11, 18, 38, 150–1, 156, 160, 236, 239
identity type 207–8
identity work
   as cost-benefit grounder 150, 154
   as emotional work 150, 157
   as enabling resource 21
   explicit 85, 219
   as facework 148, 232, 234, 239
   generative mechanism of 3, 218, 224
   implicit 85, 219
   as interactional goal facilitator 150, 159
   locus of 33–4, 218
   process of 33, 42, 52, 218
   as rights-obligations rationalizer 150, 156
   salience of 46
   as stance work 150, 158
identity work dimensions 99
   attribute 99
   doer 104
   identification 101
   image 107
   membership 101
   personality 109
   role 103
   stance 106
   status 105
identity work directions 85
   challenging ix, 31, 85, 89, 90–3, 115, 143, 153–4, 156–7
   (co-)construction 2–7, 11, 13, 30, 38, 41, 43, 50, 57–60, 62, 64–5, 67–70,

74–8, 80–1, 85, 88–9, 92–3, 99, 138, 149, 175–6, 178, 181, 184, 188, 193–5, 198–200, 202, 204–5, 210–12, 214, 217, 219, 224–5
  deconstruction ix, 13, 85, 92–3, 138, 235
  questioning 48, 67, 85, 89–93, 95, 115, 125, 153, 156–7, 181, 183–4, 186, 188–90
identity (work) strategies 119
  alignment 128
  backgrounding 125
  de-identification 125
  deviation 28, 47, 139, 202, 224
  disalignment 130
  distancing 135, 198, 219
  elevating 134
  endearing 131
  fictionalizing 136
  foregrounding 119–20, 125, 136, 219
  highlighting 6, 25, 31, 37, 86, 123–4, 153, 155–6, 158, 168, 170, 223
  shadowing 125
  verification 25, 149
identity work targets 7, 20, 26, 93, 117, 218, 221
  hearer-oriented 95
  speaker-oriented 94
  third-party-oriented 95
implicature 48, 141, 212, 214, 233
(im)politeness vii, 25, 68, 76, 145–9, 230, 232–3, 238
  assessment vii, 25, 38, 52, 54, 55, 145, 148–9, 184–5, 225
  formulae 76, 79
  (in)directness 58, 76
  Manifestation 26, 149
in-group membership 131, 134
institutional power 167, 170–2, 194–5
interaction structure 58
interactional conflict 22
interactional detachment 143
interactional effect 22
interactional event 20
interactional involvement 143
interactional mode 21
interactional resource 30
interactional result 18, 22
interactional sociolinguistics 2–3
interactional space 4

interactional target 20
interactional wants 143
intercultural communication 84
interpersonal rapport 7
interruption 78, 136, 236
intracultural communication 84

jargon 59, 61, 68, 74, 176, 178, 181–3, 188–9

kinship term 63, 220–2, 230, 237
  family term 63
  generalized kinship term 133, 222, 230

language-external 58
language-internal 58
language selection 58
language variation 10
legal mediator vii, 178–9, 181–8, 193, 225
linguistic adaptability 54
linguistic choice ix, 33, 38, 46, 52, 58, 144, 146
linguistic choice-making 58
linguistic competence 55
linguistic device 40, 205
linguistic reference 12
linguistic resource 21, 35, 51, 59–60
linguistic structure 2, 58–9
  macro 58
  micro 58, 88, 131
listener response 78

management of identity 31
  attribute 1, 9, 10–15, 17–19, 21, 25, 31, 36, 55, 99–100, 111–13, 115–16, 118–20, 128, 130, 136, 145, 147, 149
  doer 11, 13–15, 31, 34, 99, 104, 112, 114–15, 118, 145, 147, 152
  identification 10–11, 13–16, 31, 80, 99–103, 111–12, 114–15, 118, 125, 145, 147, 157–8, 164, 215, 218
  image 11–15, 17, 31, 37, 41, 99, 107–9, 111–12, 114–16, 118, 120, 129, 145, 147–8, 150–2, 164, 197, 199–203, 206, 214–15, 220, 237
  impression 7, 130, 155–6, 165
  membership 9–10, 13–15, 31, 46, 93, 99, 101, 111–13, 115–16, 118, 120, 131, 134–5, 145, 147–8, 224, 228, 233

personality 13–14, 17, 55, 109–11, 120, 150, 215, 227
public image 199
rapport vi, 7, 59, 64, 68, 78, 80, 83, 85, 96, 110–21, 128, 130–1, 133, 135–8, 141–4, 146–7, 150, 156–9, 164–5, 218, 220–1, 229, 238, 241
relationship vi, 4–5, 10–11, 14, 16–17, 25–6, 28, 35–6, 38–9, 48, 50, 55, 57–9, 63, 71–3, 78, 80, 93, 96–8, 107–8, 111–13, 115–18, 120–1, 124–6, 129, 134, 136, 138–9, 147–9, 151, 155–8, 164–5, 171–2, 188–9, 191–2, 201–2, 204, 212, 224–5, 231–2, 238
role 9, 11–17, 20, 31, 51, 53, 57, 78, 81, 83, 95, 99, 103–5, 111–12, 114–16, 118, 120, 128, 130, 136, 143, 145–7, 151, 153, 164, 171, 202, 206, 215, 224, 234–5, 239
stance 11–13, 14–15, 31, 42, 58, 83, 99, 106–7, 111–12, 114–16, 118, 128, 130, 145, 147, 150, 158–9
status 12–16, 21, 31, 34, 45, 49, 51, 53, 63, 86, 99, 105–6, 111–12, 114–16, 118, 123, 128, 145, 153, 198, 218, 225
manipulation of identity 119
closeness of identity 219
salience of identity 46
similarity of identity 219
truthfulness of identity 136–8, 219
maxims of conversation 6
manner 5, 13, 21, 66–7, 71, 79, 107, 202
quality 6, 35, 39, 58, 60–1, 66–7, 80, 111, 142, 146, 154, 170, 193–4, 199, 206–7
quantity 6, 48, 66–7
relation/relevance 6, 66–7, 230, 238–40
maxims of politeness 49, 142
agreement 83, 120, 127–8, 144, 177, 184, 187
approbation 144
feeling-Reticence 144
generosity 142, 144, 154
modesty 106, 144, 221
Obligation of O to S 144
Obligation of S to O 144
Opinion-Reticence 144
sympathy 35, 144

Tact Maxim 144, 154
meaning-making 19
metapragmatic awareness 46, 49, 50, 51, 218, 239
  metacognitive 49
  metacommunicative 49
  metarepresentational 49
  reflexive awareness 49
metapragmatic competence 49
modal particle 29, 60, 77
mode of reference 41
moral order 28, 52, 144, 146
mutual rapport 96, 131, 136, 137, 138, 157, 158

narrative 58
negative deviation 28, 29

optimal relevance 54
other-party-addressing 31, 37, 43, 44
out-group membership 135

paralinguistic device 40
paralinguistic resource 35, 60
participant resource 2
participation footing 15
  addressee 5, 17, 30, 31, 50, 51, 62, 89, 107, 117, 118, 119, 120, 121, 123, 128, 129, 130, 134, 137, 144, 146, 151, 163
  addresser 15, 16, 18, 29, 31, 50, 51, 117, 118
  animator 15
  author 15, 62, 111
  bystander 15, 144
  eavesdropper 17, 144
  figure 15, 203
  indirect participant 17
  interpreter 53, 54
  overhearer 15
  principal 15
  questioner 11, 13, 14, 79
  responder 13, 79, 217
  side participant 15
  third-party-addressing 15, 30, 31
  unexpected hearer 17
  utterer
personal value 15, 53, 54, 82, 225
person-referencing 17
persuasion 7, 37, 197, 198

politeness evaluation 25, 146, 147, 148, 149, 150
positioning 11, 39, 41, 47, 120, 148, 172
positive deviation 28
positive pragmatic strategy 28
postmodern turn 1
power relations 149, 169, 175
pragmatic awareness 46, 49
pragmatic balance 38, 39
pragmatic cognition 55
pragmatic competence 19, 22, 38, 40, 46, 49, 150, 224
pragmatic efficacy 204
pragmatic effort 35, 38
pragmatic failure 22, 222, 224
pragmatic force 36, 38
pragmatic imbalance 38
pragmatic resource 35, 38, 39, 40
pragmatic strength 6
pragmatic theories
   Adaptation Theory 33
   Balance Principle 6
   Cooperative Principle 6, 48, 66
   Face Theory 142
   Identity Maxim 6, 40, 46, 47, 48, 49, 218
   Politeness Principle 48, 49, 142
   Pragmatic Identity Theory 204, 214
   Rapport Management Model 142, 147
   Speech Act Theory 23
pragmatic turn 3
pragmatics 1, 3–5, 10, 33, 46, 59, 103–4, 112, 142, 150, 200, 212–13, 221–2
   critical 28–9, 200, 204, 212–13, 225
   interpersonal 142
   variational 221
presupposition 60, 65, 115, 205, 211–12, 214
propositional content 23, 58, 60
psychological positioning 191–2
psychotherapeutic mediator 176, 178, 181, 188, 190–5
public communication 197, 199, 201, 203, 205, 207, 209, 211, 213, 215, 225
   declaration 8, 64, 67
   notice 8, 17, 29, 43, 94, 131, 197, 200–1
   notification 200
   public slogan 8
public sphere 7, 197, 200, 214

rapport management 7, 59, 64, 68, 78, 80, 83, 119, 141–4, 146–7, 150, 157, 164–5
   association 18, 25–6, 129, 143–4, 160–1, 225
   autonomy-imposition 154
   cost-benefit 142–3, 146, 150, 154, 225
   equity 143, 154, 225
   face sensitivities 143
rapport challenging 111, 147
rapport enhancement 110–11, 147
rapport-enhancing 146
rapport impairment 116, 147
rapport maintenance 110, 112
rapport management 7, 59, 64, 68, 78, 80, 83, 119, 141–4, 146–7, 150, 157, 164–5
rapport neglecting 111, 113, 147
rapport orientation 7, 85, 110, 118, 143–4, 146–7, 218, 221
rapport-threatening 64
sociality rights and obligations 142–3
reference 12, 15, 36, 41, 45–6, 49–50, 59, 72, 98, 101, 103–7, 109, 118, 121, 126, 131–3, 164, 181, 203, 214
referential expression 59, 61–62, 68, 133
relating 7, 141, 143
relational work 59, 141–2, 145, 148–9
rhetorical resource 38
role identity theory 11

self-addressing 61, 62, 188
self-referencing term 181–3, 189
social deixis 29, 61, 63, 68
social distance 13, 64, 73, 77, 129
social group 10, 84, 221–2
social hierarchy 12
social interaction 2, 39, 107, 113
social positioning 11
social practice 15, 141, 149
social relationship 11, 48, 72–3, 204
social status 12, 45, 53, 63
social structure 10–11, 14
social value 142, 151, 225
socio-psychological effect 49
sound of speech 58, 178
speech act 1, 10, 23, 41, 58–60, 64, 66–8, 85, 124, 130, 141–2, 150, 181–6, 188–92, 194, 213, 225

assertive 64–5
commissive 65
declaration 64, 67
directive 64–5
expressive 41
speech event 50, 58, 218
stance marking 58
style 58, 60, 68, 71–3
style switching 72–3, 224

toasting 7, 163
transactional need 37–8, 43, 52
turn-taking 60–1, 78

types of communication
  institutional 149, 167–74, 176, 194–5, 197, 222
  interpersonal 110, 141–3, 167, 174, 197, 222, 225
  public 7–8, 19, 197–8, 204, 214, 222, 225

verbal communication 19, 34, 50, 57–8, 119, 141
verbal strategy 57

www.ingramcontent.com/pod-product-compliance
Lightning Source LLC
Chambersburg PA
CBHW062134300426
44115CB00012BA/1920